Two Medieval Outlaws

EUSTACE THE MONK AND FOUKE FITZ WARYN

Two Medieval Outlaws

EUSTACE THE MONK AND FOUKE FITZ WARYN

by

GLYN S. BURGESS

D. S. BREWER

First published 1997
D. S. Brewer, Cambridge
Reprinted in paperback 2009

ISBN 978 1 84384 187 6

D. S. Brewer is an imprint of Boydell & Brewer Ltd
PO Box 9, Woodbridge, Suffolk IP12 3DF, UK
and of Boydell & Brewer Inc.
668 Mount Hope Avenue, Rochester, NY 14620, USA
website: www.boydellandbrewer.com

A catalogue record for this book is available
from the British Library

The Library of Congress has cataloged the hardcover edition
as follows: 96–45609

This publication is printed on acid-free paper

Printed in Great Britain by
CPI Antony Rowe, Chippenham and Eastbourne

CONTENTS

For my wife, Janet

PREFACE

Some time during the early months of the year 1204 a certain Eustace the Monk, a peer of the Boulonnais (he had acted for a time as its seneschal), broke with his lord, Renaud de Dammartin, Count of Boulogne. Eustace had been at one time a Benedictine monk, hence his name, and he left his order seemingly to avenge the death of his father. The man accused of the murder, Hainfrois de Heresinghen, survived, as his champion was victorious in a judicial duel, and he was later to make accusations against Eustace, who had entered the Count's service. Fearing imprisonment as a result of these accusations, Eustace took to the forests of the Boulonnais, and for a time he managed with remarkable ingenuity to score innumerable victories over the count, whom he robbed repeatedly of his possessions and his honour. Eustace eventually left the Boulonnais and thereafter devoted himself to a life of piracy, at which he showed himself to be remarkably successful. In due course he offered his services to John, King of England, and in particular he seems to have helped John to conquer the Channel Islands. But Eustace was an expert at feathering his own nest. Whilst serving John, he established a base on the island of Sark, which became a pirates' den. Such was the distaste in which he was held by the guardians of the southern ports that he required safe-conducts in order to visit King John.

Eustace's period of service to John came to an end when the Count of Boulogne decided to transfer his alliance from King Philip Augustus of France to King John of England. Eustace was in London when Renaud de Dammartin swore homage to John in May 1212. As a result, Eustace was soon to transfer his own allegiance to the French crown, more particularly to Prince Louis, Philip's son, whom he helped significantly in his attempts to secure the crown of England during the civil war of 1215–1217. Much to the annoyance of King John, Eustace used his skills as a mariner to transport men and machinery to England. When Prince Louis launched an invasion of England in 1217, Eustace was by then the admiral of the French fleet. In one of the earliest sea battles fought by the English, the battle of Sandwich on 24 August 1217, the French fleet was routed. Eustace himself, whose ship was too heavily laden to manoeuvre effectively, was captured and immediately beheaded. His head was taken to Canterbury and paraded in triumph around the south of England. A fearsome opponent was no more.

At about the time that Eustace was quarrelling with the Count of Boulogne, a reconciliation was taking place between King John and another outlaw, Fouke (or Fulk) Fitz Waryn. Fouke had broken with the king because he felt that he had been disinherited in favour of a certain Morys Fitz Roger. The territory at stake was principally Whittington Castle in Shropshire. After this rupture, which took place around the year 1200, Fouke spent three years in the forests of Britain, indulging in activities which, at least in the way they have come down to us in literary form, were similar to those of Eustace the Monk. Like Eustace, Fouke inflicted a series of embarrassing losses on his opponent. On one occasion he intercepted a quantity of rich cloth and other goods, which merchants were in the process of transporting to the king. On several occasions Fouke and his men even did battle with the king's men, and he may have been responsible for the death in battle of Morys Fitz Roger, the usurper of Whittington Castle. As in the case of Eustace the Monk, Fouke frequently came within a whisker of being caught (Eustace was once caught and then rescued), but by a combination of trickery and bravery he managed to outwit, outfight or outrun his opponents. Some of Fouke's adventures whilst an outlaw are experienced in places far away from Britain, in the northern seas around Scandinavia, on an island off the coast of Spain and in the land of Barbary in North Africa. Unlike Eustace, Fouke is actually called upon in the course of his adventures to fight a very wide variety of opponents including dragons, a pack of thieving peasants and, in a bizarre single combat with an unknown opponent, his own brother. After his reconciliation with the king, Fouke's last fight is against an Irish giant, who stood twelve feet above any of his fellow warriors.

Both Eustace the Monk and Fouke Fitz Waryn were real people and both are the heroes of romances, one written in Continental French, the other in Anglo-Norman. Indeed, it is difficult to know where the real man ends and the fictional character begins, and vice versa. In the above paragraphs I have selected some salient features of their 'lives' and in so doing have felt obliged to draw on both documentary evidence and on the literary texts translated in this volume. *The Romance of Eustace the Monk* [*Li Romans de Witasse le Moine*] is a 2300-line romance composed during the period 1223 to 1284. In view of the accuracy of much of the information conveyed, a date of composition in the period 1223 to 1235 is likely. *The Romance of Fouke Fitz Waryn* [*Fouke le Fitz Waryn*] is a prose romance based on a lost verse text from the second half of the thirteenth century.

The hero of the romance, Fouke III, died around 1258 and the text may well have been written shortly after his death. But a date later in the century cannot be ruled out. The extant prose version dates from the first half of the fourteenth century. The verse original may have been put into prose by the scribe who compiled the sole manuscript in which it survives. In this volume I have placed *Eustace the Monk* before *Fouke Fitz Waryn* because of the likely date of composition of the verse texts. But the chronological order remains uncertain.

The authors of these texts were interested in particular in the period of outlawry experienced by their protagonists. But both texts present a biography of the heroes from their birth (1170 is a possible date of birth for both men) to their death (Eustace in 1217 and Fouke in 1258). *The Romance of Fouke Fitz Waryn* has often been described as an ancestral romance. The hero's exploits are integrated into an account of the origin of his lineage and the story takes us back to the time of William the Conqueror and the arrival on the scene of Waryn de Metz himself. The real Fouke's father, Fouke II, and his grandfather, Fouke I, are merged in the *Romance* into a single personage. Both texts present us with a fascinating amalgam: historically verifiable facts, information which is not verifiable but which rings true and a wide range of material which is manifestly imaginary have been blended in a satisfying whole. The texts even share some motifs. In both the heroes disguise themselves as charcoal-burners in order to deceive their opponents. Both men reverse the shoes on their horses in order to give the impression that they are travelling in the opposite direction to the one they are actually taking. Did one author borrow elements from the other, or do the motifs stem from a general stock of literary or folkloric motifs? The universal techniques of the trickster, as exemplified in the fabliaux and the stories of Renart the fox, are present certainly in both texts. Of historical interest is the fact that both texts accord an important role to King John, and in both we encounter King Philip Augustus of France. Both texts contain elements which seem to be important in the creation of the legend of Robin Hood. J.C. Holt, in his book *Robin Hood*, links the legends of Eustace the Monk and Fouke Fitz Waryn with that of Hereward the Wake and he sees these three outlaws as having had the greatest influence on the tale of Robin Hood (p. 62). Be that as it may, both authors have the ability to tell an exciting story as if it were history and to turn history into an exciting story.

I would like to record my gratitude to a number of friends and colleagues who have helped me during the preparation of this volume, in particular to Paul Breen, who first drew my attention to the figure of

Eustace the Monk and his important role in early thirteenth-century history. I am also especially grateful to Peter Ainsworth, Denis Conlon, Jacqueline Eccles, Mike Green, Alan Harding, William MacBain, Caroline Palmer and Peter Ricketts, all of whom have made helpful comments on one or more sections of this book. My wife, Janet, as usual, has acted as my general reader and helped my considerably towards my aim of bringing the lives and legends of Eustace and Fouke Fitz Waryn to the widest possible audience.

THE ROMANCE
OF
EUSTACE THE MONK

INTRODUCTION

1. *Eustace the Monk: Man of Many Talents*

Eustace the Monk does not figure amongst the great names of medieval French history. But for his adversaries at the beginning of the thirteenth century he was undoubtedly a man to be reckoned with: 'His name was enough at one time to strike terror into the hearts of Channel seamen', writes Maurice Keen in his book *The Outlaws of Medieval Legend* (p. 54).[1] Moreover, it was not merely as a seafaring man that he managed to inspire fear in his opponents. Intriguingly, he is credited with a knowledge of the black arts, and his contemporaries saw in his apparent invincibility 'clear evidence of his magical powers' (Keen, ibid.). When he was eventually beheaded, during the battle of Sandwich in 1217, his downfall was regarded as an act of God. The author of the *Histoire de Guillaume le Maréchal* calls the day he died his feast-day, because it was the day which would thereafter be celebrated as the one which saw his end (v. 17456). Eustace's head, fixed on a lance, was taken to Canterbury and later paraded in triumph throughout southern England. The death of this fearsome opponent seems to have given rise to sermons on the edifying theme that a bad end awaits all evil-doers.

When contemplating Eustace's career, one is struck by the immense range of his activities, both on land and at sea. The title of Maurice Keen's book categorizes him as an outlaw, but as early as the first paragraph of the chapter devoted to him we find him described as a 'renegade monk', 'an outlawed knight', a 'distinguished magician' and a 'sea captain' (p. 53). Moreover, in Keen's opinion he was 'probably the greatest sea captain of his age' (p. 54). His seamanship, however, was of a somewhat unconventional kind, and he qualifies handsomely for that most enthralling of terms, pirate. Indeed, David Mitchell in his book *Pirates* calls him 'the most spectacular pirate of the early Middle Ages' (p. 33). Eustace clearly

---

[1] For full details of items cited in the Introduction and Notes see the Bibliography. Maurice Keen is echoing a comment already made in 1846 by Thomas Wright in his *Essays on Subjects Connected with the Literature, Popular Superstitions, and History of England in the Middle Ages* (II, p. 121). Wright adds that Eustace was amongst the most famous men of his day (ibid.).

had an extraordinary ability to play a number of roles simultaneously and it seems that in everything he did he was endowed with such exceptional talent that he always succeeded in impressing those around him. Charles de La Roncière, in his monumental history of the French navy, describes him as the one corsair to stand out 'in powerful relief' against his more anonymous contemporaries (p. 302). So it is not surprising that once his impressive life had come to an end, and probably even during it, legend took hold of Eustace. Francisque Michel, the first editor of *The Romance of Eustace the Monk*, refers to him as a 'sort of Robin Hood of the Boulonnais', and he has often been called the Robin Hood of the Sea.[2]

All in all, Eustace must have been a man of immense energy and ability, in whatever area of activity he set his mind on. A redoubtable fighter when circumstances required, he seems to have possessed a remarkable degree of cunning and exceptional manipulative powers. He was also highly endowed with the skills of the actor. If the literary evidence is to be believed, these skills were used for a number of purposes: to avoid capture, to exact revenge, to toy with his opponents and generally to impose his will over all those who got in his way. Our principal evidence for the almost sadistic pleasure which Eustace extracted from his victories comes from *The Romance of Eustace the Monk* [*Li Romans de Witasse le Moine*], which was written some time between 1223 and 1284. Even though we must recognize that we are not dealing with an historical document, but with a literary text with its own aims and objectives, we have no reason to doubt the fundamental accuracy of the *Romance*. Similarities to other literary texts, especially to the fabliaux, the *Roman de Renart* and the Anglo-Norman romance *Fouke le Fitz Waryn*, indicate that the author was drawing on a variety of traditional themes and motifs.[3] The *Romance* is not, however, the only form of evidence concerning Eustace. There remains a good deal of archival material, on the one hand terse references to Eustace

[2] See Michel, edition, p. iv ('espèce de Robin Hood boulonnois'), De La Roncière, I, p. 302 ('Robin Hood de la mer'), Le Goff, p. 170 ('précurseur et peut-être modèle de Robin Hood'), D.J. Conlon, pp. 9, 12, Keen, p. 53. Conlon, who edited the text in 1972, sees Eustace as a possible predecessor of Friar Tuck (p. 14). According to J.C. Holt, in his book *Robin Hood*, the legend of Robin Hood, in the form in which it has come down to us, 'drew heavily' on the romances devoted to Eustace the Monk and Fouke Fitz Waryn (p. 71).
[3] For links with other texts see especially L. Jordan, 'Quellen und Komposition von Eustasche le Moine', and B. Schmolke-Hasselmann, 'Füchse in Menschengestalt: die listige Heldin Wistasse le Moine und Fouke Fitz Waryn'. The principal link is with the Anglo-Norman romance *Fouke le Fitz Waryn*, a translation of which has also been included in the present volume.

and his activities in close rolls, patent rolls, charters, etc., and on the other hand a number of more substantial accounts, written after his death by thirteenth and fourteenth-century chroniclers. Particularly important in the latter category are the chronicles of Roger of Wendover and Matthew Paris, written in Latin, the *Histoire de Guillaume le Maréchal*, written in French verse, and the *Histoire des ducs de Normandie et des rois d'Angleterre*, written in French prose. The two French texts provide an especially useful account of Eustace's death at the battle of Sandwich.

2. *The Eustace of Legend*

Such was Eustace's power to create an enduring legend, and this power may have been fostered by the *Romance* itself, that a fourteenth-century chronicler, Walter of Guisborough (also known as Walter of Hemingford), was sufficiently confused to call Eustace a tyrant of Spain, surnamed Monachus. After acquiring great booty and conquering many lands, he is said to have set out with a huge fleet and many men to conquer England itself. The English sailors, hearing of his imminent arrival and being aware of his reputation, feared total devastation if he landed with his fleet. So they put to sea and sent a volunteer to climb the tyrant's mast in order to cut down his sail and thus deprive the fleet of guidance from Eustace's vessel. This manoeuvre worked admirably for the English and, in Walter's words, 'God gave the enemy into their hands' ('tradiditque dominus eos in manorum eorum'). They returned home with great joy and great booty. The victory was greeted thankfully by England's young king, Henry III.[4]

At about the same time, John of Canterbury, in his *Polistorie*, gave a remarkable account of the battle of Sandwich, in which a monk called

---

4   *The Chronicle of Walter of Guisborough*, ed. Harry Rothwell, pp. 159–60. Rothwell thinks that Walter began his work in 'the opening years of the fourteenth century' (p. xxxi), but he adds that it could have been started as early as 1270 (p. xxx). The chronicle stops at the year 1312, but there are jottings up to 1315. Walter's story concerning Eustace was repeated word-for-word by Henry Knighton, who wrote at the very end of the fourteenth century or the beginning of the fifteenth century (his chronicle stops at the year 1395). Henry Knighton's account of Eustace appears in a section consisting of the 'wholesale appropriation' of Walter of Guisborough (J.R. Lumby, edition, II, p. xxvii). Walter's chronicle itself was also 'mostly compilation' (Rothwell, p. xxv), so he may in fact have been drawing on a source which was a good deal closer to the date of Eustace's death. Rothwell states that in general for the period 1198–1291 Walter was 'short of materials' (p. xxvi). For the Latin text see Conlon, p. 119. Michel's edition includes a translation into French (pp. xx–xxii). See also Keen, pp. 62–63.

Eustace led a large fleet against the English. In view of his outstanding knowledge of magic, says John, the lords who accompanied Eustace were confident of success. Some of the invaders even brought their wives, their children and their oxen so that they could settle in England once Eustace had delivered it into their hands. As they approached Sandwich, the entire fleet could be clearly seen, with the exception of Eustace's own ship, over which he had cast a spell which caused it to become invisible. The English were eventually saved, partly by their prayers in the name of St Bartholomew, on whose feast-day all this took place, and partly by the intervention of a former companion of Eustace, Stephen Crabbe. Using the techniques of magic taught to him by Eustace himself, Stephen set sail and jumped aboard Eustace's ship, which was visible to him alone. Seeing Stephen standing above the water, the onlookers thought that some evil spirit had assumed his form. Finding his way to Eustace, Stephen cut off his head and at once the ship became visible. But Stephen was soon seized and killed. His body was dismembered and thrown into the sea in little pieces. Meanwhile, a hurricane was beginning to uproot trees on the shore and it destroyed the French ships as they entered port. During the storm a man in red garments appeared before the onlookers, and they heard a voice crying 'My name is Bartholomew and I have been sent to assist you: you have nothing to fear from the enemy.' The figure vanished and victory went to the English.[5]

---

[5] John of Canterbury's *Polistorie* remains unedited. The manuscript is in the British Library (Harley 636). For a text of the section dealing with Eustace's defeat at the hands of Steven Crabbe and the English (f. 201v, col. 2–202v, col. 1) see Conlon, pp. 117–19. See also Keen, pp. 61–63. John's story ends, like the *Romance*, with the comment that Eustace's fate illustrates the ultimate worth of malice for those who put their trust in it. John stresses repeatedly Eustace's subtlety and cunning and also his knowledge of necromancy and sorcery. Twice he calls him an apostate monk (*moygne apostota*). But in his account of the uprooting of trees on the shore it looks as if he has confused the battle of Sandwich in 1217 with an earlier event, the great storm of 1215, which destroyed a French fleet led by Hugh de Boves. After the battle of Bouvines in 1214 Hugh was given the counties of Norfolk and Suffolk by King John, but in order to gain independence he decided to instal his own settlers there. On 26 October Hugh was travelling from Calais with, say the chroniclers, forty thousand men, women and children, whom he was bringing to England. In the storm the ships foundered on the coast at Godwin-Sands, near Yarmouth. The coast is said to have been so covered with bodies that the air itself was tainted (see Keen, p. 63, N.H. Nicolas, *A History of the Royal Navy*, I, pp. 172–73, and H. Malo, *Un Grand Feudataire: Renaud de Dammartin*, p. 218). John completes his story of Eustace by stating that the inhabitants of Sandwich built a chapel not far from the town, with adjoining houses for poor and elderly people. Each year on St Bartholomew's Day, he says, the community holds a solemn procession to this 'hospital'. This account is by no means far from the truth. T.A. Bushell in his book *Kent*

3. *The Real Eustace: his Early Life and Travels*

What can we extract from such legendary accounts and from the entire range of evidence relating to Eustace? How close can we get to the 'facts'? First of all it can be assumed that Eustace originated from the Boulonnais region of northern France.[6] His place of birth is given in the *Romance* as 'Cors en Boulenois' (v. 305).[7] The most recent editor of the romance, Denis J. Conlon, suggests the year 1170 as an approximate date for Eustace's birth (p. 14). The place-name Cors has normally been taken to represent Courset, a village in the Vallée de la Course about twelve miles from Boulogne, but it probably refers, as Anne-Dominique Kapferer suggests, in her article 'Banditisme, roman, féodalité: le Boulonnais d'Eustache le Moine' (p. 229), to the somewhat larger village of Course, which lies to the south-west of Courset. Eustace probably lived in the Château de Course, which he would have inherited on the death of his father.[8] In the *Romance* his father's name is given as Bauduin Busquet (Bauduïns Bulkés, v. 306, Bauduïns Busqués, v. 314), and he is said to be a peer of the Boulonnais and an expert in legal matters ('Si estoit pers de Boulenois; / Molt savoit de plais et de loys', vv. 308–09). Bauduin is known to us from documentary evidence, as his name appears from time to time in the 1180s as a witness to charters.[9] But in the 1190s his name no longer

reports that as a result of the victory over Eustace 'the hospital at Sandwich, first founded for returning crusaders, was now refounded for the wounded of this battle and renamed St Bartholomew's' (p. 22). Bushell tells us that a commemoration of the battle and the refounding is still held each year in the hospital chapel on St Bartholomew's Day and that this is one of the oldest commemorations regularly held in this country (ibid.).

6 Matthew Paris states that Eustace was Flemish ('erat autem ille natione Flandrensis', III, p. 29) and this was repeated by some earlier scholars. But in Eustace's day the Boulonnais was often referred to as Flemish (see H.L. Cannon, 'The Battle of Sandwich and Eustace the Monk', p. 651, and Michel, edition, pp. vi–vii).

7 Unless otherwise stated, quotations are taken from the edition by Denis J. Conlon. The editions by Michel and Foerster-Trost have also been consulted. Conlon provides an extensive collection of the texts in Latin and French texts relating to Eustace the Monk (pp. 108–22), as do Michel (Introduction, passim, and Notes, pp. 85–118) and Foerster-Trost (Introduction). See also Michel, *Rapports à M. Le Ministre de l'Instruction Publique*, pp. 10–11. In the present notes page references to documentary material are normally restricted to Conlon's edition.

8 On the Château de Course see P. Héliot, 'Le Château de Course', p. 545. This castle has now disappeared, leaving only a mound as an indication of its existence (see Kapferer, 'Banditisme', p. 229).

9 For details concerning Bauduin Busquet see Kapferer, ibid., p. 230. For the text of

appears, and this probably indicates that he died early in that decade. He would have been one of the senior barons of the Boulonnais, coming in the hierarchy below the seneschal and other senior peers (such as the constable and the marshal), but above the *baillis*.[10] Although we do not know precisely what happened to Bauduin's estates after his death, it is interesting to note that in the 1240s the Château de Course was in the possession of a certain Guillaume Le Moine, who may have been Eustace's nephew, or even his son.[11]

It is likely that in his youth Eustace received training as a knight. The *Histoire des Ducs de Normandie* refers to him as a 'chevaliers de Boulenois' (p. 167, lines 2–3), and Guillaume le Breton in his *De gestis Philippi Augusti* describes him as a *miles* (p. 314, line 16). In v. 1627 of the *Romance* he is referred to as a *chevalier*. Eustace must also at some stage in his life have received instruction in seamanship, no doubt to a certain extent in his home territory, but perhaps also on the shores of the Mediterranean. Henri Malo in his important article on Eustace, 'Eustache Le Moine: un pirate boulonnais au XIIIe', states that 'he certainly travelled, because it was he who implanted in the Channel the methods of naval combat used by the Italians'.[12] The *Romance* tells us that he paid a visit to Toledo in

---

charters witnessed by him see Conlon, p. 108, and Malo, *Un Grand Feudataire*, pp. 239–40.

[10] For the hierarchy of nobility and administrative officers in the Boulonnais see P.-J.-B. Bertrand, *Précis de l'histoire physique, civile et politique, de la ville de Boulogne-sur-Mer*, I, pp. 49–50. Bertrand tells us that the Count of Boulogne's entourage was led by his seneschal. Then came six senior officers, four peers (including the constable and the marshal) and a number of castellans, viscounts and barons. Then followed the *baillis*, whose residences were Boulogne, Calais, Outreau, Le Wast, Wissant, Loudefort, Taples, Belle-Fontaine and Desvres. See also Henri Malo, *Petite Histoire de Boulogne-sur-Mer*, p. 48.

[11] On Guillaume le Moine see Th. Duchet and A. Giry, *Cartulaires de l'église de Thérouanne*, charter 194 (pp. 156–57), D. Haigneré, 'Supplément au recueil des chartes de Samer' (pp. 364–65) and R. Rodière, 'Chartes diverses du Boulonnais' (charters 8–13). It is known that Guillaume le Moine owned lands in Monchi, a location which is mentioned in the *Romance* (v. 1583). See Kapferer, 'Banditisme', p. 229.

[12] This comment appears as a handwritten addition to the text at p. 9 and it reads in full: 'il a certainement voyagé parce que c'est lui qui a implanté dans la Manche les méthodes de combat maritime des Italiens (à moins que ces derniers ne les lui en ont appris, mais c'est peu probable, car ceux qui venaient de là étaient surtout des commerçants)'. This addition was presumably made by the author. I have found it in the copy in the Bibliothèque Municipale in Boulogne, and Denis Conlon (p. 15) encountered the same addition in the copy in the British Library. It was in fact natural that Eustace, whether pirate or legitimate mariner, would look to the Mediterranean for ideas and techniques. René Jouan in his *Histoire de la marine française* states that 'la guerre navale était fille de la Méditerranée' (p. 14). When Eustace arrived on the nauti-

Spain, where he learned necromancy and met the Devil himself. In fact, we are told, he spent a whole summer and winter in Toledo in an underground cavern, learning the techniques and the art of deception (vv. 6–16). There exists no evidence for such a visit, but it may reflect a legend which grew up around Eustace, that he had left the Boulonnais for a time and in due course returned home, armed with a variety of ingenious devices and techniques which he later put to good use against his various opponents. Toledo certainly had the reputation of being the type of place to provide such disturbing and effective skills. Montague Summers, in his book *Witchcraft and Black Magic,* tells us that Toledo, Saragossa and the University of Salamanca 'gained throughout all Europe an evil notoriety as hotbeds of necromancy' (p. 76). These places were regarded as the 'nurseries and thriving-grounds of sorcerers'.[13]

4. *Eustace becomes Eustace the Monk*

It appears that after his travels Eustace entered a monastery. Our most detailed information on this point comes from the *Romance,* which tells us on two occasions that he became a Black Monk at 'Saint Saumer' (vv. 3–4, 221). Samer, about eight miles south-east of Boulogne, was an old Benedictine abbey, founded by St Wulmer in the seventh century.[14] The evidence from the *Romance* is supported by both Ralph of Coggeshall, who

cal scene, at the beginning of the thirteenth century, neither France nor England had a recognizable navy, and what little conflict there was in the Atlantic Ocean or the North Sea took place between pirates (Jouan, pp. 14–15). Eustace's success as a mariner certainly suggests that he was aware of techniques largely unknown to his contemporaries. See below, note 61.

13 Of all the homes of sorcery Toledo was, according to Summers, especially ill-famed: 'It is said that at one period a Chair of Black Magic was openly established there, and certainly Guazzo speaks of a seven years' course of the Black Arts and Magic at Toledo' (p. 76). Summers mentions the *Romance of Eustace the Monk* and also the thirteenth-century epic poem *Maugis d'Aigremont,* in which Maugis 'gains admittance to the secret societies of Toledo, where he completes his researches into wizard sciences, and eventually obtains the professorial chair of goety in that University' (ibid.). See the edition of *Maugis d'Aigremont* by P. Vernay (Bern: Romanica Helvetica, 1980). It is interesting to note that the figure of Maugis is mentioned by the author of the *Romance of Eustace the Monk,* who compares his cunning and magical powers unfavourably with those of Eustace (vv. 285–99). See Notes to the Translation, n. 5. For further details concerning Toledo as a centre of magic see Sylvie Roblin-Dubin, 'L'Ecole de magie de Tolède: histoire et légende'.

14 The form Samer is a contracted form of Saint Wulmer (aux bois). Only a small part of the old abbey still remains.

refers to Eustace as someone who was formerly a monk ('cum quodam Eustachio quondam monacho', *Chronicon anglicanum*, p. 185), and the anonymous chronicler of Laon, who says that 'from a Black Monk Eustace became a demoniac' (p. 719b). In addition, Eustace is consistently called The Monk [Monachus or Le Moyne] in contemporary documents.[15] We have no information about why Eustace chose this particular way of life, and in fact everything we can glean about him would suggest that he was a distinctly untypical monk. Indeed, the author of the *Romance* devotes a good deal of space to telling us what an unsuitable candidate he was for devotion to a life of prayer. He seems to have spent his time creating chaos in the monastery: 'He made the monks fast when they should have eaten and made them go barefoot when they should have worn shoes. He made them curse when they should have been saying their prayers and made them misbehave when they should have been giving thanks' (vv. 224–31). These acts are described by the author as devilry (*dyablie*, v. 222), and they are presumably intended as proof of the diabolical skills which Eustace had acquired in Toledo. The *Romance* then describes a quarrel between Eustace and the abbot of the monastery, which led to Eustace casting spells in the monastic kitchen and to his gambling in a local tavern with the abbey's collection of crucifixes and statues, etc. The monastery, we are told, was completely cleaned out, with not even a pair of monk's boots remaining (vv. 232–79). As they are presented, these monastic episodes have a literary function in that they are entertaining in themselves and they also prepare the way for Eustace's later (and better documented) clashes with authority. They provide an early indication of his fondness for the appropriation of other people's possessions. Whether these activities are authentic or not we cannot say, but it is possible that information, however distorted in the telling, came the way of the author of the *Romance* from witnesses acquainted with this period in Eustace's life.

5. *Eustace Leaves the Monastery*

For reasons which are not entirely clear, Eustace in due course renounced his order. Matthew Paris, in his *Chronica maiora*, relates that he did so in order to secure the inheritance which had fallen to him because of his brothers' decease without children (III, p. 29). But in documents relating

[15] See items 8–46 of Conlon's section entitled 'Documentation' (pp. 109–19).

to the Channel Islands his brothers are mentioned as still alive after Eustace's death.[16] It is more likely that he left his order, as the *Romance* states, for the purpose of demanding justice from the Count of Boulogne against Hainfrois de Heresinghen, who, he claimed, had murdered his father. In the *Romance*, Eustace's father is said to have been involved in a legal wrangle with Hainfrois over the possession of a fief. The author states that Hainfrois was trying to disinherit him. There may have been, as Keen suggests (p. 56), rivalry and a long-standing feud between the two of them. Bauduin exacerbated the conflict by giving Hainfrois a blow (vv. 314–17). In retaliation, and to put an end to the dispute once and for all, Hainfrois went so far as to have Bauduin killed (a not uncommon form of revenge at the time, according to Henri Malo, p. 12). Bauduin was murdered, probably in some form of ambush, near a place called Basinguehans (v. 310).[17] The upshot of Eustace's request for justice was the granting of a judicial combat. Hainfrois excused himself on grounds of age and was represented by a certain Eustace de Marquise. Eustace the Monk did not fight himself, perhaps because he had not yet fully abandoned his religious status. A young nephew of Bauduin, named Manesier, offered to undertake the battle on his behalf. The combat took place at Etaples and after a great struggle Manesier lost. But Eustace, who clearly had little faith in the justice afforded by such combats, had already stated his intention of ignoring the outcome, if it went against him (vv. 322–69). The author of the *Romance* devotes seventy lines to Eustace's father and the judicial duel, so in his opinion these matters must have had some interest for his audience and some importance for the overall structure of his text.[18]

The murder of his father and his failure to secure justice, events which

---

16 See Cannon, p. 654, and Wendy B. Stevenson, 'England, France and the Channel Islands, 1204–1259', p. 574.

17 Basinguehans (v. 310) is probably Bazinghen, north-west of Marquise, but it could refer to Bezinghen near Course. For the place of provenance of Hainfrois de Heresinguehans Conlon (p. 125) suggests Hardinghem or Hervelinghen. Keen's Meresinguehans (pp. 56, 58) seems to be an error. The difficulty of identifying such places is shown by a perusal of the lists of toponyms found in D. Haigneré's *Dictionnaire topographique . . . arrondissement de Boulogne-sur-Mer*. Hainfrois may well have been the Honfredo de Honbreuq, a fellow witness with Eustace to the gift of a charter to the town of Ambleteuse in 1209, and/or the Henfridus de Haneclingguehem who witnessed the charter exempting the bourgeois of Saint-Omer from the law of wreck in April 1206 (see Conlon, p. 110, item 15, and p. 121, item 53). See also Kapferer, 'Banditisme', pp. 229–30, and 'Mépris', p. 351, and Berger and Petit, *Contes à rire du Nord de la France*, pp. 196–97.

18 For a lengthy account of the section devoted to the judicial duel, see Malo, 'Eustache le Moine', pp. 12–14. Nothing is known of Eustace de Marquise (Wistasce de Marquise, v. 350) or of Manesier.

probably took place some time in the early 1190s, apparently did not sour the relationship between Eustace and the Count of Boulogne, Renaud de Dammartin. For shortly afterwards Eustace entered the count's service. The *Romance* says tersely: 'Then the Monk served the count and took complete charge of his accounts' (vv. 372–73). Eustace clearly impressed Renaud with his organizational and military skills, for in 1203, when he needed a replacement for his seneschal, Daniel de Bétencourt, who was to accompany him to Normandy, the count appointed him to this important administrative post. The fact that Eustace was seneschal in 1203 is confirmed for us by Lambert of Ardres in his *Historia comitum ghisnensium*, and this fact provides us with our first clear-cut date in the chronology of Eustace's life.[19] The *Romance* tells us that Eustace was 'seneschal, peer and bailiff, as was his right' ('senescaus . . . / Pers et baillius, che fu ses drois', vv. 374–75). One disastrous episode in Eustace's short term of office as seneschal is worthy of our attention and it is graphically described by Lambert of Ardres. Renaud was supporting Philip Augustus at the siege of Radepont in Normandy and Eustace had to cope with the perceived threat from Count Baldwin of Guînes, who had constructed a fortress at Sangatte. Renaud claimed that in so doing he had made considerable inroads into the vast marshlands, known as the Marais-Royal, which were regarded as the territorial boundary between Boulogne and Guînes. Eustace was given the task of securing communication between Boulogne and Calais by strengthening the road at Ales. This would have made access to Sangatte difficult for the Count of Guînes and protected nearby Marck. Eustace ordered men from Marck to make their way to Ales with tools, weapons and food for thirty days. Everyone duly arrived and they started knocking down trees, which were on the territory of Guînes, and digging a ditch on each side of the road. They turned over the earth, says Lambert, 'like a swarm of ants', shouting insults at the enemy and uttering cries of 'hu! hu!' to urge themselves on. Hearing of this, the count warned the men to cease this injustice and return home. They refused and continued working with even greater enthusiasm. The count tried again, ordering them to cease until Renaud's return. Again he met with no success. So mustering all the men he could lay his hands on, Baldwin marched against the workmen. He began with another request to them to desist, but on their refusal he attacked and the men from Marck laid down their tools and fled. There was no bloodshed, but some of them were captured and others

---

[19] Lambert of Ardres, p. 587. See also A. Du Chesne, *Histoire généalogique des comtes de Guînes*, p. 259, and Conlon, p. 109, item 8.

dispossessed of everything they had. The victors hung captured banners in the church at Ardres as a sign of their success.[20] No other information about Eustace's activities as seneschal has come down to us, but we can be certain that neither Eustace nor the count would ever have forgotten this fiasco.

During this period of Eustace's life, the quarrel with his father's murderer, Hainfrois, must have smouldered on. If the *Romance* is to be believed, Hainfrois attempted to discredit Eustace by making certain accusations against him in relation to the performance of his official duties (vv. 376–77). Eustace was in charge of the *baillies* of the Boulonnais and his post would have carried considerable financial responsibilities.[21] Hainfrois seems to have suggested that he was fiddling the accounts. There is no evidence for or against this claim, but in the light of Eustace's future behaviour one suspects that there may have been more than a grain of truth in the allegation. Summoned by the count, who asked him for an explanation of the way in which he had discharged his duties ('Se li a demandé / Des baillies k'il a tenues / Pour coi il les a detenues', vv. 379–81), Eustace claimed that he was ready to answer the charges before the count's peers and barons. But Renaud demanded that he should present himself at his castle in Hardelot, where he would not be able 'to give a false account of himself' (vv. 387–89).[22] Sensing treachery and suspecting that he would end up in prison, Eustace broke with the count and fled (vv. 390–92). He took up residence in the vast forests of the Boulonnais, only insignificant remnants of which now survive (Malo, p. 15). This was the beginning of an enmity which was to last for the rest of Eustace's life. The *Romance* indicates that the count responded by seizing his property and setting fire to his fields. Eustace swore vengeance against him, saying that he would regret this action and that it would cost him ten thousand marks (vv. 395–99).

---

20 Lambert of Ardres, pp. 587–88. See Malo, 'Eustache le Moine', p. 14, idem, *Un Grand Feudataire*, pp. 90–92, and Conlon, pp. 15–16, 109, item 8. This rout of the men of Marck took place in August or September 1203.

21 For a general indication of the roles of *baillis* and seneschals see John W. Baldwin's chapter 'Baillis and seneschals: Justice and Finance in the New Domain', in *The Government of Philip Augustus*, pp. 220–58.

22 Hardelot seems to have been Renaud's favourite seat. He was not often in Boulogne, which at the time was still 'une ville de faible importance' (Kapferer, 'Banditisme', p. 228). The oldest part of the present castle of Hardelot was built in the 1230s, after Eustace's death. It is of interest that a notice outside the present gates states that one of the principal sources of evidence for the existence of an earlier castle on the site is the *Romance of Eustace the Monk* (a text which it dates categorically to 1250!).

13

6. *Eustace as Outlaw*

There follows in the *Romance* a lengthy period of conflict between Eustace and Count Renaud. Using a multitude of disguises, as well as great ingenuity and courage, Eustace scores a sizeable number of victories over his opponent, robbing him repeatedly of both his property and his dignity. There is no documentary evidence for any specific details of the conflict, but the *Histoire des ducs de Normandie* does state that a lengthy period of hostility took place ('moult avoit guerroié le conte de Bouloigne', p. 167, lines 4–5). This is echoed by the anonymous chronicler of Béthune: 'Celui Ustace le Moine ot Rainaus de Dantmartin, li cuens de Boloigne, al tens qu'il tint Bolenois, chacié de sa terre, et cil l'ot molt guerroié' (p. 774j). Many of the episodes seem to derive from the traditional armoury of the trickster, but the opening attack on Renaud, the burning of two of his mills whilst he was participating in wedding celebrations (vv. 400–29), could well be based on reality. The author insists on the truth of his account ('Che fu la fine verités', v. 429) and on a hill not far from the upper town of Boulogne, but separated from it in the thirteenth century by a deep ravine, is a place which is still called Les Quatre-Moulins.[23]

There are two further events in the *Romance* which could perhaps be based on reality. At one point Eustace's conflict with Renaud spills over briefly into one with the King of France himself, Philip Augustus, and his son, Prince Louis. During a visit by Philip to the Boulonnais, Renaud's men acted as the rear-guard for his forces as they departed from Sangatte. Eustace, who had already angered the king by robbing and killing his men, attacked the rear-guard, capturing five knights and a number of horses (vv. 1296–365). It is possible, as Conlon suggests (p. 16), that something of this sort took place, even if the story as told retains some elements from Philip's support for Renaud against the Count of Guînes in 1209 (see below, note 42, and Notes to the Translation, n. 12). Also, at one stage during his life in the forest, according to the *Romance*, Eustace was actually captured by Count Renaud, after his saddle turned during a chase, causing him to fall off his horse (vv. 1638–46). After his capture, Eustace received the support of his relatives and friends, such as William de Montcavrel and Walet de Coupelle (vv. 1670–711), and in spite of the catalogue of misdeeds perpetrated by Eustace against Renaud, they succeeded in persuad-

---

[23] See Malo, 'Eustache le Moine', pp. 14–15, and Haigneré, *Dictionnaire topographique*, p. 272.

ing the count to send him to King Philip rather than hang him himself, as he would have liked. However, whilst he was being transported to Philip, Eustace was rescued at Beaurain by William de Fiennes (vv. 1730–41). There is no evidence for this capture, but it is interesting to note that a number of the men allegedly involved in it are known to us from contemporary documents.[24] The author was clearly keen that his account should possess at least certain elements of authenticity, and one might legitimately wonder whether this capture and escape did indeed take place.

We are told that after his escape Eustace crossed the River Canche (v. 1742), which constitutes the southern border of the Boulonnais, and that after speedily gaining a certain amount of revenge against Renaud and his men he made his way to England. Once there, he offered his services to King John (vv. 1882–83). The *Histoire des ducs de Normandie* provides a different reason for Eustace's departure from the Boulonnais. It indicates that his decision to leave was the result of Renaud's alliance with King Philip.[25] It may also be that the statement in v. 1743 of the *Romance* ('N'avoit cure d'aler en France' / 'He had no desire to go to France') can be taken as indicating that Eustace was afraid of Philip and less confident that he could escape justice if he fell into his hands. Be that as it may, there can be no doubt that, even after Eustace had abandoned the Boulonnais, the antagonism between him and Renaud persisted, and this was to have serious consequences for Eustace's future life.

---

24 The charters cited by Conlon (items 7, 52, 53, 54 and 56, pp. 121–22) mention as witnesses Guillelmus de Fiennis, Ansellus de Kaieu, Willelmus de Montcavrel and Walo de Capella. Guillaume de Fiennes was present at Ambleteuse in 1209 when, along with Eustace and others, he witnessed the charter (see above note 17). He is also mentioned by R. Rodière in his 'Chartes diverses du Boulonnais' (under the heading 'Fienles, Fienlles' in the section entitled 'Commentaires onomastiques'): 'La maison de Fiennes, l'une des plus illustres du Boulonnais, est originaire de la terre de ce nom, entre Boulogne et Guînes' (p. 195). Henri Malo tells us that Guillaume de Fiennes was one of Renaud's most faithful barons (*Un Grand Feudataire*, p. 92). The place of origin of Aufrans de Caïeu is hard to identify, but a person of that name, from the Caïeu family of Ponthieu, did accompany Hugues de Saint-Pol on the Fourth Crusade. See Geoffroi de Villehardouin, *Conqueste de Constantinople*, who mentions an Ansiaus (Ansials, Anser) de Kaeu (Kaue, Chaeo) on a number of occasions. Nothing is known of Hugh de Gannes (Huës de Gaunes), who is mentioned three times in the *Romance* (vv. 536, 1726, 1734). See Berger and Petit, pp. 194–95. See Malo, ibid., pp. 112–13, for the names of knights accompanying Renaud on military duty for Philip Augustus, and Kapferer, 'Banditisme', p. 230.
25 'Por chou que li cuens estoit deviers le roi de France' (p. 167, lines 6–7). The *Histoire* also states that Eustace waged war against the Count of Boulogne until he entered John's service: 'Tant le guerroia que il ala puis au siervice le roi d'Engletierre' (ll. 5–6).

7. *Eustace as a Servant of King John*

The duration of the initial hostilities between Eustace and Count Renaud is not clear. The *Histoire des ducs de Normandie* indicates that they lasted 'for a long time' (p. 167, line 4). Yet the period between Eustace's break with Renaud, which may have occurred early in 1204, and his departure for England may in reality have been relatively short, perhaps around a year. Eustace was certainly in England by November 1205, the date of the first reference to him in English records, and it is likely that, before presenting himself to King John, he had been at sea long enough to acquire a reputation as a skilful mariner. If the author of the *Romance* is to be believed, King John's reaction to Eustace's arrival in England was so positive that he must have been fully aware of the contribution which Eustace's abilities as a seafarer could make to his cause. In the *Romance* King John immediately supplies Eustace with thirty galleys, whereupon he heads for the Channel Islands (here called the 'isles de Genesies', v. 1915). The precise date and the particular nature of Eustace's mission are in reality unclear, but John was no doubt concerned at that time not only with the Channel Islands but more importantly with the re-conquest of Normandy, which had been lost to the French in 1204. K.E.M. Hawkes, in his book entitled *Sark*, expresses in the following terms Eustace's activities after his commitment to John: 'Commissioned by King John of England to reconquer Normandy, Eustache and his cut-throat crews of English, Flemish and even French sailors ravaged the coasts of north-west France from 1204 to 1211' (p. 96). The evidence for much of this is a little thin, but we do know that John was sufficiently impressed with Eustace's efforts on his behalf to reward him with a gift of lands in Norfolk.[26] However, there were many others, particularly the authorities of the Cinque Ports and a host of unwary sailors in the waters around Britain, whom Eustace managed to antagonize or terrify in the course of his activities. These men were far less impressed by him.

Eustace clearly had a great instinct for serving other people and at the same time catering for his own interests. It is significant that Hawkes' comment on Eustace's involvement with John is made in the context of a book on the history of Sark, where the legend of Eustace the Monk is still remembered. It appears that, whilst inflicting damage on John's adversar-

[26] See Malo, 'Eustache le Moine', p. 15. See below, note 35.

ies, Eustace captured Sark and established a pirate den on this small island. Eustace and his men seem to have settled there and used the island as a more or less independent base from which to attack selected targets. Some of these targets no doubt produced gains for John, and others for Eustace himself. Henri Malo (*Renaud de Dammartin*, p. 93) states that he had a particular liking for Flemish ships, which were laden with rich cargo. John was certainly aware of Eustace's reputation for piracy, for in April 1206 he ordered the *baillis* of the Cinque Ports to help a certain Guillaume le Petit to recover his ship, which Eustace had taken from him.[27] Thus, whilst Eustace generally remained on good terms with King John, to whom, it appears, he had given his daughter as a hostage (and perhaps also his wife), his relationship with the authorities on the south coast of England was clearly far from good. If he needed to visit England at that time, he required safe-conducts. Records show that in May 1206 and April 1207 such passes were issued to him for visits within specified periods.[28] The very fact that these safe-conducts had to be issued provides us with proof that at this time Eustace was based outside England, but they also confirm that his independent activities as a pirate had not antagonized King John himself to any great extent. Eustace clearly knew how to maintain the right balance between private gain and political advantage.

8. *The Raid against Cadoc*

The *Romance* recounts an episode in which Eustace sails up the Seine and makes a daring raid on the territory guarded by a certain Cadoc, the master of the castle of Gaillon above Rouen (vv. 1954–2125). This raid presumably took place during Eustace's period of service with John. Cadoc (his full name was Lambert Cadulque) was in real life the *bailli* of Pont-Audemer and he may have been something of a rival for Eustace. In his

---

27 'Rex omnibus ballivis portuum maris, etc. Mandamus vobis quod, si Eustachius Monachus non reddiderit Willelmo Le Petit navem suam quam cepit, sicut illi mandavimus, sitis eidem Willelmo in auxilio quod illam habeat ubicumque illam invenerit in terra nostra' ('The king to all the port bailiffs and others. We send you word that if Eustace the Monk has not restored to Guillaume Le Petit the ship which he took from him, as we told him to, you should help the aforementioned Guillaume to recover it wherever it is to be found in our territory', *Rotuli selecti ad res anglicas*, p. 26). See Conlon, p. 109, item 9. Conlon gives April 1205 as the date for this document, but it dates from the seventh year of John's reign, i.e. 1206.
28 See Malo, 'Eustache le Moine', p. 15, and Stevenson, 'England, France and the Channel Islands', p. 574. The documents are to be found in Conlon, pp. 109–110, items 12 and 13.

book *The Government of Philip Augustus* John W. Baldwin tells us that he 'commanded a celebrated band of *routiers*' (p. 167) and that he became an important lord in Normandy, participating in most of the king's major campaigns (p. 223). Cadoc may have had the same pecuniary instincts as Eustace, for Baldwin informs us that he 'profited from the unsettled conditions by extortion of victims who did not dare protest' (ibid.). He not only possessed land and a house in the town of Pont-Audemer, but also, to quote Auguste Canel, author of the principal history of Pont-Audemer, 'rich and numerous domains in Normandy' (p. 62). One of Cadoc's charming habits was the use of what Canel (p. 63) calls 'the most odious violence' to force rich heiresses to marry his mercenaries when he wished to reward them for their services. In 1219, after Eustace's death, Cadoc was put in prison by King Philip and all his goods were confiscated. He may have fancied himself as a seafaring man, for in the *Romance* he does not hesitate to set sail in pursuit of Eustace. But, having humiliated him on land, Eustace manages to do the same at sea, for there Cadoc loses five ships to Eustace and he is forced to acknowledge the latter's maritime supremacy (vv. 2118–25). There is no historical evidence for this raid, but, in the *Romance* we are told that, in order to humiliate him, Eustace manoeuvres Cadoc in such a way that he becomes stuck in an area of treacherous marshland. To this day there is a large stretch of marshland, Le Marais Vernier, not far from the town of Pont-Audemer.[29]

9. *Eustace Builds a Palace*

The *Romance* tells us that, after returning from this raid, Eustace asked the king for a residence in England and the king gave him a 'magnificent and well-constructed' palace in London (vv. 2138–45). If this corresponds to reality, it would clearly indicate that we are dealing with a period of growing pretensions and ambitions on Eustace's part. This would certainly not be contrary to the known facts. His piratical activities would have brought

---

[29] In the *Romance* Cadoc is said to be seneschal of Normandy (v. 1966). De La Roncière accepts this raid against Cadoc as factual and he dates it to 1205 (II, p. 303). For further details on Cadoc see E. Audouin, *Etude sur l'armée royale au temps de Philippe Auguste*, pp. 109–12. Audouin indicates that the statement in the *Romance* that Cadoc had with him three hundred *sergents* seems accurate, as this is 'à peu près le nombre d'hommes auquel paraît correspondre la solde indiquée par le Comte général de 1202' (p. 112). Cadoc and his merciless *ruptarii* are mentioned several times by Guillaume Le Breton in his *Philippidos* (II, pp. 135, 182, 192, 220, 260, 264, 267).

him a sizeable income and his desire to serve King John and later Prince Louis suggests that he also wanted to be respected as a political figure. He was evidently thinking on a grand scale, as, in spite of its splendour, Eustace soon had this palace torn down and a new one built in its place. Also described as 'magnificent and well-constructed' ('Qui molt ert riches e bien fais', v. 2159, see v. 2145), this building must have been quite remarkable. The *Romance* says that the foundations alone cost a thousand marks of silver and it states that the king, who was persuaded to loan Eustace four hundred marks to complete it, thought him mad to have undertaken such a monstrous task (vv. 2149–59).

10. *Eustace and the Town of Winchelsea*

There is no evidence for the building of this palace in London, but there is information which links Eustace to another location in England: Winchelsea (now in East Sussex). When the *Romance* describes the battle for the Channel Islands, Eustace's battle-cry is given as *Vincenesel* 'Winchelsea' (v. 1933), and in the *Histoire des ducs de Normandie* there is a passage which relates the difficulties experienced by Prince Louis of France in Winchelsea in early 1217 (pp. 185–86). It appears from this text that Eustace knew the town well, for we are told that he had formerly owned there a very fine galley, which could now be called upon for Louis' service. A reference to Winchelsea also occurs in the *Histoire de Guillaume le Maréchal*, which gives the name of Stephen of Winchelsea (Estienble de Winchesai, v. 17439) as Eustace's executioner. Stephen seems to have known Eustace only too well, as we are told that he seizes the opportunity afforded him to relate to him the dreadful story of all the harm he had done him on land and sea 'because of his cruel treachery' (vv. 17440–44). This Stephen is presumably the Stephen Trabbe (Estievene Trabe) who is mentioned as Eustace's executioner in the *Histoire des ducs de Normandie*. This text describes Stephen as a man 'who had been with him for a long time' (p. 202, lines 8–9).[30]

---

[30] On Winchelsea and Stephen Crabbe see below, pp. 32–34, 38–39.

11. *Eustace and the Channel Islands*

Of more general importance as regards Eustace's career in the period after he left the Boulonnais is his association with the Channel Islands. His conquest and exploitation of Sark have already been mentioned, but they have to be looked at in the context of his activities in connection with the Channel Islands as a whole. In fact Eustace had an important part to play in the history of these islands in the first two decades of the thirteenth century. He is linked to them in the *Romance* and in documentary evidence. The *Histoire des ducs de Normandie* relates that he had been so successful in securing the islands for John that the king made him a grant of rights over them (p. 167, lines 7–8). There is, however, no evidence concerning the nature of these rights or the date of their bestowal.

The available information concerning the history of the Channel Islands in the first years of the thirteenth century has been analyzed by Wendy B. Stevenson in her article 'England, France and the Channel Islands, 1204–1259'.[31] In August 1203 the Islands were definitely under the control of King John. In that month John ordered the Lord of the Islands, Peter de Préaux, to exact from all those possessing lands or rents in Jersey or Guernsey one fifth of their annual income in order to 'maintain the knights and sergeants who are protecting the said islands from foreigners'.[32] These foreigners were presumably the French, who must therefore already have been launching attacks against the islands. The next reference to the islands does not appear until September 1205 and it indicates that the islands were at that time in John's hands. But, writes Stevenson, 'at some time between August 1203 and September 1205, the Channel Islands had fallen to the French and subsequently been recovered' (p. 570). From the point of view of the biography of Eustace the Monk, it is to be noted that the evidence adduced by Stevenson for the recovery of the Channel Islands comes, not from historical documents, but from *The Romance of Eustace the Monk*. There is no precise information about the original loss of the islands to the French, but the date for the loss, according to Stevenson, is the summer of 1204. In May 1204 Peter de Préaux was in command of Rouen, the Norman capital, when it was besieged by Philip Augustus. In

---

[31] On the history of the Channel Islands in the thirteenth century see also R. Lempière, *History of the Channel Islands*, J.H. Le Patourel, *The Medieval Administration of the Channel Islands 1199–1399*, and L.J. Marr, *A History of the Bailiwick of Jersey*.

[32] Pp. 569–70. The Latin text is in the *Rotuli litterarum patentium*, p. 33b.

June 1204 Peter, who was presumably still Lord of the Islands, surrendered all his lands to Philip and then received them back in return for homage to the King of France. These lands would have included the Channel Islands.

The mission referred to in the *Romance*, for which the king provided Eustace with thirty ships (vv. 1912–15), was presumably to recover the lost islands. We are told in the *Romance* (v. 1915) that Eustace went to the Channel Islands and that when he reached them they were defended by a force under the command of a castellan named Romerel. The latter ordered his men to attack Eustace as soon as he and his forces landed. But things did not turn out as the islanders had hoped. After fierce fighting, in which Eustace struck repeated blows with a huge axe, the invaders won the day. Eustace, we are told, finally made himself 'lord and master of the battle' (v. 1945). Romerel's men were driven out of the islands, and Eustace then subjected them to considerable destruction. In the words of the *Romance*: 'There was nothing left to burn either in castle or manor' (vv. 1952–53).

Stevenson thinks that Eustace must have fled from France 'in or shortly after January 1205' and that he probably obtained control of the Channel Islands not long before September 1205, in which month a writ was issued to an unknown individual ordering him to protect the islands of Guernsey, Alderney and Jersey, to maintain peace there and not to cause any damage (p. 570). In Stevenson's opinion it is 'highly probable' that this instruction was given to Eustace the Monk (p. 571). As we have seen, Eustace had subjected the islands, after conquest, to great devastation. In November 1205, King John instructed Enguerrand of Sandwich to hand over to the Archdeacon of Taunton the money which Eustace the Monk and the Justiciar's men had seized and which was in his custody.[33] Eustace had presum-

---

[33] 'Rex, Angero de Sandwico, etc. Mandamus tibi quod denarios quos Eustachius le Moyne et homines justicie arestaverunt, quos habes in custodia, liberes dilecto nostro W. archidiacono Tantoniensi, custodiendos, quia mandavimus ei quod illos a te recipiat' ('The king, to Enguerrand of Sandwich, etc. We inform you that the money which Eustace the Monk and the Justiciar's men have captured, and which you have in your custody, should be handed over for safe-keeping to our beloved W., archdeacon of Taunton, because we have told him that he should receive it from you', *Rotuli litterarum clausarum*, p. 57). The king's order to the Archdeacon of Taunton has also survived (ibid.). See Conlon, p. 109, items 10 and 11. The Archdeacon of Taunton was William de Wrotham, who was responsible to King John for seventeen royal galleys, held mainly in the Cinque Ports. John had in all fifty-one galleys, ten of which were in the care of Reginald de Cornhill (in London, Newhaven and Sandwich) and twenty-four held on the west coast and in Ireland. In addition to these fifty-one royal galleys there were in the English navy a further fifty-two belonging specifically to the Cinque Ports (see De La Roncière, I, p. 302, and Nicolas, I, pp. 134–35, 144–45).

ably returned recently to England with his booty. Stevenson is of the opinion that this evidence 'lends considerable weight' to the story told in the *Romance*, as an expedition involving the Justiciar's men must have had official status (ibid.). We can also note that in December 1205 there was renewed hostility in the Channel Islands from the French and that John had to recover them once more in 1206, this time piecemeal, first Guernsey, then Jersey. There is no specific information about any attempt by John to recover the islands in 1204 or 1205, but we do know that in the spring of 1206 he dispatched five galleys and three large ships to the Channel Islands.[34] Everything suggests that Eustace was involved in the first recovery of the islands, but it is not impossible, as Henri Malo suggests (p. 15), that John gave Eustace the thirty galleys after the instruction to Enguerrand in 1205. If this was the case, Eustace's efforts would have been directed towards the second recovery. Whatever the precise situation with regard to Eustace, the islands were never again continuously in John's hands and he was later to lose one or more of them twice before his death in 1216.

12. *Eustace Departs for France*

One of the central facts of Eustace's life is that at some stage he broke off his relationship with King John and transferred his loyalty to France, not to Philip Augustus himself as much as to his son, Prince Louis. This break cannot have been earlier than the end of 1212, for in October of that year Eustace must have been in John's service, as the king notified the sheriff of Nottingham that he had given Eustace until the end of November to pay off a debt of twenty marks. It looks as though Eustace's lands in Norfolk had been seized for non-payment of this debt. The sheriff was told to restore the lands to Eustace and to allow him to retain them for as long as it was the king's pleasure.[35]

The latest date for Eustace's break with John is thought to be November

---

[34] 'In April 1206 John dispatched to the archipelago 275 sailors in five galleys and three large ships and writs issued to the Wardens of Jersey and Guernsey in May of the same year suggest that by then he had effected its recovery – possibly to the accompaniment of yet further rampage' (L.J. Marr, *A History of the Bailiwick of Guernsey*, p. 134). See *Rotuli litterarum clausarum*, p. 69, and Nicolas, I, p. 142.

[35] For this document see Conlon, p. 111, item 20. In February 1216 Eustace's lands, which were in Swaffham, were given to William de Cuntes (see *Rotuli litterarum clausarum*, p. 248b, and Conlon, p. 113, item 28).

1214. Shortly before then, Philip d'Aubigny, Warden of Jersey, Guernsey and Alderney, mounted an expedition against him and his men in Sark. King John and others were presumably exasperated at the difficulties which Eustace had been creating for them through his piracy and angered by the degree of independence he was enjoying. Philip's mission was partly successful. Although they did not capture Eustace himself, we are told that on 4 November 1214, Roger de Chauton and Thierry de Arden conducted as prisoners from the Island of Sark Eustace's uncle, his brother, and several knights. They were taken to Porchester Castle and the king ordered the constable of the castle to take charge of them and make them pay for their own food. On that day Roger and Thierry received forty shillings for their expenses. They had also brought fourteen men-at-arms from Sark, presumably Eustace's men, and the king ordered them to be handed over to the sheriff of Southampton, who would convey them to Winchester, where they were to be handed over to Matthew de Wallop. The names of several of the prisoners held in Porchester have come down to us: Isaac de Wyrle, Baudouin de Alvington, Baudouin de Werchin, Arnould de Azincourt and Bric de Bruneswerd. The name of Eustace's brother is given as Jacobus (James). A few months later, John's hostility towards Eustace and his men seems to have been relaxed somewhat, as he ordered the constable of Porchester to release those captured on the island of Sark.[36] Stevenson suggests that John's aim in freeing these men and thus attempting 'the restoration of Eustace and his men to favour' could have been to 'build up support' for Magna Carta wherever he could (p. 574). But in reality there can have been little chance of Eustace helping John at that time, as by then he had certainly left England and was devoting his energy to the cause of France.

The circumstances under which Eustace broke with John and left England are not entirely clear. The *Histoire des ducs de Normandie* says that he quarrelled with the king, who seized him and his wife and kept them in prison for a long time (p. 167, lines 8–10). Because of this 'hatred', says the

---

[36] The order to release six named men, including Eustace's brother, was given on 15 January, 1215. A further letter from John to the constable of Porchester, dated 20 April 1215, ordered the release of 'omnes illos qui capti sunt in insula de Serke, homines videlicet Eustachii Monachi' ('all those who were captured on the island of Sark, that is Eustace the Monk's men'). See Conlon, p. 17, Nicolas, I, p. 171, and Stevenson, 'England, France and the Channel Islands', pp. 573–74. For the full documentation relating to this expedition and the subsequent release of the prisoners see Conlon, pp. 111–13, items 21, 22, 23, 24, 26, 27. Henri Malo ('Eustache le Moine', pp. 15–16) places Philip d'Aubigny's expedition in 1207, but this is certainly wrong.

Histoire, Eustace went over to Louis ('por cele haine estoit-il venus à Looys', ibid., line 10). Other accounts tend to place the blame entirely on the shoulders of the Count of Boulogne. If this is correct, Eustace would have left England on account of Renaud's desire for an alliance with King John against Philip Augustus. Ironically, however, it seems that when Renaud began thinking in terms of defecting to John it was to Eustace that he turned as a go-between. 'As early as 1209', writes John Baldwin, 'Renaud may have been in contact with Eustache le Moine' (p. 201). It is known that in 1209 Eustace paid a visit to the Boulonnais to act as ambassador for John. He was at Ambleteuse, near Boulogne, in June 1209, where he was a witness to a charter given to the town, and when back in England he was reimbursed for the expenses relating to this journey.[37] Renaud seems to have adopted a much more positive view with regard to Eustace than he had done on many other occasions and actually to have welcomed him. But King Philip appears to have got wind of Eustace's presence in Ambleteuse and to have become suspicious of these early negotiations between Renaud and King John. For this reason Philip demanded in November 1209 that the Count of Boulogne and the Count of Ponthieu should swear an oath in which they renounced contact with Eustace the Monk. In this oath the name of Eustace the Monk is linked to other 'plunderers' (*predones terre*), including the well-known Hugh de Boves.[38]

13. *Renaud de Dammartin*

Such is the importance of Renaud de Dammartin, Count of Boulogne, to any account of the life of Eustace the Monk that a word about him is in order at this stage. Renaud (sometimes referred to as Reginald or Rainald) was the son of the Count of Dammartin. Boulogne was one of the coun-

---

[37] For the charter and the list of witnesses see E.-T. Hamy, 'La Charte de commune d'Ambleteuse', and Conlon, p. 110, item 15. Also in 1209 Eustace's brother, Jake, went to Flanders to act as ambassador for King John. Both Eustace and his brother received expenses for their services (see *Rotuli de liberate ac de misis*, pp. 119, 127, 123, and Conlon, item 14).

[38] The text (Archives Nationales, JJ, 7 and 8, f. 89v; JJ, 9a, f. 85v) reads as follows: 'Hec est forma sacramenti quod fecerunt comes Bolonie et comes Pontivi quod ipsi abjurabunt Hugonem de Bova, advocatum de Braci, Eustachium Monachum, Manessem Chauderon, Petrum de Nigella et eorum coadjuratores et alios predones terre. Illos eciam quando cicius poterunt competenter bona fide abjurati facient ab omnibus militibus et hominibus et villis suis, et quod si illi in terras eorum vel in terras domini regis venerunt, ubi habeant posse de eis arrestandis vel impediendis, de illis arrestandis vel impediendis posse suum

ties belonging to Artois, and in 1191 Renaud acquired it by abducting and marrying Ida, the heiress to the county. Shortly afterwards, Philip Augustus took possession of Artois, and as Renaud's immediate lord he regularized the situation and confirmed the marriage. Early in 1192 Philip received the homage of Renaud and his wife.[39] But Renaud demonstrated an early tendency towards disloyalty. In 1197, along with some other northern lords, he reached an agreement with Richard, King of England, who had been offering lavish gifts in order to secure some new continental alliances. During the course of 1197 Renaud angered King Philip by ravaging French lands in support of Baudouin, Count of Hainaut and Flanders. The latter had invaded the Tournaisis and then been pursued into Flanders by King Philip, who had ended up having his supply lines cut and being forced to negotiate an embarrassing peace.[40] In 1198 Renaud made peace with Philip, but this did not constitute a guarantee of his loyalty. For, when John acceded to the throne of England in 1199, he renewed his oath of commitment to English interests.[41]

In 1200, however, Renaud's position with regard to King John became difficult. In that year John reached a settlement with Philip Augustus, so Renaud no longer enjoyed John's protection. Philip took advantage of this situation and made a great effort to ensure Renaud's loyalty and to seal a reconciliation with him. In 1201 he affianced his infant son, Philippe Hurepel, to the count's daughter and heiress, Mathilde, and, in addition, as Renaud's father had died recently, he gave Renaud the county of Dammartin on payment of a relief of three thousand marks of silver.[42] For

facient, et eos tradent mandato domini regis. Isti juraverunt: comes Tontivi, comes Bolonie, vicedominus Pinquinaci, Robertus de Tornella, Radulfus de Claromonte'. See Cartellieri, IV, pp. 285, 291. See Baldwin, p. 201, and idem, *Les Registres de Philippe Auguste*, VI, no. 62, Conlon, p. 111, item 17. Robertus de Tornella is probably the Raous de la Torniele (Raoul de Tournelle), who in the *Romance* accompanies Eustace on what turned out to be a fatal crossing of the Channel (v. 2268). See below, note 71.

39 As a price for their homage, Philip 'exacted from them possession of Lens and 7,000 *livres* of Arras above the normal relief. These harsh terms were undoubtedly the price of overlooking Renaud's unorthodox methods' (Baldwin, p. 81).

40 See Baldwin, p. 92.

41 Baldwin states that Renaud was 'an especially noteworthy prize because he owed his entire position to the French king's patronage' (p. 92). For the treaty between Richard and Renaud see Ralph of Coggeshall, *Chronicon anglicanum*, p. 94, and for the renewal of the oath to John on 18 August 1199 see *Rotuli chartarum*, p. 30.

42 See Baldwin, p. 201. Renaud, says Baldwin, was 'further rewarded with three additional Norman counties acquired by conquest – Varenne, Aumale, and Mortain – and by other lands in exchange for the castle of Mortemer which Philip wanted for its strategic position between Normandy and Ponthieu. To strengthen the count's position in the neighboring fiefs, the king also arranged a marriage between the daughter of the count

most of the first decade of the thirteenth century Philip's policy of concili-
ation worked, for Renaud remained loyal to Philip during this period. But
there can be no doubt that Philip's conquest of Normandy in 1204 unsettled him, as it did other lords in the area (such as the Count of Flanders).
These northern lords had been accustomed to safeguarding their independence by playing off the Anglo-Norman monarchs against their
Capetian counterparts.

Renaud's overtures to King John at the end of the decade, seemingly
through the good offices of Eustace, were no doubt an attempt to restore
his freedom of action. J.W. Baldwin refers to Renaud's 'inveterate ambi-
tion', which made him 'susceptible to new intrigues on the part of King
John' (p. 201). In March 1211 Renaud arrived in London to conduct
negotiations with King John and Eustace was there to greet him. Also
present were Henry, Duke of Brabant, brother to the emperor Otto of
Brunswick, and William I, Count of Holland.[43] The aim of this meeting
was to form an alliance against Philip Augustus. This alliance was to come
to grief at the battle of Bouvines in 1214.

The meeting in England between Renaud and Eustace may have re-
opened old wounds. The annals of Dunstable state that on rediscovering
his old enemy the count set up ambushes for him.[44] Henri Malo suggests
that Eustace may have gone back to sea in order to escape from Renaud
(p. 16). However, the count soon had his own worries, for Philip had
discovered his treachery. Open conflict broke out between the two of them
over border castles and Renaud was dispossessed of his fiefs by the king.[45]

---

of Ponthieu and Renaud's brother in 1208, and supported Renaud's military actions
against the count of Guines in 1209' (ibid.).

[43] 'Et tunc mense Martio, venerunt ad regem in Angliam Henricus frater imperatoris
Otonis, et comes de Hotlande, et comes Boloniae' ('And then in the month of March,
there came to the king in England Henry, brother of the Emperor Otto, the Count of
Holland, and the Count of Boulogne', annals of Dunstable, p. 34). See Conlon, p. 110,
item 16. Conlon thinks that Renaud had a powerful enough influence over King John to
turn him against Eustace (p. 17).

[44] 'Et tunc Eustachius pirata, dictus Monachus, aufugit a nobis ad regem Franciae cum
quinque galeis, quia comes Boloniae insidiabatur ei' ('And then Eustace the pirate,
surnamed Monachus, fled from us to the king with five galleys, because the Count of
Boulogne laid snares for him', p. 34). It is not clear whether these ambushes began with
the visit in March 1211 or developed only after the act of homage in 1212 (see note 49
and Conlon, p. 110, item 16).

[45] 'In September 1211 Renaud resigned the county of Boulogne to Prince Louis, who, as
lord of Artois, was his immediate suzerain, and sought refuge with the count of Bar-le-
Duc' (Baldwin, p. 202). See also Baldwin, p. 207, and Roger of Wendover, *Flores historiarum*, II, p. 140.

But Philip was concerned that he might be creating too many enemies, so he soon offered Renaud a pardon, on condition that he came to Pont de l'Arche to receive it.[46] Renaud refused Philip's offer and in May 1212 he returned to England, where, in the presence of a number of witnesses, including Eustace the Monk and Hugh de Boves, he did homage to John and signed an agreement of mutual assistance.[47] He was restored to his English possessions and granted a yearly payment of one thousand pounds sterling.[48]

14. Eustace Transfers his Allegiance to France

Renaud's homage to John may have been the last straw for Eustace, who at some point made up his mind to transfer his allegiance to France. Just how he left England is not clear. The *Romance* states that John had the ports watched in order to prevent his escape, but, we are told, Eustace disguised himself as a minstrel and secured a passage to France (vv. 2166–216). An alternative explanation is provided by the annals of Dunstable, which state that Eustace fled from England to the King of France with five galleys.[49] In whatever way he departed, it seems that on leaving England Eustace did not take with him his daughter, whom he had given to John as a hostage. In the *Romance* he tells the King of France that John had her slain, having first burnt and disfigured her (vv. 2226–29).[50]

---

46 See W.H. Hutton, *Philip Augustus*, p. 84.
47 See *Rotuli chartarum*, p. 186, and Conlon, p. 111, item 18. The charter of alliance between John and Renaud, dated 4 May 1212, is followed by an oath specifically against Philip (Conlon, item 19).
48 Baldwin, p. 208. The counts of Boulogne traditionally possessed a number of territories in England. But whether they were able to enjoy possession of them depended on the vicissitudes of politics.
49 See above, note 44. There is no evidence for Eustace's arrival in France with five ships, but the annals of Dunstable also tell us that 'the King of France took all the ships of England which came to his land; and therefore the King of England took many from the Cinque Ports' ('Et res Franciae cepit omnes naves Angliae quae applicuerunt in terra sua: et ideo rex Angliae cepit multos de Quinque Portubus', p. 34). See Conlon, p. 110, item 16. Baldwin tells us that John summoned a feudal levy in June 1212 and that 'Philip countered by seizing all English ships in his ports, to which John responded in kind' (p. 208). See Cartellieri, IV, pp. 310–16. If Eustace did bring the King of France five galleys, this would have been, as Brian Levy points out, a 'dot considérable et prudente' for his new lord (p. 4).
50 From an item in the *Rotuli litterarum patentium* (I, part 1, p. 144) we learn that the abbess of Wilton was told to release Eustace's daughter (see Conlon, p. 113, item 29). Malo thinks that the daughter was probably dead, for John would not have released the

Eustace certainly did not leave John's service immediately after the homage ceremony in May 1212. We have seen that he was still on good terms with John in October 1212 and he may have remained so for as long as a couple of years after that. But there may be intriguing evidence in the *Romance* that he had gone over to the French side as early as the spring of 1213. By the end of May of that year Philip had amassed his ships at Damme, the port of Bruges, ready for an invasion of England. But he paused for a moment to march against Ypres, Bruges and Ghent in order to avenge himself on Ferrand, Count of Flanders, who, when requested to do so, had failed to present himself to the king for the purpose of pledging his support for the planned invasion of England. Whilst he was away from Damme and besieging Ghent, Philip's fleet was attacked by five hundred English ships. The English fleet, led by William Longsword, Renaud de Dammartin, Hugh de Boves and other Flemish lords, destroyed four hundred French ships. Hearing this, Philip reacted quickly and caught the enemy by surprise. Many of them were killed, but Renaud, thanks to his relatives, just managed to escape (he was to be less fortunate in 1214 at the battle of Bouvines, at which he was captured and thereafter kept in prison until his death in 1227). Philip realized that his plans for an invasion of England had now been thwarted, so he set fire to the remainder of his ships in order to prevent them from falling into enemy hands.[51]

We know that Cadoc was present at Damme. Whilst the allies were massing to attack the French ships, he was, in Baldwin's words, 'busy plundering the inhabitants of Damme' (p. 211). But a passage in the *Romance*, which seems to have been misinterpreted by the earlier editors, may indicate that Eustace was also involved, on the French side. In Francisque Michel's edition we read in vv. 2257–58:

> Od lui mena le roi Adan.
> Ses nés perdi li rois cel an.

('He [the king] took with him Adam le roi. That year the king lost his ships.') Michel (p. xxiv) was convinced that he has found in this passage the name of the author of the *Romance*, Adam le roi. But Foerster and Trost, who edited the text in 1898, saw no trace of an Adam le roi in

---

hostage of someone with whom he was at war (p. 17). The *Histoire des ducs de Normandie* mentions Eustace's wife, who is said to have been imprisoned along with her husband as a result of the quarrel between Eustace and John (p. 167, lines 8–10).
[51] See F.W. Brooks, 'The Battle of Damme', Baldwin, pp. 123, 211, Hutton, pp. 84–85, Petit-Dutaillis, pp. 41, 44.

v. 2257. In their edition the first of these two lines (their v. 2256) reads: 'Od lui mena le roi a dan' (v. 2256). For them the term *dan* is related to the Latin *damnum* 'loss' ('zum Schaden', p. 76) and they interpret the line in conjunction with the following line, which relates the loss of the king's ships: 'He [Eustace] brought the king to disaster, for that year the king lost his ships.' Denis Conlon has in my view a more plausible interpretation of this line. He reads (his v. 2258): 'Od lui mena le roi a Dan.' The meaning of the line would then be: 'He [Eustace] conducted the king to Damme.' Whatever the correct interpretation, the poet clearly felt it important to tell us that on some occasion during Eustace's period of 'support' for him, the king lost his ships. The most likely occasion for this to have happened was the disaster at Damme. The author goes on to tell us that Eustace was charged with the betrayal of these ships:

> Wistasce en fu ochoisonnés
> K'il avoit traïes ses nés. (vv. 2260–61, ed. Conlon)

Eustace, the author adds, escaped punishment because no one was brave enough to attempt to prove the charge (vv. 2262–65). This wording could be taken as suggesting that in the author's view there was some truth in the allegation. In an earlier episode in the *Romance*, we recall, King Philip is said to have experienced Eustace's powers at first hand (vv. 1294–367), and if in reality he had this or a similar encounter with Eustace he would no doubt have been unable to trust him completely thereafter. He may therefore have been a natural target for Philip's suspicions that someone had informed the English of the presence of a fleet which threatened the security of their country. Certainly, at this stage in his life Eustace was a sufficiently powerful and devious figure for any sovereign or magnate to wonder whose side he was on. Baldwin points out that in 1212 Philip was aware that there was a group of figures 'who might be persuaded to join any alliance against the Capetians if they could be convinced of its probable success' (p. 207). Amongst this group, says Baldwin, was 'the mercenary captain Eustache le Moine' (ibid.). Moreover, although there is no documentary evidence for Eustace's involvement in the disaster which overcame the French at Damme, it might be regarded as surprising if Eustace had not participated in this affair in some capacity, on one side or the other.

If Eustace had gone over to France and was involved in the disaster of Damme on the French side, he probably left England in late 1212 or early 1213. But, whatever the date of his departure, once he had left John's service and transferred his 'loyalty' to France, he and his men continued, in Stevenson's words (p. 574), 'to act somewhat independently'. During the period of the English civil war, 1215–1217, he seems to have again obtained control over one or more of the Channel Islands. The annals of Dunstable state that during this war, which was waged on land and sea, 'Eustace the Monk, a formidable pirate, and Geoffrey de Lucy, seized the king's islands on behalf of Louis and set a great deal of discord in motion for him'.[52] An approximate date for this seizure would be the summer of 1216.[53] In September 1217, after the death of both Eustace and John, Louis concluded with the new English king, Henry III, the Treaty of Kingston, in which we learn that Louis was to send letters patent to Eustace's brothers ordering them to return the islands to Henry. The brothers were threatened with the loss of their lands and ultimately with not being protected by the peace treaty. In the event the brothers responded promptly, and by the end of September 1217 Philip d'Aubigny was established as Warden of all the Islands. Henry Cannon, in his article 'The Battle of Sandwich and Eustace the Monk', expresses the view that the elaborate arrangements in the treaty for ensuring obedience to its terms confirms the 'high degree of independence' which Eustace had enjoyed from his base in the Channel Islands. These islands were certainly in Eustace's possession at the time of his death (Cannon, p. 654).

The fact that Eustace was as active in the service of Prince Louis as he had been in John's is confirmed by Walter of Coventry in his *Memoriale*.[54] But apparently neither Louis nor Philip Augustus himself was any more successful than John in gaining complete control over Eustace's maritime activities. In 1216 the papal legate, Cardinal Gualo, applied to Philip for safe-conduct through his realm, and Matthew Paris in his *Chronica majora* states that Philip responded by stating that he could not guarantee matters where Eustace the Monk was concerned: 'Through our land I shall willingly furnish you safe-conduct; but if by chance you should happen to fall

---

[52] 'Nam Eustachius dictus Monachus, pyrata fortissimus, et Galfridus de Luchi ex parte Lodowici insulas regis ceperunt, et multas seditiones ei moverunt' (p. 46).

[53] Stevenson, p. 575. The statement in the annals follows the allusion to the visit of Prince Louis to London in June 1216. The latest evidence that the islands were in John's hands dates from October 1215 (ibid.).

[54] Walter points out that Eustace changed sides as fortune dictated, that he caused maximum disturbance on both sides of the Channel and that he occupied a number of islands, presumably the Channel Islands ('Expugnatis igitur aliquot navibus eorum, occisus est Eustachius cognomento Monachus, qui nunc ad hos, nunc ad illos, ut fortuna ferebat, divertens, a multis retro diebus mare illud et littora tam cismarina quam transmarina plurimum turbaverat, insulas etiam nonnullas plurimum occupaverat', II, pp. 238–39). See also Roger of Hoveden, *Chronica*, p. 184.

into the hands of Eustace the Monk or any other of Louis' men, who guard the sea-routes, do not blame me if any harm befalls you.'[55] At this stage in his career, writes Henri Malo, 'our pirate was truly the master of the sea' (p. 17).

15. *Eustace as Servant of Prince Louis*

In the French navy Eustace seems to have risen with great speed to the position of admiral. From Prince Louis' point of view he would have been valuable on two counts. His first mission was to recover the lost Channel Islands. Hawkes states that, after quarrelling with King John, Eustace 'was given command of a large fleet by the French king, with the aim of restoring the Channel Islands to the Duchy' (p. 96).[56] In this, as we have seen, he was at least partially successful. But secondly, and more importantly, rebellious English barons had summoned Louis in 1215 and Eustace's mission was to help him secure the throne of England. The aid he afforded Louis in this enterprise was, in Cannon's words, 'considerable, indeed almost essential' (p. 654). The author of the *Histoire des ducs de Normandie* tells us that Eustace devoted a great deal of effort to Louis' cause ('Si s'estoit molt penés de cel afaire', p. 167, lines 9–10) and that he made the Channel crossing many times 'as one very skilled in such matters' ('Maintes fois en ot la mer passée, comme chil qui moult en savoit', p. 167, lines 11–12). In 1215, when Philip Augustus himself was still heavily involved in the attempt to secure the crown of England, and perhaps even before the English barons had asked Louis to take the throne, Eustace was sent to England. His aim was to supply the English barons with siege machines. He succeeded in landing them at Folkestone, and John's considerable alarm and annoyance at this are recorded by Ralph of Coggeshall.[57] Without these machines

---

55 'Per terram nostram propriam conductum libenter praestabo; sed si forte incideris in manus Eustachii Monachi, vel aliorum hominum Ludovici, qui custodiunt semitas maris; non mihi imputes, si quid sinistri tibi contingat' (II, p. 653). See Conlon, pp. 113–14, item 32, Nicolas, I, p. 174, and Petit-Dutaillis, p. 94.

56 Hawkes adds: 'They occupied Sark in 1215 and 1216, but were finally evicted in 1218 by the English Crown's Warden of the islands, Philippe d'Aubigny' (ibid.). Philip had been Warden of Guernsey and Alderney since August 1207 and Warden of Jersey since November 1212. He was made Warden of Sark in December 1214.

57 *Chronicon anglicanum*, p. 172. See Petit-Dutaillis, p. 69, Cotton, p. 655, and Nicolas, I, p. 172. Nothing is known about this landing at Folkestone, other than that Eustace was aided in his mission by a certain William de Abrincis. Having initially been angry with William, on 18 September 1215 the king offered him pardon for all his offences, 'sive

John's opponents would have been, in Maurice Keen's words, 'hard pressed in their campaign' (pp. 54–55). One could even speculate that Eustace's success in providing the English barons with French military equipment could have been a significant factor in John's willingness to issue Magna Carta on 15 June 1215. Just before his meeting with the barons at Runnymede, John tried in vain to win over Philip Augustus, and, knowing from personal experience just what Eustace was capable of, he must have been alarmed at the prospect of further arms reaching his opponents.[58]

When, on the evening of 20 May 1216 Prince Louis himself set sail from Calais in an attempt to seize the crown of England, he crossed the Channel in Eustace's own ship.[59] The entire fleet is said by the chroniclers to have contained seven or eight hundred vessels, which had been collected together by Eustace himself in Calais, Gravelines and Wissant. So Eustace was clearly at that time a man of immense power and prestige.[60] Indeed, N.H. Nicolas, in his *History of the Royal Navy*, comments that: 'During the summer of 1216, the Straits of Dover and other parts of the English Channel appear to have been filled with the vessels of Prince Louis of France, under the command of Eustace the Monk' (I, p. 174). Early in 1217 Eustace again proved his usefulness to Louis when he helped him in potentially disastrous circumstances in Winchelsea, a town with which, as we have seen, he had some familiarity. At the end of February of that year Louis was about to leave England for France when he fell into a trap. He had learned that Henry III's men, under Philip d'Aubigny, had surprised and captured the town of Rye. Intending to oust Henry's men, Louis made his way to Winchelsea. But he found the town deserted, as its inhabitants had left to join Philip and his fleet in the port of Rye. Before leaving they

pro Eustachio Monacho qui applicuit apud Folkestanum, sive pro aliis' ('both with respect to Eustace the Monk who landed at Folkestone and with respect to other things', *Rotuli litterarum patentium*, I, part 1, p. 155b).

[58] Petit-Dutaillis states that Philip's action of sending war machinery to the rebels in England 'contributed to the grant of Magna Carta' (p. 69). For the political and military circumstances surrounding the grant of Magna Carta see J.C. Holt, *Magna Carta*, especially chapters 5 and 6, and W.S. McKechnie, *Magna Carta*, especially part 1.

[59] See the *Histoire des ducs de Normandie*, p. 167, line 2, and Roger of Wendover, *Flores historiarum*, II, 2, pp. 159–160, 572, 628–29, 634. Because of the strong north-east wind, Louis' ships were dispersed and his single vessel was forced to anchor at Stonar in the Isle of Thanet. There Louis met no resistance and he proceeded with his ships to Sandwich. He succeeded in conquering the whole of Kent with the exception of Dover Castle and went on to join the rebellious barons in London. See Nicolas, I, p. 174, and Petit-Dutaillis, pp. 98–100.

[60] See the *Histoire des ducs de Normandie*, p. 167, line 1, and Roger of Wendover, *Flores historiarum*, II, p. 160.

had broken their mills, so, in spite of the availability of corn in the town, the French had no way of grinding it efficiently as a source of food. To make matters worse, bands of reckless loyalists from Sussex, under the command of Willikin de Casinghem (William of Kensham), came up behind the French and cut off all their escape routes. Louis' troups were blockaded within Winchelsea and forced to live off nuts and hand-ground corn. They were soon on the brink of starvation, with the English harassing them constantly. Eustace was either with Louis in Winchelsea when he arrived there or he joined him there by managing to get through the blockade. He constructed two stone-casters (*perrieres*), which successfully pounded the enemy ships with a hail of missiles. The French had captured some large ships which were already in the town, and Eustace began to construct on one of them a huge fortification, in the form of a castle. The castle stood high above the sides of the ship and everyone was greatly impressed by it. But the English had found out about Eustace's creation and, we are told in the *Histoire des ducs de Normandie*, just before its completion they arrived before the town one evening in their ships. They took the galley away and before the very eyes of the French hacked it to pieces (p. 185, lines 6–27). Shortly afterwards, help arrived for the French. A number of knights from Artois, who had remained in London, had gone to Romney in Kent and summoned assistance from France. Two hundred ships had immediately been sent by the prior of the monastery of Waast, who was one of the *baillis* of the Boulonnais. Before any naval battle could begin, the English, who had panicked because of the accidental loss of one of their cogs (a broadly built ship with a rounded bow and stern), fled without even defending Rye. Louis plundered the town and returned to France.[61] Cannon states that 'it was largely owing to the strenuous efforts

---

61 The principal source for the Winchelsea campaign is the *Histoire des ducs de Normandie*, pp. 183–87. The present account of the blockade is based mainly on Petit-Dutaillis, pp. 141–42, but see also Carpenter, *The Minority of Henry III*, p. 27, Norgate, *The Minority of Henry III*, pp. 21–24, and Powicke, *The Thirteenth Century*, pp. 9–10. Norgate tells us that Louis and his men had taken possession of several large ships which were lying in the harbour of Winchelsea and that one of the vessels, sent from Boulogne, had, through the bravery of the mariners, managed to evade the English fleet and reach Winchelsea (p. 23). The captain of this ship would 'in all likelihood', says Norgate, have been Eustace the Monk. It would have been after his arrival in this way that he set about building a castle on one of the large ships (p. 23). The addition of a large castle to his ship may have been a development which Eustace owed to the Italians (see above, note 12, and Jouan, pp. 15–16). We should note also that the original town of Winchelsea has now disappeared and its exact location is not precisely identifiable. It was washed away during the second half of the thirteenth century. J.A. Williamson in *The English Channel* states that 'it must have been a port of unusual size and energy' (p. 102).

of Eustace that Louis survived the Winchelsea campaign'. He adds that 'we may assume that Eustace saw him safely home from this, and was waiting for him when Louis was prepared to recross the Channel to England once more' (p. 655).

16. *The Death of Eustace*

Eustace was killed on 24 August 1217 at the battle of Sandwich. Such was his prestige that the English victory on that day signalled the end of the war itself. Information about the battle comes to us from a variety of sources. There are substantial accounts in the *Histoire de Guillaume le Maréchal*, the *Histoire des ducs de Normandie*, the *Chronica majora* of Matthew Paris and *The Romance of Eustace the Monk*.[62] The account in the *Romance* is brief and it paints a rather more positive picture of Eustace's death than we find in the chronicles. Eustace, we are told in the *Romance*, fought very hard. He was captured and killed, largely as a result of the English tactic of throwing powdered lime into the eyes of the French who, blinded, ceased to be able to fight effectively. The poet does not tell us who killed Eustace or the precise circumstances of his death. Eustace's end is swift and it is starkly related: 'Those who were tormenting them were up wind. They jumped on to Eustace's ship and treated his men very cruelly. All the barons were captured and Eustace the Monk was killed. His head was cut off and at once battle ended' (vv. 2298–307).

We can compare this account of Eustace's death with the presentation of the known facts by the naval historian René Jouan. In his *Histoire de la marine française* Jouan begins by observing that at the time of the battle of Sandwich the French were masters of the stretch of water between France and England and that it was Eustace the Monk who had brought this about. Prince Louis was in need of reinforcements and provisions, since, in

---

[62] The battle of Sandwich and Eustace's death are referred to by a large number of chroniclers. See, for example, the annals of Dunstable, III, p. 50, the annals of Waverley, pp. 205–06, the chronicle of Lanercost, p. 24, the chronicle of Laon, p. 719, the chronicle of Mailros, p. 128, the chronicle of Mortemer, p. 356, Guillaume Le Breton, I, p. 314, Matthew Paris, III, pp. 26–27, the metrical chronicle of Robert of Gloucester, p. 716, Ralph of Coggeshall, p. 185, Roger of Hoveden, p. 184, and Roger of Wendover, II, p. 165. For a version in English of the account in the *Histoire de Guillaume le Maréchal*, see H. Rothwell, *English Historical Documents*, pp. 91–93. There is a verse account of the battle in the *Chronique rimée* of Philippe Mousquet (ed. Le Baron de Reiffenberg, 3 vols, Brussels: Hayez, 1836–45, vv. 22691–718).

the aftermath of King John's death on 12 October 1216, he was having more difficulty than anticipated. John's rebellious barons were beginning to restore their allegiance to the English throne. The first convoys crossed easily, but on the night of 23 August 1217 a convoy of seventy ships left Calais. It was to convey to Louis a substantial amount of war material despatched by his wife, Blanche of Castille.[63] Ten ships with castles (*accastillés*), under the command of Eustace the Monk, acted as escort. The convoy was tempting prey for the English sailors and on 24 August a squadron of ships from the Cinque Ports hove into view. The English fleet manoeuvred to take advantage of the wind and then suddenly they attacked the escort ships. Eustace, says Jouan, had overcome these same enemies twenty times, but on this occasion his ships were too heavily laden to operate as combat ships. They were carrying a cargo which was too precious to entrust to the merchant ships. A ferocious struggle took place, but the efforts of the French were in vain. They eventually succumbed, and their leader, Eustace the Monk, was put to death. The whole convoy was taken or destroyed. The mastery of the sea passed to the English and Louis' hopes were dashed. On 11 September he abandoned his claim to the English throne.[64]

There is nothing in Jouan's succinct account of the battle which contradicts the *Romance*. Thus we have yet more confirmation of the fundamental accuracy of the Old French text. Other historians, drawing on the wide variety of sources available, fill in some of the details relating to this important naval engagement. By far the most substantial of these accounts is that by Henry Cannon in his article 'The Battle of Sandwich and Eustace the Monk'. Cannon begins by discussing the background to the battle, its personnel and the number and type of ships involved (pp. 658–62). As the battle was about to begin, 'the French had the advantage in respect to the wind, the choice of the day, the number of their ships, the number of their knights, and possibly the number of their men-at-arms' (p. 662). Moreover, they enjoyed a further advantage: 'They had the redoubtable Eustace for their pilot' (ibid.). The French, in contrast, were handicapped by their

---

63 For the contribution of Blanche of Castille to Louis' cause see Elie Berger, *Histoire de Blanche de Castille*, pp. 26–28. It was she who in Calais formed the army and the fleet which were to be despatched to help Louis.

64 Jouan, p. 18. For other accounts of the battle written by historians of the English or French navies, see De La Roncière, II, pp. 312–15, and Nicolas, I, pp. 176–84. See also Carpenter, *The Minority of Henry III*, pp. 43–44, Ellis, *Hubert de Burgh*, pp. 40–45, Keen, pp. 60–61, Petit-Dutaillis, pp. 167–69, and Powicke, pp. 12–13.

overladen ships (especially the one in which Eustace was travelling), by their lack of large vessels and by their over-confidence (pp. 662–63).

Using Cannon's account and those by other historians (especially Sir Nicholas Nicolas, the historian of the British navy), we can supplement Jouan's information with the following observations. The English fleet from the Cinque Ports was led by Hubert de Burgh, the king's Justiciar and governor of Dover Castle. He was conscious of the need to prevent the formidable French force from landing, but he faced considerable opposition from those around him. They were aware that the French fleet was commanded by Eustace the Monk and consequently were afraid of putting to sea.[65] The English squadron seems to have consisted of sixteen large, well-manned ships and twenty smaller vessels. When the English set sail, the French, who had left Calais with the intention of proceeding up the Thames to London, had completed a substantial part of their journey. The wind was southerly and the French, who were sailing in rank in close order, were going large and attempting to round the North Foreland in Kent. Although at first it appeared to the French that they were going to be attacked by the English, the latter in fact made no effort to engage with the enemy. Moreover, the French at this stage would not have been too concerned at the sight of the English ships, for in view of their recent record of success over the English they would have assumed that such a small force of fishing vessels would cause them no problem. Matthew Paris has Eustace the Monk exclaim, when he sees the English keeping their wind and seeming to be heading for Calais: 'I know that these wretches think they can invade Calais like thieves, but that is useless, as it is well defended.'[66] The *Histoire de Guillaume le Maréchal* states that when they saw that Hubert de Burgh was apparently seeking to avoid them the French sailors yelled out derisively 'The Hart! The Hart!', as if the English fleet were a deer escaping from the huntsmen (vv. 17360–61). Certainly, as Matthew Paris states, Eustace himself had no wish to attack the English at that stage, and he appears to have recommended that their ships should be allowed to proceed unhindered.

The English, however, with Hubert de Burgh out in front and the rest advancing in column behind him, had a clear-cut stratagem. They were

---

[65] For the preliminary discussions which seem to have taken place before the departure of the English fleet see Nicolas, I, pp. 177–78.

[66] Matthew Paris presents two slightly different versions of the battle. This comment by Eustace occurs in the variant version and is published by Bouquet, *Recueil des historiens de la Gaule*, XVII, p. 741. See Nicolas, I, p. 179.

attempting to gain the wind of the French, and having done so they launched a fearsome assault from behind, with the wind full in their sails. A different, and almost certainly erroneous account of the beginning of the battle is given by Guillaume Le Breton, who states that the overall French commander, Robert de Courtenay, opened the fighting by launching an attack on the English in his own ship, expecting the others to support him. None came to his assistance and he was forced to surrender.[67] It is more likely that the English, as they reached the sterns of the French vessels, hurled grapnels into them in order to fasten the ships together and prevent their escape. Several of the French ships manage to sail on and escape, but the majority of the smaller vessels were caught. They had clewed up their sails in readiness for a fight and had difficulty gaining speed. 'The action,' writes Nicolas, 'commenced by the crossbowmen and archers under Sir Philip d'Albini pouring volleys of arrows into the enemy's ships with deadly effect' (I, p. 179). Eustace's ship, the French flagship, veered and struck the second ship of the English column, which contained Richard Fitz-John (a man who has sometimes been confused with King John's illegitimate son Richard[68]). A fierce, but indecisive battle took place between Richard and Eustace. Then other English ships came up with the wind and began to attack Eustace's ship on all sides. The remaining French ships were unable to turn quickly enough to bring him any assistance. There seem to have been two reasons for this. On the one hand, the French had not been expecting a serious engagement and they seem to have underestimated the desperate nature of the predicament in which Eustace found himself. On the other hand, in Cannon's words, 'arrayed in rank in close order, with a strong wind blowing them on their course, it would have been extremely difficult so to manoeuvre to the left flank as to attack the English column effectively' (p. 664). Eustace's ship was in particular difficulty because it was laden down by the weight of a trebuchet and by the horses, knights and treasure it was carrying.

Eustace was soon grappling with four English ships, of which one was a large cog. As well as its size, the cog enjoyed the advantage of superior height and its mastheads proved an excellent base from which to hurl down missiles. According to the *Histoire des ducs de Normandie* both

---

[67] Guillaume Le Breton, *De gestis Philippi Augusti*, I, p. 314, Cannon, p. 63, and Nicolas, I, p. 180 (note c).

[68] See Matthew Paris, *Chronica majora*, III, p. 27. John's son Richard was only eight years old at the time. In addition, his name appears from time to time as Eustace's executioner, e.g. Lloyd, p. 395, and Taylor, p. 248 (see also below, note 74). The error was corrected by Petit-Dutaillis, p. 168.

stones and lime were used (p. 201, line 27). In particular, the use of finely pulverized lime, contained in great pots which, according to the *Romance*, broke on the sides of the ship, was a very effective ploy. The use of lime is also mentioned by the *Histoire de Guillaume le Maréchal* (vv. 17400–04), Roger of Wendover and Matthew Paris. The lime created a great cloud which, as the French were before the wind, completely blinded them, thus preventing them from mounting an effective defence. The *Romance* insists on how valiantly the French fought to stop the English boarding their vessel until the time came when they could no longer see (vv. 2289–99).[69] This is confirmed by Matthew Paris, who indicates that, in spite of their great bravery, the French fell because of their inexperience in naval tactics.[70] The English then charged on board and used their axes to cut away the rigging and halyards, with the result that the French were enveloped by the sails and thus greatly restricted in their movements. A huge slaughter of men took place. Only the nobles were spared, as they could be ransomed. One of the nobles known to have been taken was a certain Raoul de Tournelle. He is mentioned in the *Romance* as having accompanied Eustace on his voyage (v. 2268), yet another proof of the fundamental accuracy of the *Romance*. In all, one hundred and twenty-five knights are said to have been captured, plus more than a thousand soldiers of lower rank.[71]

A search began for Eustace and he was finally discovered in the hold (Matthew Paris says the bilge-water). According to Matthew Paris, he was found by men named Richard Sorale and Wudecoc.[72] Eustace offered a large sum of money as a ransom (ten thousand marks according to the *Histoire de Guillaume le Maréchal*, vv. 17436–37). Matthew Paris adds that he made an additional offer of faithful service to the King of England![73] As we saw earlier, the name of his executioner is given in the *Histoire des ducs*

---

[69] This use of chemical warfare seems to be without parallel in British naval history (see Ellis, *Hubert de Burgh*, p. 44).

[70] *Chronica majora*, III, p. 27. See Nicolas, I, pp. 180–81.

[71] The figures are provided by the chronicle of Mailros (p. 128) and the chronicle of Lanercost (p. 24). See Nicolas, I, p. 182. The capture of Raoul de Tournelle is mentioned in the *Histoire de Guillaume le Maréchal* (vv. 17405–24) and in the chronicle of Mailros, p. 128 (where he is called Radulphus de Tornellis). The *Histoire* gives his captor as Renaut Paien de Gernesie (Ranulf Paganus). See above, note 38.

[72] *Chronica majora*, III, p. 27.

[73] 'Optulit pro vita sua et membris inaestimabilem pecuniae quantitatem, et quod de caetero sub rege Anglorum fideliter militaret' ('He offered for life and limb an incalculable amount of money and promised henceforth to fight faithfully under the King of England', ibid.).

de Normandie as Stephen Trabe or Crave (p. 202, line 8). The *Histoire de Guillaume le Maréchal* gives the name as Stephen of Winchelsea and it states that Stephen began by recalling to Eustace the trials he had caused on both land and sea. He offered him the choice of having his head cut off on the trebuchet or on the rail of the ship. Then, however, seemingly without waiting for a reply, he sliced off his head (vv. 17436–56).[74]

Once Eustace the Monk was dead and his ship captured, the battle was virtually over. Maurice Keen observes that Eustace's men must have had a great deal of faith in him, as after his death they seem to have lost all will to fight: 'The capture of his ship was the signal for the whole French fleet to turn in retreat' (p. 61). Most of the large ships got back safely to Calais, but almost all the smaller ones were lost. The garrison of Dover Castle had been able to witness the battle, and when the conquerors returned with their spoils consisting of gold, silver, silk garments and many different types of weapons they were received by the clergy in full ecclesiastical dress. Prayers of thanksgiving were offered out of gratitude for this unexpected success. The threat which over the years Eustace the Monk had posed to the sailors in the waters around Britain is well illustrated by the fact that his head was fixed on to a lance and taken to Canterbury. It was afterwards paraded throughout the south of England, perhaps throughout the whole of England.[75] On seeing it, many people must have breathed a sigh of relief. The man whom Petit–Dutaillis (p. 99) calls 'one of the most feared men of his time', a man who 'sowed terror in the Channel', was no more. The English had won a great victory, one which Sir Nicholas Nicolas

---

[74] The story that before being beheaded Eustace was confronted with a catalogue of his misdeeds is paralleled in Matthew Paris' account, in which his executioner, here John's son Richard, calls him a foul traitor and castigates him for his false promises (*Chronica majora*, III, p. 27). Stephen Trabe (Crave or Crabbe) is known to us from contemporary documents as a notorious pirate himself. After Eustace's death he was in the employ of King Henry III. See *Rotuli litterarum clausarum*, I, p. 193, II, pp. 44, 45b, 50b, 68, 90, and *Rotuli litterarum patentium*, 1216–25, p. 96, and 1225–32, pp. 10, 11, 14, 44.

[75] 'Et la tieste Witasse le Moine fu fichie en une lance; si fu portée à Cantorbire et par le païs por moustrer' (*Histoire des ducs de Normandie*, p. 202). The anonymous chronicler of Laon (*Chronicon anonymi Laudunensis canonici*) states that Eustace's head was displayed throughout England ('caput vero Eustacii est per Angliam delatum in pilum', p. 719d). A similar statement about Eustace's head being transported throughout several locations in England ('cujus caput abscissum, delatum est per diversa loca Angliae super palum') is made by Nicholas Trevet in his *Annales* (p. 201). See also Philippe Mousquet, *Chronique rimée*, vv. 22709–10 ('Li ont jus la tieste copée. / Par le païs, sour une lance, / L'ont portée, pour sa viltance').

considers to be 'worthy of the first place' in the list of British naval successes (I, p. 183).

17. *The* Romance: *Manuscript, Date, Author*

Eustace must have been an immensely charismatic figure. 'No one would believe,' writes the author of the *Histoire des ducs de Normandie*, 'the marvels he accomplished or which happened to him on many occasions' (p. 167, lines 12–13). However frightening a figure he was, there is surely a strong element of admiration in these words. The fact that chroniclers wrote about him a hundred or more years after his death shows that he was not easily forgotten. After having been something of a legend in his own lifetime, he became a larger than life figure as the years went by. As we have seen, he was considered capable of conquering England single-handedly. Moreover, of course, one person with poetic gifts, the author of *Li Romans de Witasse le Moine*, thought that his exploits were worth relating at some length. He presumably expected them to be both entertaining and instructive.

Li Romans de Witasse le Moine is a text of 2307 lines, written in octosyllabic rhyming couplets, the traditional metre for medieval French romance. It is extant in just one manuscript: Paris, Bibliothèque Nationale, fr. 1553, ff. 325v, col. b – 328v, col. b. In addition, two further versions of the *Romance* are known to have existed at one time. When an inventory of the library of King Charles V of France was made by Gilles Malet in 1373, and repeated in 1380 by Jean Blanchet, two manuscripts containing the *Romance* were found in the collection. Clearly their presence in such a library confirms that at that time the *Romance* enjoyed a certain popularity at the highest level.[76] Charles V's collection of books, which forms the nucleus of that now housed in the Bibliothèque Nationale, was soon to be pillaged and dissipated, and the Eustace manuscripts remain lost. The text, as it has been preserved in MS 1553, is not likely to have been composed

---

[76] For the inventories see J. Barrois, *Bibliothèque protypographique ou librairies des fils du Roi Jean*, items 71 and 81, and L. Delisle, *Recherches sur la librairie de Charles V*, II, items 1103 and 1223. The entries in Delisle read: 'Du bel Ascanor de la Montangne et de Wytasse le Moyne, avec de grans truffes' (item 1103); 'Vuitasse le Moyne, rymé, en ung meschant cayer sans nulles couvertures' (item 1223). It may be that one of the manuscripts was taken by the Duke of Bedford on the occasion of the English invasion in 1424 and the other given by Charles VI to his wife Isabeau of Bavaria in 1390 (see Conlon, pp. 11–12).

before 1223, since in v. 1298 and v. 2254 Louis, son of Philip Augustus, is called King Louis ('Li roi Phelippe od lui mena, / Qui toutes ses os i mena, / Et son fil le roi Loëy / Molt mena biele gent od li', vv. 1296–99; 'Le roi Loëy fist passer / A grant navie outre la mer', vv. 2254–55). Louis was not crowned king until his father's death in 1223.[77] In the manuscript the *Romance* is preceded by the *Roman de la Violette*, which has been copied by the same hand. At the close of the *Roman de la Violette* we read: 'Chi define li Roumans de Girart de Nevers et de la Violete / Qui fu escris l'an de l'incarnation nostre signour Jhesu Crist Mil. cc. et iiij. xx. et quatre / El moys de fevrier' ('Here ends the Romance of Girart de Nevers and the violet, which was written in the year of the incarnation of our Lord Jesus Christ 1284, in the month of February').

A date around 1284 is normally taken to be the latest by which *The Romance of Eustace the Monk* could have been written. From the way in which the story is told, however, a date in the region of 1284 seems too late. Even if the legend of Eustace was still going strong towards the close of the thirteenth century, it is unlikely that an author writing at that time would have included such a wealth of detail or that the detail would have been so accurate. Everything suggests that fairly soon after Eustace's death the author wrote down what he knew, with the aim of providing as detailed a biography of Eustace as he could muster. He almost certainly invented the opening sections which relate Eustace's adventures in the south of France, knowing nothing much more than the fact that Eustace had travelled and that he had a reputation for sorcery. He may not have known much about how or why Eustace became a monk and what his real behaviour had been like in the monastery. But he no doubt knew a great deal about the Eustace of the Boulonnais, about Count Renaud and the nobility of that region. His knowledge of Eustace's time as a servant of King John, of his conquest of the Channel Islands and of his piracy was distinctly sketchy, but he knew enough to provide the basic outline of Eustace's life during this period. His acquaintance with the precise details of Eustace's period of service to Prince Louis was also not extensive, but what he says seems broadly to be true.

Thus, we are dealing with an author who came from the Boulonnais, or from not too far away from this region. The number of place names relating to the Boulonnais or the surrounding area is considerable (over thirty such toponyms are found in the text). Some of the medieval forms

---

[77] However, in 1215, the English barons, as a way out of the impasse in their conflict with King John, recognized Louis as King of England (Holt, *Magna Carta*, p. 147).

are difficult to identify clearly (e.g. Basinguehans, v. 310, and Heresingue-hans, v. 311, see above, note 17), but the author would certainly have expected his audience to have known where these places were and to have been interested in the topographical detail he was conveying. There was clearly no absolute need for an author attempting to relate the story of the legendary Eustace the Monk to provide so many references to precise locations. Even more significant perhaps is the presence in the story of the vassals of Renaud de Dammartin and the relatives of Eustace the Monk, men who were in many cases one and the same. In this regard two passages from the *Romance* are of particular interest. When Eustace, disguised as a White Monk from Clairmarais, sits down beside the count and asks for a cessation of hostilities between himself and Eustace, the count, who is still intent on capturing Eustace, refuses. One of the count's servants tells him to capture Eustace there and then, because he is sitting beside him. At that point a series of supporters intervene and confuse the issue by confirming the identity of the fake monk and providing a contradictory description of the real Eustace (vv. 430–543). These men are: William de Montcavrel, Hugh de Gannes, Hugh de Belin, Aufrans de Cayeux and Walet de Cou-pelle.[78] Later, when Eustace is finally captured by the count, a similar group of individuals makes a plea that he should not be dealt with sum-marily by Renaud himself, but sent to the King of France for a proper trial (vv. 1638–741). On this occasion the names of the men are: William de Montcavrel, Ansiaus de Cayeux (presumably the same as Aufrans de Cayeux), Hugh de Belin, Walet de Coupelle and Bauduin d'Aire.[79] Hugh de Gannes is put in charge of transporting Eustace to the king, but he lets Eustace's supporters know what is happening and indicates the precise place, 'be-neath Beaurain', where they can rescue him. The rescue party is led by William de Fiennes (v. 1738). On both occasions the dialogue between Count Renaud and Eustace's supporters is vivid and convincing and one has the impression that the author is making a genuine attempt to recon-struct these scenes. He may have wished to involve imaginatively men with whom he was acquainted and who were indeed involved historically.

Where, then, did he get the names and the details of the conversations?

---

[78] The forms of the names in the text are Guillaumes de Montquarrel (v. 533), Huës de Gaune (v. 536), Huës de Belin (v. 538), Aufrans de Caieu (v. 540) and Wales de la Capiele (v. 542).

[79] On this occasion the forms are Guillaumes de Mont Chavrel (v. 1670), Ansiaus de Caieu (v. 1686), Huës de Belin (v. 1690), Wales de la Chapiele (v. 1696) and Bauduïns d'Aire (v. 1708). See above, note 24. Walet de Coupelle died before 1231 and William de Moncavrel between 1216 and 1218.

No doubt from one or more of those present, unless he was present himself. We note that four men were present on both the occasions mentioned above: William de Montcavrel, Aufrans (Ansiaus) de Cayeux, Hugh de Belin and Walet de Coupelle. One name in particular stands out, Walet de Coupelle (Walo de Capella). He was also present in London in May 1212 when Renaud de Dammartin did homage to King John.[80] No doubt he could have given the author specific details of what went on in the conversations in the Boulonnais and also told him how Eustace had reacted to Renaud's arrival in London. He seems to have died around 1231. The *Romance* tells us that Eustace wanted to leave England as soon as he saw Renaud: 'Dont s'en vaut revenir li Moigne / Quant il vit Renaut de Bouloigne' ('Then the Monk decided to return home when he saw Renaud de Boulogne', vv. 2164–65). Walet could have given the author this information, as well as an outline of Eustace's other activities whilst serving John. This information could have been picked up by Walet whilst he was in London, probably to a certain extent from Eustace himself.[81]

If the wealth of topographical and personal detail in the *Romance* was to have any value and to make an impact on the public for whom the text was destined, one cannot but think that the text was composed fairly soon after Eustace's death. Was it written during the reign of Louis VIII (1223–1226) or in the decade or so after his death? If it was written between 1223 and 1226, the references to Louis as 'King Louis' would make perfect sense. One might object that, whilst he was still alive, it may have been unwise to remind Louis of the French defeat at the hands of the English in 1217. But in fact the battle as described in the *Romance* contains no reference to Louis or to Eustace's role in an attempted invasion of England. The battle is presented as another episode in Eustace's life, one which happened to go badly wrong. There is only one reference to the English in the account of the battle and that is to say what a great slaughter of them took place (v. 2278). The only precise reference to King Louis in the later stages of the text (the first occurs when Eustace is still in the forest, v. 1298) is to his successful crossing of the Channel, thanks to Eustace the Monk (vv. 2254–55).

Another possible objection to a date of composition within Louis's reign derives from the fact that Renaud de Dammartin was still alive

---

[80] See *Rotuli chartarum*, p. 186.
[81] One should not overlook the possibility that William de Fiennes could have been the informer. He certainly met Eustace in 1209, and he too was present at Renaud's homage ceremony in 1212. See above, note 24.

(albeit in prison, where he died, chained to the wall, in 1227). Relatives or former vassals of Renaud would no doubt have formed part of any audience in the Boulonnais region for a romance about Eustace the Monk, a man they would all vividly remember. But we have to be aware that Renaud was not originally from the Boulonnais, which had a string of heiresses and no male heir, and that since the battle of Bouvines in 1214 he had been dishonoured. Eustace the Monk, however, was a native of the area, and after his spectacular death in 1217 he may have acquired heroic stature. Although he repeatedly calls him a master of cunning and trickery, the author of the *Romance* never condemns Eustace outright. The rather moralistic final couplet in the text ('Nus ne puet vivre longhement / Qui tos jors a mal faire entent' / 'No one can live a long life if he always attempts to do harm', vv. 2306–07) is probably no more than a traditional authorial ploy, similar to those used by the writers of fables and fabliaux, to bring a text to its conclusion. Authors may not have wanted to seem to be adopting too positive a view of heroes who were clearly also villains. But for the author of the *Romance* Eustace was evidently more of a hero than a villain. More importantly he was a man about whom one could tell a good story.

Be that as it may, a date between 1223 and the early 1230s is likely for the composition of *The Romance of Eustace the Monk*. The name of the author of the text is, of course, unknown to us. As we have seen, Francisque Michel thought that he had found his name in v. 2257, which he prints as 'Od lui mena le roi Adan' ('He took with him King Adam'). This line, in Michel's view, contains an allusion to the well-known thirteenth-century author, Adam le roi, also known as Adenet le roi. Adam / Adenet is the author of four works, *Beuvon de Conmarchis*, *Les Enfances Ogier*, *Berte aus grans piés* and *Cleomadés*. But Adam le roi was not born until around 1240, and his principal period of literary activity, as Albert Henry has established, was 1269–85.[82] Moreover, his biography is 'remarquablement connue' (Henry, p. 11), and if he had composed *The Romance of Eustace the Monk* we could expect that this information would have come down to us. Adam was born in the Brabant, and after the death of his protector, Henry III, Duke of Brabant, in 1261 he turned for support to Guy de Dampierre, Count of Flanders. He had no known contacts with the Boulonnais, nor did his patron, Guy de Dampierre, have any clear reason to be interested in Eustace or Renaud de Dammartin.

---

[82] See A. Henry, *Les Oeuvres d'Adenet le roi*. 5 vols, Bruges: De Tempel, 1951–71, I, p. 47.

Denis Conlon suggests Gerbert de Montreuil as a possible author of the *Romance* (p. 13). Gerbert is known to us as the author of the *Roman de la Violette*, the text which immediately precedes *The Romance of Eustace the Monk* in the extant manuscript (but one of the lost versions of *Li Romans de Witasse le Moine* was next to the *Escanor* of Girart d'Amiens).[83] The date of composition of the *Roman de la Violette* is 1227–29, so Gerbert's period of literary activity is ceratainly more appropriate than that of Adam le roi. However, until further discoveries shed new light on the problem, *Li Romans de Witasse le Moine* must remain anonymous.

18. *The Structure of the Text*

(i) *The Prologue*

The text opens with a thirty-eight line Prologue. In it we learn that Eustace entered the Benedictine monastery of Saint Samer and that he paid a visit to Toledo, where he acquired knowledge of necromancy. In Toledo, we are told, he spent a whole winter and summer communing with the Devil in an abyss and learning a wide range of magic tricks and techniques of deception. The Devil informed him that he would do a great deal of harm during his lifetime and that he would end up dying at sea, after having waged war against kings and counts.

(ii) *The return from Spain*

There follows a section in which, during his return journey from Toledo to the Boulonnais, Eustace and his two travelling companions wreak havoc in and around the town of Montferrant (probably Clermont-Ferrand). This section occupies 182 lines (vv. 39–219) and it can be divided into two main episodes. The first (vv. 39–159) concerns the tricks played by Eustace and his aged companion on a tavern-keeper's wife and the unsuspecting inhabitants of the town. They have no local money on them and the woman refuses to accept the coins minted in Tours and Paris which Eustace is carrying. She makes them pay double for the meal and to gain revenge Eustace makes her bare herself and then release the wine from her barrels. The townspeople come running up and they too bare themselves, before

---

83 See *Le Roman de la Violette ou de Gerart de Nevers par Gerbert de Montreuil*, ed. D.L. Buffum. Paris: Picard (SATF), 1928.

finally realizing that Eustace and his companions are responsible for what has happened. Their attempts to follow the travellers come to grief when the old man casts a spell which causes a river to appear between the pursuers and the pursued. The townspeople are forced to retreat, but Eustace continues his revenge by returning to the town and getting the old man to cast another spell. This one causes a fight to break out between the inhabitants of the town. Finally, his honour satisfied, Eustace throws an ear of grain between them and all is well again. Even the wine returns to its barrels.

The second episode (vv. 160–219) concerns a carter who accepts, for an agreed sum of money, to transport Eustace and his companions a few leagues on his cart. But the journey is too bumpy and uncomfortable for the travellers and they ask the carter to slow down. His refusal to do so is the signal for a spell to be cast on him whereby he has the impression of travelling backwards whilst in reality still moving forwards. The carter eventually asks the passengers to get down and he waives the fare. Then, seeing that in fact he has not been going backwards, he realizes his mistake. But the travellers have succeeded in obtaining free transport.

(iii) *Eustace in the Boulonnais*

The third section of the *Romance* is by far the longest. It occupies seventy-two per cent of the text (vv. 220–1881) and recounts Eustace's experiences as a monk, his emergence from the monastery as a result of the murder of his father, the subsequent judicial duel, his period of service to the Count of Boulogne, the charges of malpractice made against him, his break with the count and his spell as an outlaw in the forests of the Boulonnais. This section could also be divided into two parts, one before and one after the break with the count. Eustace's life in the forest is clearly the centre-piece of the entire text, and it could be said that everything before it acts as an introduction to it and that everything which follows is a consequence of it. The divisions of the pre-forest section are:

1. vv. 220–279   Eustace as a monk; general disruption in the monastery
2. vv. 280–303   Eustace and the abbot; a specific example of Eustace's powers
3. vv. 340–369   Eustace's early life; his father, the murder and the judicial duel
4. vv. 370–399   Eustace serves the count; accusations against him; the rupture

The episodes relating to Eustace's skirmishes with Renaud are mainly brief sketches, culminating in his capture and escape. They are:

1.	vv. 400–429	The burning of the count's two mills
2.	vv. 430–549	Eustace, in disguise, sits beside the count
3.	vv. 550–579	Eustace steals the count's horse, Morel
4.	vv. 580–639	Eustace disguises himself as a shepherd; capture of the monks
5.	vv. 640–659	Eustace cuts out the tongue of one of the count's servants
6.	vv. 660–741	Eustace, betrayed by one of his young spies, takes vengeance
7.	vv. 742–775	Eustace cuts off the feet of four of the count's servants
8.	vv. 776–853	The count, captured by Eustace, refuses the offer of peace
9.	vv. 854–899	Eustace escapes from the count disguised as a straw seller
10.	vv. 900–929	Disguised as a penitent, Eustace steals the count's horses
11.	vv. 930–993	Eustace sends a merchant to the count with his tithe
12.	vv. 994–1068	Eustace escapes from the count disguised as a charcoal-burner
13.	vv. 1069–1141	Eustace escapes disguised as a potter
14.	vv. 1142–1171	Eustace climbs into a tree and imitates the nightingale
15.	vv. 1172–1185	The count arrests everyone on sight
16.	vv. 1186–1283	Disguised as a woman, Eustace dupes one of the count's servants
17.	vv. 1284–1293	Eustace is betrayed by a priest on whom he takes revenge
18.	vv. 1294–1365	Eustace in conflict with King Philip; he attacks the rear-guard
19.	vv. 1366–1395	Hainfrois stumbles upon Eustace, but is allowed to leave
20.	vv. 1396–1422	Eustace, disguised as a leper, steals the count's horse
21.	vv. 1423–1493	As a one-legged man, Eustace again dupes the count
22.	vv. 1494–1545	Eustace escapes capture by reversing his horse's shoes
23.	vv. 1546–1637	Eustace, disguised as a carpenter, escapes and steals a horse
24.	vv. 1638–1717	Eustace is captured, but supported by some of the count's vassals

25. vv. 1718–1743   Eustace is rescued by William de Fiennes
26. vv. 1744–1777   Eustace takes his revenge by robbing the abbot of
                    Jumièges
27. vv. 1778–1819   Eustace steals four horses in payment for his
                    mackerel
28. vv. 1820–1881   Eustace deceives the count's men with inedible
                    pastries

(iv) *Eustace as pirate and mariner*

He becomes a servant first of King John, then of Philip Augustus and
Prince Louis.

At this point there is a sudden shift in the narrative. The fourth and last
section of the *Romance* (vv. 1882–2305) begins when Eustace leaves the
Boulonnais and makes his way to England. The subsequent episodes are as
follows:

 1. vv. 1882–1910   Eustace goes to King John and enters his service
 2. vv. 1911–1953   Eustace conquers the Channel Islands
 3. vv. 1954–2125   Eustace humiliates Cadoc
 4. vv. 2126–2135   Acts of piracy by Eustace
 5. vv. 2136–2159   Eustace builds a palace in London
 6. vv. 2160–2216   Renaud comes to England and Eustace escapes to
                    France
 7. vv. 2217–2250   Eustace enters the service of the King of France
 8. vv. 2251–2265   Eustace serves Louis and is implicated in the
                    disaster at Damme
 9. vv. 2266–2305   Death of Eustace at sea whilst crossing the Channel
10. vv. 2306–3207   Epilogue

The author evidently had no wish to compose a romance containing
sections of equal length. If we divide the text into three episodes, the first
would consist of 182 lines, the second of 1661 lines and the third of 424
lines. A division into four parts would split the second episode (Eustace in
the Boulonnais) into a section of 180 lines (the pre-forest section) and one
of 1497 lines (Eustace as outlaw). Whichever division we choose, our
decision will point to the fundamental intent of the author: to contruct a
story which is dominated by a description of Eustace's period as outlaw,
the period in his life which is overwhelmingly concerned with his struggle
against Renaud de Dammartin, Count of Boulogne. We can also note that
the count's role in the pre-forest section (his failure to exact justice in
respect of the murder of Eustace's father and his reaction to Hainfrois'

accusations) is crucial to the rupture which leads to Eustace's period of outlawry. In the final section the count's homage to King John is given as the reason why Eustace leaves England and offers his service to the King of France. *The Romance of Eustace the Monk* is in many ways *The Romance of Eustace and the Count.*

19. *A Note on the Translation*

This translation is based on the edition by Denis J. Conlon: *Li Romans de Witasse le Moine: roman du treizième siècle, édité d'après le manuscrit fonds français 1553 de la Bibliothèque Nationale, Paris,* Chapel Hill, North Carolina: University of North Carolina Press, 1972. The verse text has been rendered as faithfully as possible in English prose. The text could not be described as difficult, but there are passages in which the meaning remains unclear. On the whole I have avoided extending the notes by drawing attention to linguistic problems. I have not followed the author's changes in narrative tense, preferring to render the text in the English past tense. When translating dialogue, the problem of when to use the shortened forms 'wouldn't, couldn't, weren't', etc., was encountered and the decision taken to render each case on its merits in order to ensure a smooth flow to the text.

The Romance of Eustace the Monk

I SHALL TELL YOU briefly the tales I know about the Monk. He went to Samer, about eight leagues away from the sea, and there he became a Black Monk.[1] When he returned from Toledo, where he had learned necromancy, there was no one in the kingdom of France who was so skilled in the arts of magic and sorcery. He played many tricks on many people. He had spent a whole winter and summer in Toledo under ground, in an abyss where he spoke to the Devil himself, who taught him the tricks and the ruses by which everybody is deceived and taken in. He learned a thousand spells, a thousand magic tricks and a thousand incantations. He found out how to look into a sword and how to recite the psalter backwards, and from the shoulder of a sheep he had many a lost object returned to its owner. He knew how to look into a basin in order to restore losses and thefts, how to bewitch women and how to cast spells over men.[2] There was no one from there to Santiago de Compostella who knew as much about the zodiac, the firmament or the vault of heaven. He could imitate the chimera, the beast which no one can get to know, and he caused monks to fart in the cloister. When Eustace had learned enough, he took leave of the Devil. The Devil told him he would go on living until he had done a great deal of harm. He would wage war against kings and counts and be killed at sea. (1–38)

Eustace came back to France, where he later performed many a vile deed. One night he came to Montferrand, where he accomplished a most devilish act. The day after his arrival, he had a copious meal prepared before he left by a wealthy inn-keeper's wife, a very arrogant and haughty woman. It was at grape-harvest time, and Eustace had three companions who were returning with him from Toledo. The must from the grapes was all around the house in thirty barrels. Eustace ate and drank with the inn-keeper's wife, and when they had eaten, I believe, and it came to paying the bill, Eustace had no money from that locality, only coins minted at Tours and Paris.[3] The woman overcharged them considerably and refused their money. For the three sous they had actually spent they had to pay six sous or more. Eustace, who was an expert in craftiness, cast a spell over the woman as he was about to leave the town. He threw down on to the threshold an ear of grain over which he had made an incantation, and the woman immediately bared herself as far as her girdle and pulled out all the spigots from the first barrel she could lay her hands on. She put all her wares on the market, crying: 'Come along now, gentlemen!' (39–73)

The wine ran all over the house and men and women came running up. When they had crossed the threshold, the men lowered their breeches and the women stripped to the girdle or the navel. You have never heard such an infernal commotion as they created in that house. They removed the spigots from the barrels and the wine ran all over the streets. Everyone came running up, but no one dared go into the house without showing their bum to everyone else who entered. For that reason no one else dared go in. Eventually they realized that the travellers who had eaten there were responsible for all this. The townsmen made haste and went charging after Eustace, catching up with the travellers three leagues away from Montferrand. The townsmen yelled at them: 'My lords, you will pay for this!' Eustace looked around and said to his companions: 'There is someone following us. What are we going to do about it?' 'By my head,' said a bearded old man who had spent twenty years in Toledo, 'do not be alarmed. I shall create so much fear amongst them that there's no cleric, townsman or priest who would want to remain here, not even for five marks.' The old man cast a spell, and a river came down between the clerics and the townsmen, huge and broad, deep and dark, wider than the Seine or the Loire. The frightened townsmen retreated, but the river kept following them, always hard on their heels. They went backwards, being afraid of drowning, and the travellers followed them. (74–118)

The townsmen returned to Montferrand and the travellers went in after them. When Eustace entered the town, he started his tricks again. The townsmen raised the alarm, and Eustace winked at the old man as a sign that he should cast another spell to frighten these people. The tocsin started to ring, and as the people began to assemble the old man immediately launched his spell. They all grabbed each other by the hair and a great uproar set in amongst them. For a squabble without the use of club or sword you have never seen the like. As each one came up, he gave the first person he encountered a thump on the neck. Many a blow was administered, and throughout the town of Montferrand two thousand inhabitants came to blows with each other. Some were pushing, others pulling; one fell like a cow, another sent his companion flying, and another yelled: 'Ladies! Gentlemen!'⁴ No one entered the fray without receiving some sort of blow.

Eustace threw an ear of grain down between them and separated them at once. They departed immediately and peace was restored as before. None of the wine had been lost and everything was just as it had been. All the women who had earlier undressed put their clothes back on, and the men who had taken down their breeches pulled them up again. Everyone went home, and Eustace continued on his way. No one followed him. (119–59)

Eustace caught up with a carter, who was driving a cart pulled by his four horses. He was going for a barrel of wine six leagues away. Eustace and his companions asked the carter how much he would charge to carry them to the town he was heading for. He replied: 'Twelve pence'. 'You will have them willingly.' When the deal had been done, they climbed up and off they went at a good pace. The carter struck the horses and they bounded forward down a path. Eustace's bum was grazed, for the cart jolted along, taking them at too fast a pace. He said to the carter: 'May God soon put some hindrance your way! You are driving us much too fast. May God send you some misfortune!' 'Fair lord,' said the carter, 'there can be no delay. I have to complete my journey and I think it is already past nones[5].' Eustache saw that it was to no avail: 'Go slowly, scoundrel,' he said, 'a curse on you, for you have taken the skin off our bums!' (160–90)

The peasant struck his horses forcefully and the bearded old man immediately began to cast a spell: the more the peasant advanced, the more it seemed that he was going in reverse. The old man began his spell and the carter began to go in reverse. He began to strike his horses and they retreated angrily. He began to curse God and to threaten his horses: 'Come on now, Martin! Come on now, Fauvel! By my bowels and my brains! Gee up! Move forward, by my teeth! I'm not far off breaking all your bones. Come on now! You stubborn old mare! I'm never going to get any help from you.' The carter began to go out of his mind, for he thought he was constantly going backwards. 'My lords,' he said, 'get out, because you brought me bad luck when you climbed up! I'll let you off the fare entirely.' When they all saw that he was letting them off and that they had paid their debt, they jumped out of the cart, and the carter, who realized that he had been deceived, found out that he had not gone backwards, but rather constantly forwards. (191–219)

Eustace came to the Boulonnais. He became a monk at Samer, where he performed many devilish acts before leaving the abbey. He made the monks fast when they should have eaten and made them go barefoot when they should have worn shoes. He made them curse when they should have been reciting the office and made them misbehave when they should have been giving thanks. (220–31)

One day the abbot was in his chamber. He had been bled after a journey, and a plentiful supply of food and drink had been prepared for him, pork and mutton, wild geese and venison. Eustace, who has since mocked many a worthy man, came before the abbot: 'Lord,' he said, 'here I am. Are you going to invite me to stay for a while? If I thought I could get something to eat, I would tell you my business.' The abbot said: 'You are a fool. A curse on me if you do not get a good beating tomorrow and if you are not held captive in the chapter house.' Eustace said: 'People who are threatened go on living! They struggle on for a long time.' Eustace went into the kitchen and saw in front of him a tub which was full of water. He stared at it and began to cast a spell over it. The water began to change colour, becoming as red as blood. Eustace sat down on a bench and spotted half a pig. In everyone's hearing, he cast a spell over it, first to the right, then to the left, and it took on the appearance of an old woman, ugly, hump-backed and sour-faced. The cooks took to their heels and went to tell the abbot, who came there and saw the hideous old woman. In the hearing of all the monks, he yelled: 'In the name of God, let us get out of here. This man is a demon.' Eustace cancelled the spell and carried the meat to one of his neighbours, an inn-keeper who thought very highly of him. All night long he ate and drank there and gambled everything at backgammon. The bell was left with no means of ringing. Eustace wagered everything, the cruci-fixes and the statues. Not even a pair of monk's boots was left. Eustace the Monk stole everything. (232–79)

May it not be displeasing for you to hear this. This very night I shall tell you something which will make you laugh. You will soon hear me tell and relate it. Some people, I believe, tell tales of Basin and Maugis. Basin swindled many a town and Maugis performed many a deceitful trick. For Maugis stole the crown of France by necromancy, and also stole Joyeuse, Courte and Hauteclaire, and Durendal which shone so brightly.[6] Basin also robbed Maugis and Maugis robbed Basin. But no more about Maugis; I shall tell you about Eustace the Monk, who was, I believe, much more skilful than Maugis or Basin. Neither Travers, nor Barat, nor Haimet ever knew so many tricks. Now hear about Eustace the Monk, who waged war against the Count of Boulogne for a very long time. This was how it began. (280–303)

Eustace, of whom you hear me speak, was born in Course in the Bou-lonnais. We know for certain that his father was called Bauduin Busquet and that he was one of the peers of the Boulonnais. He was very learned in trials and in the law, and he was killed near Bazinghen. Hainfrois de Heresinghen had him killed and put to death there, because he wanted to get hold of his property. Bauduin Busquet was causing him difficulty in respect of a fief, which was being contested in court, and he gave him a blow which led to the quarrel. Eustace had become a monk at Samer, near Boulogne, and on the death of his father he left the abbey and presented himself before the Count of Boulogne, saying: 'Lord, Hainfrois has murdered my father. Grant me justice, I beg you.' So Hainfrois was summoned to court and Eustace rose to his feet: 'Lord,' he said, 'listen to me. My father has been killed and murdered, and Hainfrois is the man who killed him and put him to death. He is my mortal enemy.' 'I deny this,' said Hainfrois. 'In God's name, in the name of mankind and in my own name, there was no witness to this and no one has heard tell of it. But I call upon my friends for support.' (304–35)

Commitments were soon made and pledges and hostages handed over. Together with thirty members of his family Hainfrois gave his age on oath. He swore that he was sixty years old and even more, he thought. So it was immediately agreed that one of his relatives, or a man-at-arms, could fight on his behalf. But he had no relative or friend who dared to undertake the battle for him or to defend his person. So a certain individual named Eustace de Marquise, who was tall, bold, strong and handsome, was suggested to him.[7] So the battle was agreed. A nephew of Bauduin Busquet, a young man named Manesier, got up. He was a tall youth, handsome and strong. He accused Hainfrois of the murder of his uncle, whom he had killed, and said that he would prove it. So the battle was joined, Eustace against Manesier; each man had a high opinion of his own ability. Both were strong and fierce. The battle took place at Etaples and the contest between the two vassals was keen. Then Eustace the Monk came before the Count of Boulogne: 'Lord,' he said, 'I shall have you know without fail that I disassociate myself from this battle and that I shall never make peace. I shall avenge my father's death.' (336–69)

The Monk left the battlefield and Manesier was soon killed. Then the Monk entered the count's service and took complete charge of his affairs. He was seneschal of the Boulonnais, peer and bailiff, as was his right. Hainfrois denounced him to the count and made things very difficult for him. The count summoned Eustace immediately and asked him about the offices which he held and why he had discharged them badly. Eustace said without delay: 'Here I am, now that you have summoned me, quite ready to explain myself before your peers and your barons. I am a peer of the Boulonnais.' The count said: 'You must come to Hardelot to explain things to me. There you cannot lie to me.' Eustace said: 'This is treason; you want to put me in prison.' The Monk left there and departed from the count on bad terms. He was later to cause him distress on many occasions. The count seized his lands and set fire to his fields. Eustace the Monk swore that he would regret burning his fields and that it would cost him ten thousand marks. (370–99)

One day Eustace the Monk came to two mills outside Boulogne, which the count had built. He made his men stay back and in one mill he found a miller, whose head he threatened to cut off if he did not go immediately to the celebrations being held for the marriage of Simon de Boulogne: 'You will tell everyone that Eustace the Monk has come to provide them with light, because they haven't enough light to eat by. I am going to make them such a pair of candles that the mills will be lit up.' The miller went to the count and told him about Eustace the Monk. The count jumped up at once from his meal and yelled with great urgency: 'Come on now, after Eustace the Monk!' The mayor jumped up, as did the provost, and the tocsin[8] soon began to ring. When Eustace heard it ringing, he started to leave. They began to pursue him, but could not catch up with him. At the marriage of Simon de Boulogne, Eustace the Monk set fire to these two mills you have just heard about. That was the pure truth.[9] (400–29)

One day, Eustace, who knew many a trick, was at Clairmarais. There he learned that the count was going to Saint-Omer, so he donned a white cloak and a broad-sleeved gown. He borrowed two monks from the abbot and all three mounted their horses at once. Eustace set off with stirrups made of medlar wood. Between two valleys he met up with the count, who was leading three mettlesome horses. The count greeted Eustace and Eustace bowed to him. The count arrived at one of his properties and Eustace made up his mind to go and speak to him. He began to retrace his steps at once and arrived just as the count had dismounted. Then Eustace the Monk sat down beside the Count of Boulogne. Now what an absolute fool he was to have sat down beside him, knowing that if he were captured he would be burned or hanged! 'Lord,' he said, 'in God's name, have mercy. I beg you to abandon your anger against Eustace the Monk.' The count said: 'You should say no more. If I can get my hands on Eustace, I shall have him skinned alive. Eustace came like a crusader to burn down my two mills. He is launching a war against me. From now on I shall be on the look-out for him. If I can get my hands on him, he will die a wretched death. I shall either have him tortured or else hanged, burned or drowned.' (430–69)

Eustace said: 'By my cloak! Peace would be an excellent thing. For Eustace has become a monk and you are Count of Boulogne, so you should show him mercy. In God's name, lord, I beg you to stop being angry with him and he will become your close friend. Lord, make peace with him; one should show mercy towards a sinner!' The count said: 'Hold your tongue and don't speak to me about this again. Get out of here, get away. I have no wish to talk to you. I cannot put my trust in a monk where peace with Eustace the Monk is concerned. By the Virgin Mary's bowels! I think this monk is spying on me. There is no worse tyrant on earth. I am very much afraid he will cast a spell over me. Lord monk, what is your name?' 'I am called brother Simon. I am a cellarer from Clairmarais. Eustace came to our house yesterday, together with thirty men, fully armed, and he begged the lord abbot to seek peace on his behalf with you.' The count said: 'Your abbot had better not agree to give him lodging, for I would go and tear him to pieces. He would be no friend of mine, if he housed my enemy. I should soon have his tonsured head off. Lord monk, where were you born?' 'At Lens, lord, where I spent twenty years.' 'Upon my word,' said the Count of Boulogne, 'you look like Eustace the Monk in appearance and facial features, in body, looks and stature, in eyes, mouth and nose, apart from the fact that you are tonsured. But you have a broad tonsure, red shoes, a white gown and a pale face. If it were not purely out of respect for God, I would have taken all three of you hostage. Get out of here! Be on your way!' (470–517)

The other two monks were terrified and Eustace did not feel safe. With the count there were some of his relatives and his own people. The count had made all the peers in the Boulonnais swear three times that they would hand Eustace over to him and not fail to do so just because they were related to him. A man-at-arms came to the count and told him about Eustace the Monk. 'Lord,' he said, 'what are you waiting for? Eustace is sitting beside you. Capture him and you will be acting wisely. It is he, I tell you in truth.' 'Listen to this son of a whore, this good-for-nothing,' said William de Montcavrel. 'He is Dom Simon the cellarer. I can recognise him as easily as I can a penny.' 'That is true,' said Hugh de Gannes. 'Eustace is not so yellow.' 'No,' said Hugh de Belin. 'He was born in Lens near Hénin.' 'Upon my word,' said Aufrans de Cayeux, 'Eustace is not yellow or blue.' 'No,' said Walet de Coupelle, 'he is rather reddish around the cheeks.' (518–43)

The two monks trembled with fear. Eustace said: 'A lot of people look alike.' They were all saying their *miserere*; each man's heart thumped. Eustace took his leave of the count. All three set off, and Eustace, who knew so many devilish tricks, went into the stable and had a serving-boy saddle one of the count's horses called Morel, a magnificent and handsome animal. Then he mounted and rode off at a great pace. As he left, he told the boy to announce to the count that Eustace was taking away Morel, and the serving-boy yelled out at once: 'Help, help! Virgin Mary!' The count and the rest of his household jumped up. 'What's the matter?' said the knights. 'A devilish, enemy monk is leaving here on Morel.' 'Get going,' said the count, 'by my brains, by my bowels and by my heart and lights! After him, as quick as you can!' 'Since he's on Morel, he'll never be caught. For Morel runs like the wind and the man taking him has the Devil in his head. I know in truth that I shall never manage to catch him.' 'God,' said the count, 'why didn't I capture him when he was sitting beside me?' The serving-boy said: 'I did tell you, but you didn't believe what I said.' (544–77)

The count had his household, his men-at-arms and his knights mount their horses, and they charged off after Eustace. They set off in pursuit of Eustace, who came to a hamlet. There he left Morel with a man he knew, and realizing that he was being pursued took off the clothes he was wearing and put on some others. He donned a light cloak, hung a club round his neck and went to guard a flock of sheep, which were grazing on a stretch of moorland. The Count of Boulogne came that way and said: 'Young fellow, which way did a white monk on a black horse go?' 'Lord, he went right through that valley, on a horse as black as a mulberry.' The count departed without delay and pursued Eustace at top speed. Feeling himself to be in danger, Eustace left his sheep and entered the forest once more. The count spurred his horse like a madman, leaving all his companions behind. He saw the two monks fleeing and yelled to them angrily: 'By the legs of God, you will not get away. You will never escape me like this.' The monks prayed that God would save them from prison, and from harm and cruelty: 'Oh! Oh! Our Lady, Virgin Mary, make the count desire to do us no harm or shame! Eustace the Monk, the Devil, the Enemy, has been captured and the count wants to take us as well. I'm afraid he will hang us. He is close to us now, here he is! In God's name, let's beg him for mercy.' (578–619)

You have never seen two monks who so lost their source of strength. They were very distraught and thought they had lost everything. They had dismounted in a valley and the count did the same and seized them by their hoods. They got down on their knees. 'In God's name, have mercy,' said Dom Vincent. 'By the legs of God,' said the count, 'you will not escape me like that. You will be hanged from a tree.' 'Lord, have mercy! Lord, have mercy!' 'By St Honorius, you will not escape me like that,' said the count. 'For you are proven thieves. You will give me back my horse, Morel, or you will soon be put to death.' The count had them both bound and left lying in a garden. Eustace, who was in the forest, was carefully watching the count's harness. A serving-boy was leading a pack-horse, and Eustace knocked him to the ground, cut out his tongue and sent him to the count. He went running to the count and told him about the Eustace the Monk, as someone unable to speak. He began to stutter. 'What the devil's the matter with you?' said the count. Having had his tongue cut out, he replied: 'Belu, belu'. He could not tell his story. A squire said to the count: 'He is the one who was leading our packhorses. He has fallen into bad hands and lost his tongue at least. Eustace has got his hands on him and held on to our pack-horse.' (620–59)

The count made his way back towards Eustace and passed through the forest of Hardelot, taking many different paths. Eustace had two spies who spied for him night and day, never staying long in the same place. He had brought up and raised the two boys. The count continued in pursuit of Eustace, and one of the boys came up to him, saying: 'Lord, what would you give me if I told you where my lord was? I belong to Eustace the Monk.' 'Upon my word,' said the Count of Boulogne, 'if you tell me where he is, you will be doing yourself a favour. You will become one of my retainers at court.' 'Lord, he is sitting eating. If you follow me, you will soon have caught him.' 'Get going,' said the count, 'I'll follow you and come behind you at a good distance. But mind he does not suspect anything. I'm afraid he might play a trick on you.' The other spy heard what this boy said. He realized his treason and that he had betrayed his lord, who had brought him up. He went to Eustace and told him that the other spy had sold him to the count. Eustace said: 'Get away from here. When the boy comes here to deceive and betray me, I shall string him up, for he has fully deserved it.' (660–92)

The spy left Eustace and his other spy came back. Eustace said: 'You have got to help me to cut this branch'. 'Willingly,' said the boy. He cut the little branch. 'Twist it well and make it into a rope.' He twisted the rope, very much afraid, and Eustace slipped it round his neck. He put the little rope round his neck. 'In God's name, have mercy on me,' said the boy. 'Lord, why do you wish to hang me? Could you not wait until I have confessed my sins?' Eustace said: 'You know a lot of evil tricks, but here am I, and I know even more. You have fallen into bad hands. You thought you could make me wait here until the count could capture me. I have no time to confess you. Get up there and speak with God! You will climb up that tree and be closer to God when you speak to him. Get on up and tell me how you sold me to the count.' 'Lord,' he said, 'by St Remi! I did sell you and betray you. What devils told you that? There will never be anyone who can kill you. Get going, there is no time to lose.' Eustace said: 'Before I go, I

58

shall see you hang. Go on up and do it yourself.' The boy climbed up the tree at once and hanged himself by the little rope. The count came along, spurring his horse at top speed. Eustace got back on Morel and saw the count coming after him: 'Lord,' he said, 'do I need to watch out? Take care of that boy for me who has been hanged. With your permission, I'm off.' The count followed him in a great rage. Both the count and his men pursued him hotly, arresting two of his men and putting their eyes out. When Eustace heard what had happened, he swore by the Virgin Mary that for the four eyes put out four of the count's men would lose their feet. (693–741)

The count went to Saint-Omer. He was unable to catch Eustace, who began to keep watch in order to see if somewhere, be it wood, road or path, he could find four men whose feet he could cut off. Very soon he encountered five men-at-arms, who belonged to the count. They were taking the two monks from Clairmarais to prison. Eustace said to the men: 'Get down off your horses; you will not be taking these two monks any further. You will come and speak to us; if you think this is bad, things will soon get worse for you.' Eustace brought them to a halt and cut the feet off four of them. To the fifth he said: 'Go to the count and tell him about Eustace the Monk who has taken the feet belonging to four men in return for four eyes he has put out.' 'Lord,' he said, 'most willingly.' He did not forget his trotters. He went rushing off to the count and told him at once that in exchange for four eyes which he had put out Eustace had taken four men's feet. 'In faith,' said the count, 'by the legs, by the body and by the bowels of this wretched, truant monk, who has caused me so much shame and humiliation!' Twenty knights were then sent to search thoughout the forest, and they rode up and down for a long time. This cost the count dearly. (742–75)

One day they were in the forest. Eustace the Monk dressed in a hair-shirt and a hooded cloak and made his way along a path, where he came upon the twenty knights. He acted in a most pitiful fashion and greeted them humbly. They responded gaily: 'Tell us where you have come from and where you are going'. 'Lords, I am going straight to the Count of Dammartin and I come from Boulogne. I am going to make a complaint about a wicked monk. He has robbed me in this land, saying that he was at war with the count. What he has taken from me was worth a hundred marks, and now I am a beggar and an object of scorn. He refused to give me any of his bread either in the morning or at supper-time. Lords, tell me without delay where I shall find the count.' One of them replied: 'In Hardelot. That is where you should go and what I advise.' Eustace made his way to Hardelot and approached the count as he was eating. He said: 'May God be here so that he can give me justice over the Devil! Lords,' said Eustace the Monk, 'which one is the Count of Boulogne?' A man-at-arms said: 'There he is.' (776–804)

Eustace went up to him and said: 'Lord, in God's name, have mercy on me! I am a townsman from Andely. I was on my way from Bruges in Flanders, bringing silk hose and thirty pounds in pennies. A drunken madman, who was was tonsured like a priest and looked just like a monk, and who said he was your enemy, robbed me of gold, silver and precious furs and he took my horse and my clothing. I make my complaint to you about this mad monk who has robbed me; grant me justice. He is not far from here (he was right, for he was there, talking to the count himself!). The treacherous monk of low birth made me put on this cloak, and then he made me swear I would come and talk to you. You can be certain that he is not far away from here. I saw him enter a copse.' 'What sort of man is he?' said the count. 'Is he black or white, large or small?' Eustace said: 'He is my size'. The count immediately jumped up, saying: 'Take me to him at once and I shall avenge you'. Eustace said: 'Come on then, I shall hand him over to you. Come and take him.' The count followed him with six companions, and Eustace, who had thirty men with him, led the count in amongst his own men and gave him hospitality. The count did not feel safe, but Eustace said to him: 'Do not be afraid. I want to make peace with you. In God's name, fair sweet lord, let us talk about this peace.' The count replied: 'Leave me in peace. This is all to no avail; in God's name, you will never be reconciled with me.' Eustace said: 'Get going, since things cannot be otherwise. You came under my safe-conduct and you will not be deceived.' The count returned home and Eustace himself departed. (805–53)

One day the count armed himself and summoned all his men. He had been informed that Eustace had gone into a fortified town. The count made his way there, but Eustace, who knew so many tricks, began to work out how he could escape. With a worthy fellow he exchanged his dark-brown robe for a poor cloak and managed to get away from the town. On his way he met a man laden down with straw. Eustace immediately bought the straw and carried it over towards his enemies, crying: 'Hay for sale!' He was faltering beneath the weight and had one eye closed and the other open. The straw had hidden him well and he went hobbling along past the Count of Boulogne: 'Good fellow,' said the count, 'tell me whether Eustace the Monk is still in there. I think he has already escaped me.' Eustace said: 'I can tell you in truth that he spent last night at my house and left this morning. You can capture him now that he is on his way.' The count said:

'Mount your horses and get after him!' The horses were close-by and they all set off at once. Eustace, who was so cunning, wasted no more time. He put down the straw and set off after them. A serving-boy was leading a horse, and Eustace took it from him and jumped into the saddle. In everyone's hearing he yelled: 'Here is the Monk and he is just leaving'. When the Count of Boulogne heard him, he shouted: 'After the Monk!' But the Monk escaped them all; no one captured him or caught up with him. The count must have been beside himself that Eustace had escaped him. (854–99)

The count and his men went one day to Hardelot. Disguised as a pilgrim Eustace set off after him, together with ten companions. The count got down off his horse and Eustace came up to him: 'Lord, in the name of the pope in Rome, we are penitents. We have sinned against many men and have repented in God's name. We have entered upon a long period of suffering.' He got the count, once he had heard what he said, to give him three sous. The count went into the castle, leaving the horses outside. Eustace took all the horses and set fire to the town, sending word to the count through a man-at-arms that the penitents to whom he had given three sous had done this. 'Upon my word,' said the count, 'I am mad not to have captured these rogues, these wretches, these false pilgrims! If I wanted to leave here, I would have no horse to ride. He certainly knows how to go about his business. There has never been such a devilish monk! If I can get my hands on him, it will not be long before he dies.' (900–29)

One day Eustace was journeying and he met a merchant who was on his way from Bruges in Flanders and carrying sixty pounds in coin with him. The merchant was from Boulogne and he recognized Eustace the Monk. He did not feel very secure and was very much afraid for his money. Eustace said to him at once: 'Tell me how much money you have'. 'Lord,' he said, 'I shall tell you and not lie to you. I am carrying sixty pounds worth in a bag and have fifteen sous in my purse.' Eustace immediately stripped him and took him into a copse, where he counted all the money. He gave it all back to the merchant, saying: 'Be on your way. I commend you to God. If you had told me any lies, you would not have taken a penny from here. Rather you would have lost everything and not got back a single penny.' The merchant thanked him and Eustace said: 'Get going and promise me you will go to the Count of Boulogne and take him this palfrey.[10] This represents the tithe from his horses. I am keeping nine of them, the plump and handsome ones.[11] Yesterday evening, someone came and told me that the count had nothing to ride. Last night, when I left him, I took all his horses away from him, and now I want to provide him with

61

his tithe. You must take him this palfrey. Also take him three deniers and a farthing, for that represents without doubt the tithe from the three sous of good Angevin money, which he gave to the pilgrims who took away the ten horses and set fire to his town.' (930–71)

The merchant promised him he would go to the Count of Boulogne, and Eustace gave him three pennies, the farthing and the saddled palfrey. 'Tell him that Eustace sends him the tithe from all his spoils.' The merchant took his leave and departed from the Monk happily. He went straight to the count and told him about Eustace the Monk. At once the count had the merchant seized and held prisoner. He was absolutely convinced that it was Eustace the Monk. 'Lord,' said the merchant, 'I have come here to you from Boulogne. Eustace made me swear that I would come and talk to you, and I came to you in order to keep my word.' The count replied: 'I believe you.' When the count heard what he said, he immediately let him go, and without delay the merchant gave him the horse and the three pennies and the farthing. (972–95)

One day the count went hunting and a spy came and informed him that Eustace was in the forest. Then the count and all his household dressed in a garment of homespun cloth and followed his spy on foot. They lay in wait in a ditch. Eustace's spy came upon them, and realizing it was the count went to Eustace and told him. Eustace immediately went to see a charcoal-burner, who had an ass which he used for carrying the charcoal he had for sale. Without more ado, Eustace dressed in the charcoal-burner's clothing, donning his black hood and blackening his face, his neck and then his hands. He was quite remarkably stained and the ass was laden with charcoal. Eustace held a goad and made his way towards Boulogne. The count did not pay the slightest attention to him when he saw him passing and he did not even bother to speak to him. Eustace yelled out to them: 'Lords,' he said, 'what are you doing there?' The count was the first to reply: 'What business is it of yours, peasant?' Eustace replied: 'By St Omer, I am on my way to explain to the count how the men belonging to Eustace the Monk are causing us shame and humiliation. I did not dare bring my *ronci*[12] to carry the charcoal I have for sale, in case Eustace stole it from me. At this moment he is lying contentedly beside a good charcoal fire with plenty of meat and venison. He has set fire to all my charcoal, which cost me so much labour to collect.' 'Is that near here?' said the count, and Eustace replied: 'It is right in there. If you wish to speak to him, just follow this path to its end.' (996–1041)

Eustace spurred on Romer, and the count started to enter the forest with his men. The charcoal-burner had put on the Monk's clothing and the count found him sitting there. He was severely beaten and injured. They thought, without the word of a lie, that he was Eustace the Monk. 'Lords,' he said, 'have mercy, for God's sake! Why are you beating me like this? You can have these clothes. I can tell you that I have nothing else. The clothes belong to Eustace the Monk who is now on his way to Boulogne. He is taking my ass and my charcoal and has completely blackened his hands, face and neck with charcoal. He put on my black hood and made me get undressed and put on his clothes.' The count said: 'Listen to this, lords. Now capture him if you wish. By God's teeth, this living Devil has made me angry so many times! He is the charcoal-burner on the road who spoke to us just now.' The count added: 'Quickly! Get after him!' Their horses were nearby and they mounted. Spurring on their horses at once, they charged off after Eustace. Eustace had washed his face, and he met a potter who was crying: 'Pots! Pots!' Eustace was no fool. He knew he would be pursued, so he quickly made a bargain with the potter, and in exchange for his ass and his charcoal he got pitchers and pots, large and small. So Eustace became a potter and the potter a charcoal-burner. The latter was a fool to abandon his profession, as he had no need of this new one. Eustace cried: 'Pots! Pots!' The count emerged from the wood and asked the potter if he had seen a charcoal-burner. 'Lord,' said Eustace the Monk, 'he is heading straight for Boulogne, leading an ass laden with charcoal.' (1042–90)

The count spurred on his horse, as did his men-at-arms and his knights, and they caught up with the charcoal-burner. They beat him severely and injured him. They rained blows on him and bound him hand and foot. Then he was loaded on to a *ronci* with his head towards the crupper. The peasant yelled and bawled and shrieked: 'Lords,' he said, 'in God's name I beg you to have mercy on me. Tell me why you've captured me, and if I've done you any wrong I'll gladly put it right.' 'Ha, ha, wretch!' said the count, 'do you think you can escape? I shall soon have you hanged.' A wise knight, who looked at the potter and recognized him easily, said that he knew where he hailed from. 'How the devil did you become a charcoal-burner? You used to be a potter. No one can survive if he takes on so many jobs.' 'Lord, have mercy,' said the good fellow, 'in exchange for this ass and this charcoal I gave away my pots to the charcoal-burner, on whom may God send down some hindrance! For it's because of him that I'm being treated in this way. I think he must have stolen them. So help me God, I didn't steal them. I gave up my pots for the ass. He's heading quickly for the wood, crying "Pots, pots!" as he goes.' The knight said to the count: 'Eustace knows so many shameful tricks! Just now he was a charcoal-burner, now he's become a potter.' 'Get going,' said the count, 'by my heart and lights! Get after him now at top speed! Bring me everyone you meet, today and tomorrow. I shall never have done with this Monk unless I take everyone prisoner.' (1091–135)

Then they let the charcoal-burner go and returned to the forest to renew the pursuit. Eustace had thrown away his pots, breaking them all into little pieces in some marshy ground. He had carried them far too long. Then Eustace the brainless climbed into a kite's nest and there he became a nightingale, for he considered the count a fool. When he saw him pass by, he began to cry out: 'Kill, kill, kill, kill,' and Count Renaut replied: 'I'll kill him, by St Richard, if I can get my hands on him.' 'Hit, hit,' said Eustace the Monk. 'Upon my word,' said the Count of Boulogne, 'I'll do it, I'll do it, but I shall never catch him here.' Eustace felt reassured and let out another few words: 'He hadn't got it, yes he had, no he hadn't, yes he had!' When the Count of Boulogne heard him, he said: 'He certainly had. He's taken all my good horses from me.' Eustace called out: 'Today, today!'[13] 'You're right,' said the count, 'today's the day I'll kill him with my own hands, if I can get my hands on him.' 'The man who takes a nightingale's advice,' said the count, 'is no fool. The nightingale has taught me to avenge myself on my enemies, for it has called out to me that I should hit him and kill him.' Then the Count of Boulogne set off in pursuit of Eustace the Monk. He arrested four monks and took them straight off to prison. Then he sent to prison four merchants and a dealer. He captured three poulterers and two ass-drivers, and afterwards sent directly to his prison six fishermen and their fish. Then four clerics and an archpriest had to be put in prison. That day more than sixty companions were in his gaol. (1136–85)

The count went to Neufchâtel, where he began a new trial. Eustace, who knew so many tricks, followed him into the town. He put on a woman's garments and looked remarkably like a woman. He was clad in a linen dress and his face was well covered. At his side he had his distaff. Then Eustace the Monk did some spinning! He went straight up to a man-at-arms, who was holding one of the count's horses, and said: 'Let me get on this horse and I'll let you have a fuck.' 'Willingly,' said the man, 'up you get, young lady, on this good, ambling palfrey. You shall have four deniers from me if you let me have a fuck.' 'I'll teach you how to use your bum,' said Eustace, 'better than any man had ever been able to do so.'[14] The young man raised Eustace's leg and he let out a fart. 'Ah, young lady, you are farting!' Eustace said: 'Don't worry! My fair, sweet friend, don't be upset. It's this saddle which is making the noise.' Eustace the Monk mounted the horse and he and the youth, side by side, spurred on into the forest. The youth said: 'Let's not go any farther. I've got my lord's horse and you have his best palfrey. I'll be punished,' he added, 'if this affair is not soon over. Let's do our business here.' (1186–222)

'Young man,' said Eustace the Monk, 'you are very keen to fuck. I shall soon teach you to use your bum. Just come a little farther now, so that no one will come spying on us.' 'Young lady,' said the youth, 'mind there is no trickery. By the bowels of the Virgin Mary, I would soon have your life.' Eustace said: 'Fair, sweet friend, don't upset yourself so. My dwelling is here ahead of us. Just come a little farther.' Foolishly the youth followed him and Eustace reached his own men. He grabbed the youth by the neck. Now he could only consider himself a fool! He knew that the peasant was right to say: 'The goat scratches so hard that it has difficulty lying down'. Eustace said: 'Get down off the good horse, you are not taking it any farther. This very fine palfrey is staying here and never again will the count ride it.' Then they both dismounted and there was a great deal of merriment. (1223–47)

'Lords,' said Eustace the Monk, 'this young man will do his business, for I have given him my word on that.' Eustace took him a bit farther on and led him into a bog: 'Young man,' he said, 'don't concern yourself. Now take off all your clothes. I know very well that you like a fuck.' The youth entered the bog, not daring to contradict him. Eustace said: 'Now use your bum! You've got plenty of time for a fuck. Make full use of your bum or you will get such a good beating that you will never be able to walk. You thought you could fuck me. You ought to be ashamed for wanting to fuck a black monk.' The youth said: 'In God's name, have mercy! Spare me this humiliation. Lord,' he said, 'by our Lady, I thought you were a woman.' Eustace was not an heretic, nor was he an arse-fucker or a sodomite, and he said: 'Now come along and get going. You will tell the count from me just how I have treated you.' 'I'll tell him that for you at once,' said the youth. Then he set off. But, not daring to return to the count with his message, he fled to a foreign land. After that, the hostilities between Eustace the Monk and the count lasted a long time. Eustace continued to cause him a great deal of humiliation. (1248–83)

One day, Eustace, who was aware that the count was looking everywhere for him, was at Coupelle. He had put his trust firmly in a priest, who was rich and comfortably off, and he was staying with him. The priest denounced him to the count and Eustace then caused him great humiliation. He bound the priest hand and foot and threw him into a ditch. One day the Count of Boulogne came to Genech on business, taking with him King

Philip, who was accompanied by his entire army and also by his son, King Louis, who had some fine men with him. The king had a fine company of men and that night he stayed at Coupelle. Whilst there, he assembled his forces at Sainte-Marie-au-Bois, which was near Coupelle.[15] There Eustace the Monk, who had done the count a lot of harm, had a fine company of men with him, and outside the wood he had a spy. Eustace captured a townsman from Corbie and left him with nothing other than his tunic. He sent him to the king at Coupelle and then killed a knight. The king became angry and said to the Count of Boulogne: 'Count, hear what Eustace the Monk, who robs and kills my men, has done.' The count replied: 'So help me God. I cannot avenge myself on him. He is a devilishly warlike monk.' Then the king had him pursued, but he never managed to get hold of him. (1284–321)

The king went to Sangatte, and when he was on his way back from there the count formed the rearguard so that the king's men would have no reason to worry. Eustace, who knew so many tricks, was in a town nearby. The Count of Boulogne's spy told him that Eustace the Monk was in that town keeping watch on the king's army, which was passing that way. The count made his way there, and Eustace, who was so artful and who had been warned of this by his spy, caught sight of a new fence. A peasant was putting nails into this fence and Eustace came straight up to him. The peasant had on an old cloak, which Eustace very quickly took from him, giving him in return his good robe and sending him to his lodgings. The fence was easy to nail, so Eustace then set about the task. He was wearing an old bonnet and holding a cloth, with which he was rubbing down the stakes and battens. The count emerged from a valley and headed straight for Eustace, who was furiously nailing the fence: 'Peasant,' said the Count of Boulogne, 'is Eustace the Monk in here?' Eustace replied: 'In truth I do not know, lord, and I do not want to lie to you. He left the town just now and took flight because of the king's army. He was speeding along with great urgency, right up there. He is not far away. You can easily catch up with him.' (1322–58)

The count began to spur his horse, and Eustace, who wanted nothing else, attacked the rear of the army. There he captured five knights, six palfreys and five war-horses, for he had a large company of men close by. They went to hide in the wood and then sat down to eat. Eustace's mortal enemy, Hainfrois, suddenly turned up whilst he was eating. He had entered the wood to urinate and did not think he would ever get away; he was greatly afraid and terrified. Eustace rose to his feet, saying: 'Now get off your horse and come and eat with us.' Hainfrois dismounted in great fear, as he had little faith in Eustace. When the meal was over, he began to beg Eustace for mercy fervently and Eustace said: 'Be on your way. You have killed and put an end to my father and my cousin german and caused trouble for me with the count. I shall not go into detail now, but, even if I were given the whole of France, I would not make peace with you. But because you have eaten with me, you will have no further reason to concern yourself with me today. Now go quite freely, and tell the count from me that just now I was erecting the fence when he asked me which way Eustace the Monk had gone or whether he was still in there.' (1359–95)

Hainfrois left Eustace and told the count the whole story. The count immediately made his way there and Eustace departed. Then Eustace dressed like a leper, with his goblet, his crutch and his clapper. When he saw the count pass by, he began to shake his clapper and succeeded in getting twenty-eight pence off both the count and his knights. When the count had passed by, a young lad remained behind, leading a very fine war-horse. Eustace knocked him off the horse, jumped into the saddle and set off. The lad went to the count: 'Lord, upon my word, a leper has robbed me of one of your horses.' 'Look here,' said the count, 'by my bowels, by my belly and legs! The man with the clapper was the Monk who deceives us so much.' 'Upon my word,' said Count Renaut, 'he looked very much like a leper. His fingers were all crooked and his face pock-marked.' The count had a search made for him everywhere. (1396–422)

Eustace made himself one-legged. He had bound his leg to his buttock and knew exactly how to walk with a crutch. Having cut up a cow's lungs and tied them to his thigh with a blood-stained bandage, he went into the church. The Count of Boulogne was there and the prior was singing mass. The church was full of people, including knights and men-at-arms. Eustace came up to the count and told him about his illness. He showed him his leg and his buttock and begged him to do right by him. The count held out twelve pence to him and Eustace took the money. Then he came straight up to the prior as he was taking the offerings and raised his thigh, showing him his buttock. 'Lord,' said Eustace, 'see what a bad state I am in. My thigh is completely withered. In the name of God and the Virgin Mary, do beg these knights to give me money to have my thigh cured.' The prior said: 'Let the offerings come in and then I shall say something. I shall gladly ask them to help you.' When the offerings were all in, the prior without delay begged on behalf of Eustace the Monk, who had humiliated so many people. 'Lords,' said the prior, 'listen to me. This poor man you can see has a completely withered thigh. In the name of God and the Virgin Mary, he greatly needs others to do right by him. He has only one foot and a crutch. In God's name, lords, give him alms. I beg you above all things.' (1423–65)

Eustace was no fool. He acquired eight sous there and then slipped away from the church before mass was over. He had no desire for the kiss of peace, as he preferred war to peace. He came up to the count's horse and immediately mounted it with his crutch hanging down. The children cried out loudly: 'The one-legged man is taking away a horse. See how he spurs on through the valley!' Then the knights dashed out and there was no one left in the church. They were all astounded at the one-legged man, who had taken flight on the magnificent Spanish horse. Eustace was speeding through the countryside. 'Come on,' said the count, 'by my bowels! How treacherous this Monk is who can cause me so much harm and humiliation! Now he has taken my horse again. It would be no use my chasing him, for I would never catch up with him.' Then the count made everyone swear that if they could capture him, wherever it might be, wood, town or path, they would hand him over as a prisoner. (1466–93)

One day it had snowed very hard. Eustace had been spotted in a hamlet, where he was living, and the count went straight over there with thirty fully-armed men. Eustace would soon be captured and caught. But William de Montcavrel had him warned by a young boy. Eustace mounted Morel, and with two companions he fled without any weapons. The count followed his tracks, which showed up in the snow. But Eustace went into a smithy and had his horse's shoes turned round. Once this had been done, he set off, with the result that the further forward he went the more his tracks made it appear to the count as if he were retracing his steps. The count set off along the trail. By his tracks it appeared to him that Eustace was going in the opposite direction. (1494–515)

The count retraced his steps, and the tracks led him to the smith who had turned the shoes round. He would soon be in a sorry plight. The count summoned the smith. and I think he intended to make him suffer. He ordered him without more ado to hand over to him Eustace the Monk. The smith said: 'I don't have him, may the Virgin Mary help me.' The count said: 'You will hand him over. By these tracks which have led us here you are proven guilty.' The smith said: 'Lord, have mercy! Three squires passed here and had their horseshoes turned round, but I don't know why they did it. They left here just now and followed the path by which you have come back.' The count said: 'By the legs of the saints! This Monk is so treacherous. Because he has reversed the shoes we have come back here. Smith, you who reversed the shoes, you will part with twenty pounds. Either you give me twenty pounds or you will be strung up high.' The

smith promised twenty pounds and handed over guarantees and a hostage.
(1516–45)

The count followed Eustace through the forest of Hardelot. Eustace was
sitting eating outside, in a derelict church. Three carpenters were there
working on the construction of a new church. The count passed by and
one of his men-at-arms ran over towards the church. When he saw the
man approaching, Eustace became a carpenter. With a cudgel round his
neck he quickly emerged from the church: 'May God protect you, lord,'
said Eustace, 'who is it who is passing over there?' The man replied: 'They
are men who have sworn an oath of private vengeance and been banished
from their land. They have come looking for a man in this land who is very
skilled in warfare. They have heard about the Monk, who was born near
Boulogne, and have sought him far and wide, for he is very brave and
bold.' 'Brother,' said Eustace the Monk, 'you have embarked upon a task
which will turn out to be worthless. He is a complete idiot, a good-for-
nothing. Over there, eating in this church, is a devilish, enemy monk. May
he suffer misfortune! He has made us all go hungry. Get down off your
horse and go and see the man sitting in that corner over there. He is the
Monk, don't doubt it.' The man got down off his horse at once, saying to
the Monk: 'Hold my *ronci* for me. There is none so good from here to
Monchy. Mind he doesn't strike you, for he kicks with his rear hoof.' The
Monk said: 'I find you trustworthy. He won't kick me if I can help it.' The
young man entered the church, but he did not find the Monk, and when
he did not find him he considered himself tricked. He was wasting his
efforts. Eustace mounted the horse immediately and shouted out to him in
a loud voice: 'Carpenter, here is your cudgel. I am off and I commend you
to God.' 'By God's teeth,' said the man, 'get down off my horse and bring
him back to me.' 'I shall not, because he is such a fine one. The count will
not catch me today and in fact I am going to take this fine horse away.'
Eustace said: 'Lord vassal, go back on foot and tell the count from me that
he would have been well supplied and fed if he had stopped off here.'
(1546–607)

Eustace went into the forest, and the other man, grief-stricken and
distraught, went on foot. That day he was in a sorry plight. He frequently
stumbled in the snow and was dying of hunger and thirst. He was walking
in such a pitiful state that his teeth were chattering. The count was sitting
at table when his squire suddenly appeared, soiled all over, right down to
his breeches. The count said: 'May things turn out well for you! You have
followed close behind me. Did you catch up with the Monk?' The squire
was distressed and could not utter a word. So the count said once more:

'Say something, you devil! May you get a toothache!' 'Lord,' said the squire, 'the Monk is a fine knight, for he often takes what is yours. He is good at teaching you your *paternoster*. He robbed me of my *ronci* and put my life at risk.' 'Go on!' said the count, 'by my legs, by my belly and by my bowels! By my throat and teeth! How this man deceives everyone! By God's legs, he will not get away. Lords, men-at-arms, let this be quite clear!' (1608–37)

Eustace was in the forest and the count went straight there. Eustace was riding Morel, but he had no saddle-girth. The count pursued him like a madman. Now he would soon be caught! Eustace spurred Morel and the horse darted forward. But the saddle turned. Eustace fell off and the count captured him. He defended himself ferociously and cast the count's shield down in front of him. The count immediately grabbed Eustace with his two hands and Eustace, who would gladly have humiliated him, hit out at the count. One pulled one way, one another. You have never seen such a struggle as there was when Eustace was captured, for he defended himself with great skill. But Eustace was captured and held prisoner. He was then well guarded and restrained. They bound him hand and foot and loaded him on to a *ronci*. The count wanted to hang him at once, but Eustace had his supporters. Blows would have been exchanged before he was hanged or killed. 'Lords,' said the Count of Boulogne, 'I have captured Eustace the Monk. Now advise me what to do with him. I shall act according to your advice. Do you advise me to hang him or to hand him over to the King of France?' (1638–69)

William de Montcavrel said: 'That would not be to our liking. He is our relative and our friend. You would have too many enemies.' The count said: 'I shall soon hang him and I shall see who will take him from me! Or else I shall send him to the king. No one on earth will stop me, and he will have him hanged or drowned, or make him suffer real pain.' William said: 'Fair, sweet lord. Just keep your anger in check. Hand the Monk over to us as a pledge against everything we hold from you.' 'By God's bowels,' said the count, 'I shall not!' Instead it is my intention to finish him off.' Aufrans de Cayeux said: 'Lord, do hold your anger in check. You could easily harm his friends if you attempted to finish him off.' 'Lord,' said Hugh de Belin, 'do you want to finish him off completely?' 'Yes, by St Peter of Rome. He will never deceive anyone again,' said the count. 'He has caused a great deal of harm and he is such a treacherous monk.' Walet de Coupelle replied: 'He will not die today, by my brains! You are a very evil man, Lord Count. You will not be acting to your advantage in this way. He has behaved in hostile fashion. You took his land off him. Now have him tried in court, or otherwise you will come off badly. If you hanged the Monk, you would have a large number of enemies, and if you do not treat him well swords will soon be drawn.' (1670–707)

'Lord,' said Bauduin d'Aire, 'just take my word in this matter. Send him to the king in Paris and he will be judged by right and by law.' The count said: 'If he were allowed to go on living for a single day, he would escape.' 'Have him so tightly bound then that he cannot escape justice.' The count said: 'I shall send him to the king and rid myself of him.' Each man replied: 'That is my advice to you.' The count sent him to Hardelot, and when night fell he summoned a carter to take Eustace to the king. The carter gave him his word that without anyone knowing he would take him to the King of France. Hugh de Gannes mounted his horse with thirty fully-armed men. They were responsible for taking him to the king, but they preferred to help him rather than harm him. Eustace was put on the cart and at night they set out. Eustace's friends were grief-stricken. They made their way past Montreuil, and Hugh de Gannes warned them, telling them that if they were ready and equipped to help Eustace the Monk they could rescue him beneath Beaurain. William de Fiennes armed himself and with thirty companions went to Beaurain, where they rescued Eustace the Monk in spite of the Count of Boulogne. (1708–41)

The Monk crossed the Canche, having no desire to enter France. Before the count knew a word about it, he had extracted his payment. The Abbot of Jumièges came along, and Eustace looked at him and saw who he was: 'Abbot,' he said, 'stay where you are! What are you carrying? Do not conceal it from me!' The abbot replied: 'What business is it of yours?' Eustace almost struck him. 'What business is it of mine, idiot? By my head! I shall have my share of it. Get down off your horse at once and say no more, or you will get such a beating that you would give a hundred pounds to avoid it.' The abbot thought he was drunk and said to him in kindly fashion: 'Be on your way! You will not find what you want here.' Eustace said: 'Do not treat me with scorn. Be quick and get down off your horse or you will be in a sorry plight.' Terrified, the abbot dismounted and Eustace asked him how much money he had with him. The abbot said: 'Four marks in truth. I have four silver marks with me.' Eustace searched him immediately and found thirty marks or more. He gave him back the four marks, the amount he said he had. The abbot was rightfully upset. If he had told the truth, he would have had all his money back. The abbot lost his money merely for having lied. (1742–77)

One day the count was in Boulogne, and Eustace the Monk came there and entered the town. He had bought mackerel and sold them to the count's men-at-arms. To get his payment and settle the account Eustace went to eat at court, but he did not manage to get a penny. He asked for his payment, but did not receive a single drop of silver. The men merely set a date for payment. Then Eustace left. The count got ready to go out and had his horses saddled. Eustace came over to the horses and took hold of four of the very best, as if to take them to water. He got three serving-boys to go with him and they led the horses for him. He took them out of Boulogne, where he had his own men. He made the boys dismount and his men took the horses away from them. The boys made their way back and Eustace informed the count, through a man-at-arms whom he met, that he was taking away the four horses by way of payment for his mackerel. The man went running to the count and told him about Eustace the Monk, who had sold him forty-four mackerel, even more. 'As payment he has taken four good horses, I believe, and he ate at your court.' 'By God's feet! He keeps me on a very tight rein. By the Virgin Mary's bowels, I'll shorten his life!' The count began to pursue him, but he never managed to get his hands on him. Eustace became a flan seller, a pastry seller and a cake seller. (1778–819)

One day the count was in Calais, and Eustace, who knew so much about evil and guile, came there at top speed, accompanied by a squire. He built a huge, blazing fire in a house outside the town and made waffles, newly-baked tarts and very fine dumplings. Inside he had the tarts cooked with tow, pitch and wax and saw to it that they were all very well and master-fully made. The count was sitting at table when Eustace took up his wares and brought them to him. He came to the count and told him that a young nobleman, who held his fief from him and had a case to plead before him, was making him a present of them and was going to come and eat with him. The present was accepted. But that day they would consider them-selves tricked. Eustace had written a letter and placed it in one of the tarts. It related the true story of the joke. (1820–45)

Eustace took leave of the count, and when the meal was completed the present was quickly brought before the count. They brought in the tarts, and the man who had brought them in, a knight who was the count's constable and one of his closest advisers, took one of them. He became so embedded in a tart that he could not open his mouth or get his teeth back out of it. Before he managed to extricate himself, he said to his com-panion: 'Have a taste. You have never eaten such tarts and never tasted anything like them in your life.' So he too took one of the tarts. He had large teeth and became so severely stuck that he could not get his teeth out. He began to sweat with anguish, and when he did manage to extricate himself, he began to swear profusely: 'By God's teeth! I'm dishonoured. I've eaten the Devil, that's my belief.' All those who had eaten the tarts were severely deceived. No one failed to become stuck as soon as he had taken a bite. In one of the tarts they found the letter which told them that Eustace the Monk had done this: 'Upon my word,' said the Count of Boulogne, 'this Monk is very treacherous. He is leading us a merry dance. May he be commended to the Devil! For he will never be caught or apprehended.' (1846–81)

Eustace went to England and begged King John for mercy. In the guise of a Hospitaler he went and prostrated himself at the feet of the king, who asked him why he was doing this. Eustace said: 'Have mercy, lord.' 'Get up from there,' replied the king, 'since you are a Hospitaler, you will gladly receive mercy.' Eustace said: 'Hear my business. Eustace the Monk sends word to you and begs you, with pleas for mercy, to retain him in your household.' The king replied without delay: 'He will be retained, if he is willing to swear that he will serve me in good faith and never let me down. I shall want hostages from him.' Eustace said: 'If you wish, you will have my daughter as a pledge, or my wife, if you like.' The king said: 'Are you the Monk, you who are speaking about this matter?' 'Yes, lord, my name is Eustace.' The king said: 'By St Edmund, who is my true lord, I shall retain you willingly. You are very welcome.' (1882–910)

So Eustace was retained and the king gave him galleys. Eustace set sail with thirty galleys and came to the Channel Islands. The islanders were armed and assembled, with a castellan leading them. When he saw this fleet coming, he said to his men: 'Now wait until they have landed. When we see them ashore, we shall destroy them immediately.' When Eustace had landed, he was the first to disembark and all his companions jumped out after him. The inhabitants of the islands attacked them and Eustace advanced towards the castellan, who was right out in front of his men. No matter who complained, he led all those under his command right up to Eustace's ships.[16] 'God is here,' cried Romerel. 'Winchelsea,' cried Eustace.[17] Heavy fighting took place there and many men were unhorsed, for one side attacked very fiercely and the other side defended very well. Then a great melee began, savage, violent and arduous, and Eustace held a huge axe with which he struck great blows on the battlefield. He splintered many a helmet, and many a warhorse lost its shoulder. He struck blows to the right and blows to the left, making himself lord and master of the fighting. Eustace said: 'Go to it! You'll soon see them take flight.' There was a great and fierce battle there, and that day many biers had to be constructed. Eustace threw everyone out of the islands, which he destroyed with the result that there was nothing left to burn in either castle or dwelling. (1911–53)

One day, at floodtide, Eustace was at Harfleur, where the Seine flows into the sea. He anchored his galleys and got into a small boat with thirty of his closest companions. He began to row up the Seine and they reached land without undue delay. He arrived at Pont-Audemer, where he went to stand on the bridge. Eustace had donned a surplice, and standing before him he saw Cadoc, the seneschal of Normandy, who had three hundred men-at-arms in his household to guard the bridges of the Seine and prevent the Monk from getting past. Eustace summoned a barber and had himself shaved on the bridge. He said to Cadoc: 'What would you do to him if you caught up with the Monk?' Cadoc replied: 'I would make sure I handed him over to the King of France, who would have him crucified, hanged, burned or drowned.' Eustace said: 'By St Winnoc! If you gave me your cape, I would soon give you information about him and then I would show you where he is.' Cadoc replied: 'You will have my cape, if you hand the Monk over to me.' Eustace said: 'You will see him. Take off your cape and give it to me.' (1954–85)

Cadoc gave him his cape, which would soon be called 'escape'. It was lined with grey squirrel fur, and Eustace put it on saying: 'Mount your horse quickly! He is close by, in the meadows.' Cadoc mounted with thirty of his men and Eustace himself took them to the meadows near Pont-Audemer. He would soon make Cadoc furious. In the meadows there was a reaper who was mowing one section nearby. Eustace said: 'By St Winnoc! If this reaper escapes you, you will never catch the Monk.' Spurring their horses, Cadoc and his men went over towards him. They encountered a huge quagmire and they all fell in. Each of them became dreadfully stuck and the horses sank right up to their bellies. Eustace, meanwhile, came up to Cadoc and greeted him, saying: 'Lord, what are you doing there?' 'By my entrails,' said Cadoc, 'may God bring down some misfortune on you this day, since you brought us here! You have tricked us terribly!' From beneath his hood Eustace laughed heartily at Cadoc, who was thoroughly deceived when he fell into the quagmire. He and fifteen of his comrades were completely stuck, and he swore like a renegade, as did his companions. Eustace said: 'By St Remi! You will never get out of this quagmire unless you follow my advice.' Cadoc yelled out: 'Son of a whore, wretched swine! You've got us into this mess! May tomorrow be an evil day for you! You'll have one if I get my hands on you!' Eustace said: 'As long as you are in this mire, I am not afraid of you. You can lie there until Easter. Unless you take my advice, you will never get out of the mire. All hold hands together and climb on to your saddles. If you can jump with your feet together, you will ease the weight on your horses and be freer. Do it now, if you believe me.' (1986–2039).

They followed Eustace's advice and each of them hauled himself up on to his saddle. They held hands and Cadoc was the first to jump. He fell into the mud right up to his armpits. The others clung on to their saddles and were up to their waistbands in mud. Eustace was not at all upset by this. He almost fainted with laughter and said: 'You are captured! You will never get out of here unless you are pulled out with ropes.' 'By my thighs,' said Cadoc, 'by my belly and bowels! By God's teeth! How humiliated I am!' Eustace yelled out and called to the reaper in a loud voice. He came running up and jumped into the mud next to Cadoc. He did so in order to help him and became stuck in it right up to his waist. Eustace said: 'Now there is more!' Cadoc was absolutely convinced that the reaper was Eustace the Monk, who had attacked him. Immediately he attacked the reaper, striking him on the ear with his fist. The reaper was astonished and his whole ear tingled. Cadoc hit him again on the ear, and the reaper, thinking he was drunk, tried to get away from him. He had clearly fallen into bad hands and was being severely injured and beaten. (2040–73)

Eustace cried out: 'Let him be. He has done nothing wrong. He left his reaping to come and help you. His good turn is being badly rewarded when you behave shamefully and harmfully towards him. My name is Eustace the Monk and I have got you into this plight. From now on you can just keep on treading mud, for I'm going off towards the sea. You have given me your cloak and had a poor reward from me for doing so. I had my beard trimmed in your sight and now I'm making you do some fishing here. Now don't be stingy or mean with your effort. Do a lot of stamping in this muck, for there are a great many eels in it. But you are in a sorry plight. You have caught so many big fish that you can't get them all ashore.' Cadoc said: 'If I were out of here, you would very soon die. No one would ever be deceived or tricked by you any more.' Eustace said: 'People who are threatened go on living! They struggle on for a long time.' He left there and returned to his boat. Cadoc immediately hailed the people on the bridge at Pont-Audemer to come and get him out of the mire, in which Eustace had made him go fishing. When Cadoc had been pulled out, he had three hundred men arm themselves. He charged off towards Boulogne, having sent a hundred men on ahead. He was convinced he could catch Eustace there. But Eustace, without more ado, created a floodtide to protect himself and came to Barfleur.[18] He had extorted thirty marks as protection money from the islands and the rest of the region. He arrived at Barfleur and received a further three thousand marks. Cadoc began to pursue him, but could not catch him up. He pursued him and his ships, but Eustace turned round and took five ships from him. Cadoc had no desire to pursue him further. He came back, for the sea was too cruel to him. (2074–125)

Eustace raised his sail, and off the port of Croufaut he caught up with a very fine and valuable ship, which was sailing calmly in front of him. He jumped on to the ship and attacked those on board. Then he dealt with them in such a way, and reduced them to such a state, that he was able to exact two hundred marks from them. As a result they considered themselves deceived. (2126–35)

Eustace, who had performed many evil acts on land, came to England and went straight to King John. He addressed him promptly: 'Lord,' he said, 'I want to request a home in your land.' The king replied: 'You shall have it. Take one wherever you wish. In London I can give you a palace which is magnificent and well constructed.' Eustace thanked him for this, but he had not been there long before he had the palace knocked down. He set more than four [hundred] workmen to work building foundations there which cost a good thousand marks of silver, before the building rose above ground level.[19] Then the King of England came to him and said he was mad to have begun such a project. He lent him four hundred marks to help him accomplish all his desires, and Eustace finished the palace, which was magnificent and well constructed. (2136–59)

Whilst the Monk was in England, the Count of Boulogne arrived. He had quarrelled with the King of France and come quickly to King John. When he saw Renaud of Boulogne, the Monk made up his mind to come back home. The king had the sea watched to prevent Eustace from getting across. Eustace, who had a way with words, took a bow and a vielle.[20] Covering up his short cloak, he set off disguised as a minstrel. He had a hood with stripes of orphrey[21] and a cane covered in leaves, and he came straight to the coast where he saw a merchant ship about to set sail. Everyone had gone aboard the ship, and Eustace, thinking deeply, waited. He put his feet together and jumped in. The pilot said: 'Minstrel, you'll get off, so help me God.' Eustace replied: 'Yes, indeed, when we get to the other side. I don't think you are being very sensible. For my passage I shall give you five silver pennies or my vielle.' 'What stories have you told?'[22] 'I am a jongleur and a minstrel and you will find very few like me. I know all the songs. In God's name, fair lord, get me across. I come from Northumberland and I have spent five years in Ireland. I have drunk so much beer that my face has turned pale and wan. Now I am going to go back and drink the wines of Argenteuil or Provins.' (2160–97)

'What is your name, and no joking?' 'Lord, my name is Mauferas. I am an Englishman from Ganstead. Ya, ya, codidouet.'[23] The sailor said: 'You are English? I thought you were French. Do you know any songs at present?' 'Yes, I know about Agoulant and Aymon. I know all about Blancandin and I know about Florence of Rome.[24] There is no song on earth of which I have not heard either the tune or the melody. I would have entertained you well, but at present I would not sing for anything, for this sea frightens me a great deal. I could not put my mind to saying anything worthwhile.' No one made any more requests of him, so the Monk got his way. In the evening he arrived at Boulogne and then set off at once, running like a messenger-boy. He was carrying with him a large box containing a letter, and he went to the king and showed it to him. The king looked at the letter and saw that the Monk had come to France and was sending him greetings. The Monk was angry with King John and would never be at peace with him because of his daughter, whom he had killed, burned and disfigured, and also because the Count of Boulogne was there. That was the reason why Eustace the Monk had come. He had no intention of betraying the king, rather he wished to serve him very well. The king said: 'If he is on this side of the water, get him to come and speak with me; he can come and go in safety. He can come here very easily, because no one will be on the look-out for him as far away as this.' Eustace said: 'Here I am.' 'Are you he?' said the king. 'You are not much like a Frenchman. You are not big, but small, yet you are so brave and bold. You know a great deal about guile and cunning and do not need any cat's grease to help you. You will not serve me unless you can behave well.' Eustace said: 'By St Simon! I shall do nothing other than good.' Thereafter the Monk was a good warrior. (2198–250)

Eustace was very bold and fierce, and later he performed many devilish acts in the islands on the other side. With a large fleet of ships he helped King Louis to cross the Channel, and single-handedly and by his own efforts he conquered the Boulogne ship.[25] He accompanied the king to Damme, and in that year the king lost his ships.[26] Eustace was arraigned for this on the grounds that he had betrayed his ships. Eustace denied it completely, so that there was no one bold enough to prove it in any way. So they let the matter drop. (2251–65)

On another occasion Eustace set sail across the Channel with a large fleet of ships. With him he had Raoul de Tournelle, and Varlet de Montagui was there too.[27] Eustace, who was very brave and courageous, reached the open sea; more than twenty ships passed in front of him, and they attacked his fleet very fiercely with huge bows and arrows, for they had set out in light ships. Eustace and his men defended themselves by hurling and throwing missiles and firing arrows. They slaughtered a great many Englishmen and defended themselves courageously. Eustace knocked down a good number of them with an oar which he was holding. Some had their arms broken, others their heads smashed. This one was killed and that one laid out; one was knocked down and another wounded, whilst a third had his collar-bone shattered. But the enemy attacked him from all sides and tormented him very severely, striking the side of the ship with great axes. But Eustace's men defended themselves so strenuously that their opponents could not get on board. Then they began to hurl well-ground lime in large pots, which they smashed to pieces on the ship's rails. The powder rose in great clouds, and it was this which caused them the most damage. After that, they could no longer defend themselves, for their eyes were full of powder. Those who were tormenting them were up wind. They jumped on to Eustace's ship and treated his men very cruelly. All the barons were captured and Eustace the Monk was killed. He had his head cut off and at once the battle ended. No one who is always intent on evil can live for a long time. (2266–307)

NOTES TO THE TRANSLATION

1. The Black Monks were Benedictines. Later Eustace will be found in the company of Cistercians (White Monks) from Clairmarais (vv. 430ff).

2. Cf. this passage from Chaucer's *The Parson's Tale*: 'But lat us go now to thilke horrible sweryng of adjuracioun and conjuracioun, as doon thise false enchauntours or nigromanciens in bacyns ful of water, or in a bright swerd, in a cercle, or in a fir, or in a shulder-boon of a sheep' (*The Riverside Chaucer*, ed. L.D. Benson and F.N. Robinson, 3rd ed. Oxford: Oxford University Press, 1988, p. 307; 'Let us now consider this horrible profane practice of adjurations and conjurations, as in the common use, of these vile enchanters or necromancers scrying in basins full of water, or in a bright sword, in a circle, or in a fire, or in the shoulder-bone of a sheep'). Chaucer and the author of the *Romance of Eustace the Monk* are referring to various types of divination and incantation. Divination by looking into a basin is hydromancy, or more specifically lecanomancy: 'The seer, or it may be the inquirer himself, by gazing fixedly into a pool or basin of still unruffled water, will see therein reflected as in a mirror an exact picture of that which it is sought to know' (Montague Summers, *Witchcraft and Black Magic*, p. 77). The act of 'looking into a sword' is a form of crystal-gazing (crystallomancy), the use of burnished steel 'to see reflected therein passing events or to glimpse the shadow of futurity' (Summers, p. 78). See also the chapter entitled 'Divination' in Charles J.S. Thompson, *Mysteries and Secrets of Magic* (pp. 142–50). The examination of a sheep's shoulder is spatulamancy, a form of extispicy. The diviner would 'draw conclusions from the lines and dots found on the shoulder blade of a sheep after it had been dried in the sun' (Thompson, p. 144). See Beryl Rowland, *Blind Beasts: Chaucer's Animal World*, Kent, Ohio: The Kent State University Press, 1971, pp. 149–51. The allusion to 'turning the psalter round' ('le sautier faire torner', v. 20) seems to prefigure the rituals of the Black Mass of which inversions of various sorts are a feature. See Summers, pp. 208–13, and Thompson, pp. 137–41.

3. This passage reads: 'Wistasces n'avoit nul denier / De la monnoie dou païs / Fors que tornois et paresis' (vv. 56–58). Coinage was reformed and standardized by Charlemagne, but in the centuries following his reign minting rights tended to become increasingly localized. The basis for most European coinage was the *denier* 'penny', but its value and silver content varied from one minting authority to another, even though all mints used the same accounting system. The *sou/sol* 'shilling' and the *livre* 'pound' were not actual coins but money of account. The terms *tornois* 'minted at Tours' and *paresis* 'minted at Paris' were substantives, or adjectives used with *denier* and *livre*. Four *livres parisis* were equivalent to five *livres tornois.*

4. For v. 144 Conlon follows Michel and reads 'Cil s'escrie: "Dame! Baron!" ' I have taken the form *dame* to be feminine here. But Foerster-Trost have 'Dame baron!' ('lord barons') in which *dame* derives from *dominum* 'lord'.

5. Nones were the ninth hour of the day (around 3.00 p.m.).

6. Joyeuse is Charlemagne's sword (e.g. *La Chanson de Roland*, vv. 2501, 2508, etc., ed. F. Whitehead, Oxford: Blackwell, 2nd ed. 1946, revised ed. by T.D. Hemming, Bristol: Bristol Classical Press, 1993). Durendal is Roland's sword (ibid. vv. 926, 988, etc.) and Hauteclaire that of his companion, Oliver (ibid., vv. 1363, 1463, etc.). Courte or Courtain is the sword belonging to Ogier le Danois, hero of a lost twelfth-century

poem and of the *Chevalerie Ogier*, a thirteenth-century *chanson de geste*. Maugis and Basin are thieves and sorcerers who are found in a number of texts. One text which seems to be have been important for the author of the *Romance of Eustace the Monk* is the early thirteenth-century epic *Renaut de Montauban* (also called the *Quatre fils Aymon*), in which Maugis is a leading figure. In this text we find allusions to all four swords mentioned in the *Romance*, as well as to Basin, Aymon (who is mentioned later in the *Romance*, v. 2205), Toledo and a horse called Morel (see below, v. 552, etc.). The manuscript tradition relating to *Renaut de Montauban* is complex, but in this text Maugis is a both a thief and an *enchanteor*, and he is associated with Toledo, where he acquired his training in magic. In *Renaud de Montauban* Maugis uses magic to put Charles and the peers of France to sleep and then, as he is said to have done in the *Romance* (vv. 287–90), steals their swords (vv. 10502–524, ed. Jacques Thomas, Geneva: Droz, Textes Littéraires Français, 371, 1989). On Maugis see P. Verelst, 'Le Personnage de Maugis dans *Renaut de Montauban* (versions rimées traditionnelles)', *Romanica Gandensia*, 18 (1981), pp. 73–152. One can also note that Basin appears in the epic *Jehan de Lanson*, as do Courtain, Durendal, Hauteclere, Agoulant (who is mentioned later in the *Romance*, v. 2205), the city of Toledo and a personage called Malaquin, an enchanter from Nubia (ed. J.V. Myers, Chapel Hill, North Carolina: University of North Carolina Press, 1965). On *Jehan de Lanson* see also *Histoire Littéraire de la France*, 22, pp. 561–82, especially p. 570. Maugis and Basin are also mentioned in the same line of the *Roman de Fauvel* (ed. A. Långfors, Paris: Firmin Didot, 1919), v. 1183.

7. Foerster and Trost give the name of Hainfrois' champion as William not Eustace ('Willaume ot non de Maraquise', v. 349).

8. The tocsin was a bell used to sound an alarm.

9. On this episode see Introduction, p. 14. It has been suggested that Simon de Boulogne was Count Renaud's favourite minstrel (Conlon, p. 128). But Renaud had a brother called Simon, who married Marie, the heiress of Ponthieu and niece of King Philip Augustus. However, this marriage did not take place until 1208. See Introduction, n. 42.

10. A palfrey is a saddle-horse which was used for ordinary riding and particularly favoured by women.

11. The tithe was originally a levy of one tenth of income for the support of the clergy and the Church, but increasingly it was appropriated for secular purposes. It was especially a tax paid in kind. By stealing ten horses and returning one, Eustace sees himself as fulfilling this obligation.

12. A *ronci* (or *roncin*) is a packhorse or hack of little value (cf. *La Chanson de Roland*, v. 758: 'Nen i perdrat ne runcin ne sumer').

13. In the text, the forms representing Eustace's efforts to imitate the nightingale are 'ochi', 'fier', 'non l'ot, si ot' and 'hui' (vv. 1148–62).

14. The terms I have translated as 'to fuck' and 'to use one's bum' are *bareter* (vv. 1199, 1204, 1224, 1259) and *culeter* (vv. 1205, 1207, 1225, 1258, 1260). It seems that *bareter* is not attested elsewhere with this meaning. The verb *foutre* 'fuck' appears in vv. 1255 and 1265 and in the phrase *fout-en-cul* in v. 1270.

15. Berger and Petit (p. 196) may well be correct in interpreting *Genos* in v. 1295 as Guînes rather than as Genech (Conlon, p. 125, gives Genech (Nord) or Gennes-Ivergny (Pas de Calais)). They point out that in 1209 (i.e. several years after Eustace's period of outlawry), the King of France went to Guînes in order to assist the Count of Boulogne. The king's expedition was directed against Count Arnaud of Guînes and it passed through Sangatte, a location which is mentioned in vv. 1322–23. See Baldwin, *The Government of Philip Augustus*, p. 201. In v. 1303 *Sainte Marie au Bos* is presumably, as Berger and Petit indicate, Sainte-Marie-au-Bois de Ruisseauville (Pas-de-

Calais), an old abbey near Coupelle-Vieille (a location which appears in the text as La Capiele or La Chapiele) rather than Sainte-Marie-au Bosc (Seine-Maritime), as Conlon suggests (p. 127). See Berger and Petit, pp. 198–99.

16. Vv. 1930–31 ('Parmi ses tres, ki ke s'en plaigne, / Li a conduit toute s'ensaigne') are difficult to interpret. In this passage there is a general difficulty in interpreting the subject of the various verbs. *Tres* in v. 1930 could mean 'tents' or 'masts, sails', but Foerster and Trost (p. 73) correctly point out that neither interpretation is satisfactory. They suggest replacing *ses tres* by *son cors*. Berger and Petit translate the lines as 'Et, s'en plaigne qui voudra, il [Eustace] amena contre lui tous les hommes qui combattaient sous son enseigne.'

17. Michel (p. 108) interprets *Godehiere* in v. 1932 as the Anglo-Saxon for 'good lord' (= God help). He sees *Vincenesel* in v. 1933 as being composed of *(St) Vincent* and *help*, whereas it is certainly to be interpreted as 'Winchelsea'. For Eustace's link with Winchelsea see Introduction, pp. 19, 32–34, 38–39.

18. V. 2112 reads 'Si fist a lui tenser .I.flue.' Berger and Petit translate this line as '[Eustace] provoqua un raz-de-marée pour se protéger', and they are of the opinion that Eustace is again demonstrating his powers as a magician (p. 187).

19. The text states that Eustace employed 'more than four' workmen ('Des ouvriers i mist plus de quatre'), but this is too small a figure. Berger and Petit translate as 'avec une-main-d'oeuvre abondante'. The mark was money of account and a denomination of weight for precious metals. It represented two thirds of a pound sterling and half a Parisian pound.

20. A vielle was a fiddle, a bowed instrument with four or five strings.

21. Orphrey was originally Phrygian gold embroidery (*auriphrygium*). It was later used for any gold or rich embroidery, and also more particularly for the ornamental strip on an ecclesiastical vestment.

22. It is not entirely clear who speaks v. 2187 ('De coi fesistes or faviele?'). Conlon attributes it to the mariner, but Forester and Trost award it to Eustace. Berger and Petit, who translate the Foerster-Trost text, render it as 'Pourquoi faire des histoires?'

23. The form *codidouet* (v. 2201) is rendered by Berger and Petit as 'Godidouet' and, following Foerster-Trost, they explain it as 'God it wot.'

24. Agoulant is a pagan king, who appears in a number of *chansons de geste*, especially the *Chanson d'Aspremont*. Aymon, son of Renaud de Montauban, is found in *La Mort Maugis d'Aigremont* and in *Renaut de Montauban* (see above, note 5). Blancandin is perhaps the hero of the idyllic romance *Blancandin et l'Orgueilleuse d'Amour*. Florence de Rome is the eponymous heroine of an early thirteenth-century *chanson de geste*.

25. Conlon states that the Boulogne ship ('la nef de Boulogne', v. 2256) was a huge ship in the form of a castle, which Eustace had built in Calais with the intention of frightening the English (p. 18). The Boulogne ship could perhaps have been the one on which Eustace managed to reach Louis in Winchelsea. See Notes to the Translation, n. 61.

26. On the loss of the ships in Damme see Conlon, pp. 12 and 18, and Introduction, pp. 28–29. Conlon thinks that it was probably during the attack on the ships by the English in Damme that Eustace lost the Boulogne ship (see note 25).

27. On Raoul de Tournelle see Notes to the Introduction, n. 38 and n. 71. Varlés de Montagui has not been identified.

BIBLIOGRAPHY

Editions

Conlon, Denis J. *Li Romans de Witasse le Moine: roman du treizième siècle, édité d'après le manuscrit fonds français 1553 de la Bibliothèque Nationale, Paris.* Chapel Hill, North Carolina: University of North Carolina Press (University of North Carolina Studies in the Romance Languages and Literatures, 126), 1972, 142pp.

Foerster, Wendelin, and Johan Trost. *Witasse le Moine: altfranzösischer Abenteuerroman des XIII. Jahrhunderts, nach der einzigen Pariser Handschrift von neuem herausgeben.* Halle: Niemeyer (Romanische Bibliothek, 4), 1898, xxxi + 88pp, reprint, Geneva: Slatkine, 1976.

Michel, Francisque. *Roman d'Eustache le Moine: pirate fameux du XIIIe siècle, publié pour la première fois d'après un manuscrit de la Bibliothèque Royale.* Paris: Silvestre – London, Pickering, 1834, xlv + 118pp.

Translation

Berger, Roger, and Aimé Petit. In *Contes à rire du Nord de la France.* Troesnes: Corps 9 Editions (Trésors littéraires médiévaux du Nord de la France), 1987, pp. 149–99.

Chronicles and Archival Material

(i) In Latin

Annals of Dunstable (*Annales prioratus de Dunstaplia*). In *Annales monastici*, ed. H.R. Luard. 4 vols, London: Longman etc. (Rerum britannicarum medii aevi scriptores), 1866–69, I, pp. 3–420.

Annals of Waverley (*Ex annalibus Waverleiensis Monasterii*). In M. Bouquet, *Recueil des historiens des Gaules et de la France.* 24 vols, Paris: Imprimerie Royale, 1734–1904, XVIII (1822), pp. 187–210.

Chronicle of Lanercost. In *Chronicon de Lanercost 1201–1346*, ed. J. Stevenson. Edinburgh: Maitland Club, 1839.

Chronicle of Laon (*Ex chronico anonymi Laudunensis canonici*). In M. Bouquet, *Recueil des historiens des Gaules et de la France.* 24 vols, Paris: Imprimerie Royale, 1734–1904, XVIII (1822), pp. 707–20.

Chronicle of Mailros. In *Chronica de Mailros, e codice unico in bibliotheca cottoniana servato.* Edinburgh: Edinburgh Printing Company (for the Bannatyne Club), 1835.

Chronicle of Mortemer (*Ex chronici coenobii Mortui-Maris*). In M. Bouquet, *Recueil des historiens des Gaules et de la France.* 24 vols, Paris: Imprimerie Royale, 1734–1904, XVIII (1822), pp. 354–52.

Guillaume Le Breton. *Gesta Philippi Augusti* and *Philippidos*. In *Oeuvres de Rigord et de Guillaume Le Breton, historiens de Philippe-Auguste, publiées pour la Société de l'Histoire de France*, ed. H.F. Delaborde. 2 vols, Paris: Renouard, 1882–85.

Matthew Paris [Matthaei Parisiensis], *Chronica majora*, ed. H.R. Luard. 7 vols, London: Longman, etc. (Rerum britannicarum medii aevi scriptores), 1872–84. For the variant readings for Matthew's description of the battle of Sandwich see M. Bouquet, *Recueil des historiens des Gaules et de la France*. 24 vols, Paris: Imprimerie Royale, 1734–1904, XVII, p. 741.

Henry Knighton. *Chronicon Henrici Knighton vel Cnitton, monachi Leycestrensis*, ed. H.R. Lumby. 2 vols, London: Her Majesty's Stationery Office, etc. (Rerum britannicarum medii aevi scriptores), 1889–95 (see I, Book 2, pp. 205–06).

Lambert of Ardres. *Historia comitum ghisnensium*. In (i) *Chronique de Guines et d'Ardre par Lambert, curé d'Ardre (918–1203) / Lamberti ardensis ecclesiae presbyteri chronicon ghisnense et ardense (918–1203)*, ed. Denis-Charles de Godefroy-Ménilglaise. Paris: Renouard (Société des antiquaires de la Morinie), 1855, and (ii) M. Bouquet, *Recueil des historiens des Gaules et de la France*. 24 vols, Paris: Imprimerie Royale, 1734–1904, XVIII (1822), pp. 584–88 (extract).

Nicholas Trevet. *Annals*. In *F. Nicholai Triveti, de ordine frat. praedicatorum, annales*, ed. Thomas Hog. London: English Historical Society, 1845.

Ralph of Coggeshall. *Chronicon anglicanum*, ed. J. Stevenson. London: Longman (Rerum britannicarum medii aevi scriptores, 65), 1875 (see pp. 172, 185).

Roger of Howden (or Hoveden). In *Chronica magisteri Rogeri de Hovedene*, ed. W. Stubbs. 4 vols, London: Longman, etc. (Rerum britannicarum medii aevi scriptores), 1868–71.

Roger of Wendover, *Flores historiarum*, ed. H.R. Luard. 3 vols, London: Longman, etc. (Rerum britannicarum medii aevi scriptores), 1890 (see II, pp. 160, 165).

Rotuli de liberate ac de misis et praestitis regnante Johanne, ed. Sir Thomas Duffus Hardy. London: Eyre and Spottiswoode, 1844.

Rotuli litterarum clausarum in Turri Londinensi asservati, ed. Sir Thomas Duffus Hardy. 2 vols, London: Eyre and Spottiswoode, 1834–44.

Rotuli litterarum patentium in Turri Londinensi asservati, ed. Sir Thomas Duffus Hardy. London: Publications of the Commissioners of the Public Records, 1835 (I, part i, 1201–1216).

Rotuli selecti ad res anglicas et hibernicas spectantes, ex archivis in domo capitulari westmonasteriensi, deprompti, ed. Joseph Hunter. London: The Commissioners of the Public Records of the Kingdom, 1834 (p. 26).

Walter of Coventry. In *Memoriale fratris Walteri de Coventria (The Historical Collections of Walter of Coventry)*, ed. William Stubbs. 2 vols, London: Longman, etc. (*Rerum britannicarum medii aevi scriptores*), 1872–73 (see II, pp. 238–39).

Walter of Guisborough (or of Hemingford). In *The Chronicle of Walter of Guisborough, previously edited as the Chronicle of Walter of Hemingford or Hemingburgh*, ed. Harry Rothwell. London: The Royal Historical Society (Camden Series, 89), 1957.

(ii) In French

La Chronique de l'anonyme de Béthune. In M. Boúquet, *Recueil des historiens des Gaules et de la France*. 24 vols, Paris: Imprimerie Royale, 1734–1904, XXIV, part 2, ed. L. Deslisle (1904), pp. 754–75 (extract).

Histoire des ducs de Normandie et des rois d'Angleterre, publiée en entier, pour la première fois, d'après deux manuscrits de la Bibliolthèque du Roi, ed. Francisque Michel. Paris: Renouard, 1840, reprint New York – London: Johnson Reprint, 1965.

John of Canterbury, *Polistorie*. Unedited. MS London, British Library, Harley 636 (see f. 201v, col. 2 – 202v, col. 1).

L'Histoire de Guillaume le Maréchal, comte de Striguil et de Pembroke, régent d'Angleterre de 1216 à 1219: poème français, ed. P. Meyer. 3 vols, Paris: Renouard, 1891–1901.

(iii) Written in English

Robert of Gloucester, in *The Metrical Chronicle of Robert of Gloucester*, ed. William A. Wright, Part II, London: Her Majesty's Stationery Office (Rerum britannicarum medii aevi scriptores), 1887 (see p. 716, v. 10616).

Items Devoted in Full or in Part to Eustace the Monk

Cannon, Henry line 'The Battle of Sandwich and Eustace the Monk', *English Historical Review*, 27 (1912), 649–70.

Carpenter, David A. 'Eustace the Monk', in *Dictionary of National Biography, Missing Persons*, ed. C.S. Nicholls. Oxford – New York: Oxford University Press, 1993, pp. 212–13.

Deseille, Ernest. *Eustache le Moine, chronique boulonnaise*. Boulogne-sur-Mer: Aigre, 1878.

Jordan, Leo. 'Quellen und Komposition von *Eustache le Moine* nebst Analyse des *Trubert* und Nachweis der Existenz mehrerer Robin Hood-Balladen im 13. Jahrhundert', *Archiv für das Studium der neueren Sprachen und Literaturen*, 113 (1904), 66–100, 116 (1906), 375–81.

Kapferer, Anne-Dominique. 'Banditisme, roman, féodalité: le Boulonnais d'Eustache le Moine', in *Economies et sociétés au moyen âge: mélanges offerts à Edouard Perroy*. Paris: Publications de la Sorbonne (Etudes, 5), 1973, pp. 220–40.

———. 'Mépris, savoirs et tromperies dans le roman boulonnais d'Eustache le Moine (XIIIème siècle)', in *Actes du colloque des 5 et 6 mai 1978, littérature et société au Moyen-Age*. Amiens: Université de Picardie – Paris: Champion, 1978, pp. 333–51.

Keen, Maurice. 'The Romance of Eustace the Monk', in *The Outlaws of Medieval Legend*. London – Henley: Routledge and Kegan Paul – Toronto – Buffalo: University of Toronto Press, 1961, revised ed. 1977, pp. 53–63.

Levy, Brian. 'Eustache le Moine, ou le combattant à la recherche d'un combat?', in *Le Monde des héros dans la culture médiévale*. Greifswald: Reineke (*WODAN*, 35), 1994, pp. 161–70.

Malo, Henri. 'Eustache le Moine: un pirate boulonnais au XIIIe siècle', *La Revue du Nord*, 1893, 15–19, 41–46, 82–86, 117–20. Also in separate print, Paris: Bibliothèque de la Revue du Nord, 1893. A lecture given in Boulogne, 12 March, 1893 (page references are taken from the copy in separate print).

Paris, Gaston. Review of Foester-Trost edition, *Romania*, 21 (1892), 279–80.

Schmolke-Hasselmann, Beate. 'Füchse in Menschengestalt: die listige Heldin Wistasse le Moine und Fouke Fitz Waryn', in *Third International Beast Epic, Fable and Fabliau Colloquium, Münster 1979, Proceedings*, eds. J. Goossens and T. Sodmann. Cologne: Böhlau (Niederdeutsche Studien, 30), 1981, pp. 356–79.

Wright, Thomas. 'Eustace the Monk', in *Essays on Subjects Connected with the Literature, Popular Superstitions, and History of England in the Middle Ages*. 2 vols, London: John Russell Smith, 1846, II, pp. 121–46.

Other Items Consulted

Ahier, Philip. *Stories of Jersey Seas, of Jersey's Coast and of Jersey Seamen*. Huddersfield: Adventurer Press, n.d.

Appleby, John T. *John, King of England*. New York: Knopf, 1959.

Audouin, Edouard. *Etude sur l'armée royale au temps de Philippe Auguste*. Paris: Champion, 1913.

Baldwin, John W. *The Government of Philip Augustus: Foundations of French Royal Power in the Middle Ages.* Berkeley – Los Angeles – London: University of California Press, 1986.

Barrois, J. *Bibliothéque protypographique, ou librairies des fils du Roi Jean, Charles V, Jean de Berri, Philippe de Bourgogne et les siens.* Paris: Treuttel and Würtz, 1830.

Berger, Elie. *Histoire de Blanche de Castille: reine de France.* Paris: Thorin, 1895 (see pp. 26–28).

Bertrand, P.-J.-B. *Précis de l'histoire physique, civile et politique, de la ville de Boulogne-sur-Mer et de ses environs, depuis les Morins jusqu'en 1814.* 2 vols, Boulogne: chez tous les libraires, 1828, reprint, Marseille: Laffitte, 1975.

Bougard, Pierre, and A. Nolibos. *Le Pas-de-Calais, de la préhistoire à nos jours.* Saint-Jean-d'Angély: Editions Bordessoules, 1988.

Brooks, F.W. 'The Battle of Damme – 1203', *The Mariner's Mirror*, 16 (1930), 263–71.

Bushell, T.A. *Kent.* Chesham, Buckinghamshire: Barracuda Books (The Barracuda Guide to County History, 1), 1976.

Canel, A. *Histoire de la ville de Pont-Audemer.* 2 vols, Pont-Audemer: Imprimerie Administrative de l'Hospice, 1885.

Carpenter, David A. *The Minority of Henry III.* London: Methuen, 1990.

Cartellieri, Alexander. *Philipp II. August, König von Frankreich.* 4 vols, Leipzig, 1921–22, reprint, Aalen: Scientia Verlag, 1969.

Cooper, William D. *The History of Winchelsea: One of the Ancient Towns added to the Cinque Ports.* London: John Russell Smith – Hastings: Harry Osborne, 1850, reprint East Sussex County Library, 1986.

D'Hauttefeuille, A., and L. Bénard. *Histoire de Boulogne-sur-mer.* 2 vols, Boulogne-sur-mer, 1860.

Delisle, Léopold V. *Recherches sur la librairie de Charles V.* 2 vols, Paris: Champion, 1907.

———. *Recherches sur les comtes de Dammartin au XIIIe siècle.* Nogent-le-Rotrou: A. Gouverneur (Mémoires de la Société Impériale des Antiquaires de France, 4th series, 1), 1869.

Derville, Alain et al. *Histoire de Calais.* Westhoek: Editions des Beffrois (Collection Histoire des villes du Nord – Pas de Calais, 8), 1985.

Dictionnaire historique et archéologique du Département du Pas-de-Calais: arrondissement de Boulogne. 3 vols, Arras: Sueur-Charruey, 1880, reprint, Brussels: Editions culture et civilisation, 1978.

Dinaux, A. *Trouvères, jongleurs et ménéstrels du Nord de la France et du Midi de la Belgique.* 3 vols, Valenciennes, 1834–42.

Duby, Georges. *Le Dimanche de Bouvines: 27 juillet 1214.* Paris: Gallimard, 1973. Also in English as *The Legend of Bouvines: War, Religion and Culture in the Middle Ages*, trans C. Tihanyi, Cambridge: Polity Press, 1990.

Du Chesne, André. *Histoire généalogique des maisons de Guines, d'Ardres, de Gand et de Coucy, et de quelques autres familles illustres, qui y ont esté alliées.* Paris: Cramoisy, 1631.

Duchet, Th., and A. Giry. *Cartulaires de l'église de Thérouanne.* Saint-Omer: Fleury-Lemaire (Société des antiquaires de Morinie), 1881.

Ellis, Clarence. *Hubert de Burgh: a Study in Constancy.* London: Phoenix House, 1952.

Haigneré, Abbé Daniel. *Dictionnaire topographique de la France comprenant les noms de lieux anciens et modernes: arrondissement de Boulogne-sur-Mer.* Boulogne-sur-Mer: Aigre (Mémoires de la Société Académique de l'arrondissement de Boulogne-sur-Mer, 11), 1882.

———. 'Supplément au recueil des chartes de Samer', *Mémoires de la Société Académique de l'arrondissement de Boulogne-sur-Mer*, 13 (1882–86), 361–76.

Hamy, Ernest-Théodore. 'La Charte de commune d'Ambleteuse', *Bulletin de la Société Académique de Boulogne*, 1 (1864–66), 139–46. Also in separate print, Boulogne: Aigre, 1866.

Héliot, Pierre. *Histoire de Boulogne et du Boulonnais*. Lille: Raoust, 1937, reprint, Marseille: Laffitte, 1980.

———. 'Le Château de Course', *Bulletin de la Commission des monuments historiques du Pas-de-Calais*, 6 (1939), 544–48.

Holt, J.C. *Magna Carta*. Cambridge: Cambridge University Press, 1965.

———. *Robin Hood*. London: Thames and Hudson, 1982.

Hutton, William H. *Philip Augustus*. London and New York: MacMillan, 1896.

Jamieson, A.G. (ed.). *A People of the Sea: the Maritime History of the Channel Islands*. London – New York: Methuen, 1986.

Jouan, René. *Histoire de la marine française des origines jusqu'à la Révolution*. Paris: Payot, 1932.

La Roncière, Charles de. *Histoire de la marine française: I, les origines*. Paris: Plon, 1899.

Le Goff, Jacques. *La Civilisation de l'occident médiéval*. Paris: Arthaud (Collection Les Grandes Civilisations), 1964.

Le Patourel, John. 'Guernsey, Jersey and their Environment in the Middle Ages', *La Société Guernesiaise, Reports and Transactions*, 19 (1971–75), 441–50.

———. *The Medieval Administration of the Channel Islands 1199–1399*. London: 1937.

Lindsay, Jack. *The Normans and their World*. London: Hart-Davis, MacGibbon, 1973.

Lloyd, Alan. *King John*. Newton Abbot: David and Charles, 1973.

Lottin, Alain et al. *Histoire de Boulogne-sur-Mer*. Lille: Presses Universitaires de Lille (Collection Histoire des villes du Nord – Pas de Calais, 5), 1983.

McKechnie, William S. *Magna Carta: a Commentary on the Great Charter of King John*. Glasgow, 1905, 2nd ed. 1914, reprint, New York: Burt Franklin, 1958.

Malo, Henri. *Un Grand Feudataire: Renaud de Dammartin et la coalition de Bouvines. Contribution à l'étude du règne de Philippe-Auguste*. Paris: Champion, 1898.

———. *Petite Histoire de Boulogne-sur-Mer*. Boulogne-sur-Mer: Société Typographique et Lithographique, 1899.

Marr, L. James. *A History of the Bailiwick of Guernsey: the Islanders' Story*. London and Chichester: Phillimore, 1982.

Michel, Francisque. *Rapports à M. Le Ministre de l'Instruction Publique sur les anciens monuments de l'histoire et de la littérature de la France qui se trouvent dans les bibliothèques de l'Angleterre et de l'Ecosse*. Paris: Imprimerie Royale, 1838 (see pp. 10–11).

Mitchell, David. *Pirates*. London: Thames and Hudson, 1976.

Mollat du Jourdin, Michel. 'Philippe Auguste et la mer', in *La France de Philippe Auguste: le temps des mutations: actes du colloque international organisé par le C.N.R.S. (Paris, 29 septembre – 4 octobre 1980)*. Paris: Editions du Centre National de la Recherche Scientifique (Colloques internationaux du Centre National de la Recherche Scientifique, 602), 1982, pp. 605–23.

Nicolas, Nicholas H. *A History of the Royal Navy, from the Earliest Times to the Wars of the French Revolution*. 2 vols, London: Richard Bentley, 1847.

Norgate, Kate. *The Minority of Henry the Third*. London: MacMillan, 1912.

Petit-Dutaillis, Charles. *Etude sur la vie et le règne de Louis VIII (1187–1226)*. Paris: Bouillon, 1894.

Powicke, Sir Maurice. *The Thirteenth Century: 1215–1307*. Oxford: Clarendon Press, 1953, 2nd ed., 1961.

Rodière, Roger. 'Chartes diverses du Boulonnais', *Mémoire de la Société Académique de l'arrondissement de Boulogne*, 24 (1906), 1–241.

Roblin-Dubin, Sylvie. 'L'Ecole de magie de Tolède: histoire et légende', in *Histoire et littérature au Moyen Age: actes du colloque du centre d'Etudes Médiévales de l'Université de Picardie (Amiens 20–24 mars 1985)*, ed. D. Buschinger. Göppingen: Kümmerle, 1991, pp. 419–33.

Rothwell, Harry. *English Historical Documents: 1189–1327.* London: Eyre and Spottis-woode, 1975.

Stevenson, Wendy B. 'England, France and the Channel Islands, 1204–1259', *La Société Guernesiaise, Reports and Transactions,* 19 (1971–75), 569–76.

———. 'English Rule in the Channel Islands in a Period of Transition, 1204–1259', *La Société Guernesiaise, Reports and Transactions,* 20 (1978), 234–58.

Summers, Montague. *Witchcraft and Black Magic.* London – New York – Melbourne – Sydney: Rider, 1946, reprint London: Senate, 1995.

J. Taschereau. *Catalogue des manuscrits français de la Bibliothèque Impériale, Département des manuscrits,* 1 (1868), 248–52 (description of contents of MS 1553).

Thobois, Abbé B.-J. *Le Château et les seigneurs de Mont-Cavrel, commune d'Alette (P.de-C.).* Arras: Répessé-Crépel, 1901.

Thompson, Charles J.S. *Mysteries and Secrets of Magic.* London: Lane, 1927, reprint London: Senate, 1995.

Williamson, James A. *The English Channel: a History.* London: Collins, 1959.

THE ROMANCE
OF
FOUKE FITZ WARYN

INTRODUCTION

1. *Fact and Fiction*

'The whole affair of Fulk fitz Warin', writes the historian Sydney Painter in his book *The Reign of King John*, 'is extremely curious. A simple knight of meagre landed power defies the king, rises in revolt, gathers a band of outlaws, and wanders about a realm for three years. Then he is pardoned at the request of two of the king's most intimate friends, given what he had originally wanted, and later allowed to marry a rich widow' (p. 52).[1] This 'extremely curious' affair is the subject of the Anglo-Norman romance *Fouke le Fitz Waryn*, originally a verse romance from the thirteenth century, but surviving only in a fourteenth-century prose version, which is translated below under the title *The Romance of Fouke Fitz Waryn*. Also extant is the synopsis by the sixteenth-century antiquary, John Leland, of a lost English verse romance. As in the case of *The Romance of Eustace the Monk*, *The Romance of Fouke Fitz Waryn* contains information concerning the hero's life and activities which can be substantiated from documentary evidence. It also makes statements which may well be historically accurate but which lack documentary support. In addition, it contains material which is clearly invented. This invented material no doubt derives in part from the author's individual creativity and in part, again in a fashion similar to *The Romance of Eustace the Monk*, from a general stock of romance or folklore motifs. Painter categorizes the entire text as 'a weird mixture of accurate information, plausible stories that lack confirmation, and magnificent flights of pure imagination' (p. 50). This point of view has recently been echoed by Janet Meisel in her book *The Barons of the Welsh Frontier*. She describes *The Romance of Fouke Fitz Waryn* as a 'peculiar combination of fantasy, error and fact' and also as a text which contains a 'strange combination of the commonplace and the bizarre' (p. 132). However, it is important to recognize that, although it can be condemned for its

---

[1] For full details of items cited in the Introduction and Notes see the Bibliography. All references to the text of *Fouke le Fitz Waryn* are taken from the edition by E.J. Hathaway, P.T. Ricketts, C.A. Robson and A.D. Wilshere, Oxford: Blackwell, 1975.

occasional inaccuracies, the *Romance* is an important source not only for the history of the Fitz Waryns as a family but for the history of the Welsh Marches in the twelfth and early thirteenth centuries.

In the *Romance* the story of Fouke Fitz Waryn (I shall use the French form Fouke rather than the anglicized Fulk and the form Waryn rather than Warin) is presented to us in three parts of disparate length. It opens with some family history, which centres first on the area surrounding Ludlow then expands to cover north Shropshire and the Welsh Marches. The central section, which for many readers provides the text with its principal interest, tells of Fouke's period of outlawry. Here we are told how Fouke quarrels with King John and how, until his pardon, he is hunted and hounded by a variety of pursuers. Like the writer who gave us an account of the successes enjoyed by Eustace the Monk, the author delights in narrating the notable victories which Fouke scores over King John and the anger and frustration which he repeatedly causes him. In the third section the tale is brought to a swift conclusion by means of a brief account of Fouke's later years, which are dominated by his blindness and his feeling of sorrow for the sins he has committed.

2. *Fouke as a Historical Figure*

Like Eustace the Monk, Fouke Fitz Waryn was a real person. His historicity is amply conveyed by a wide range of documentation. Unfortunately, however, the documentation relating to his period as outlaw is distinctly slender, and unlike those of Eustace the Monk his activities did not give rise to lengthy descriptions or provoke vituperative comments in the works of contemporary chroniclers. When compared with the known facts, the *Romance* offers us a good deal which is true or broadly true. But it has to be admitted that there are also historical inaccuracies. The opening section, which deals with the background to the hero's life and adventures, displays a certain amount of confusion. As the editors of the Anglo-Norman Text Society (ANTS) edition tell us, there are in this section 'many errors in the chronology, the genealogy and the identification of historical persons' (p. xxviii). The author begins with an account of the decades following the Conquest, but some of the knights presented as companions of William the Conqueror actually flourished during the reign of Henry I. Moreover, although the hero of the *Romance* is Fouke III, the author devotes a good deal of space to his grandfather, Fouke I, and his father, Fouke II, confusing the two in the process. In fact, not only are some of Fouke I's attested activities transferred to his son, Fouke II (also known as Fouke le Brun), but he is also confused with the founder of the family himself, Waryn (Gwaryn) de Metz. The final section of the text is, from the standpoint of history, not so much inaccurate as incomplete. Fouke III did not die until around 1258, yet the period of his life which followed his pardon in 1203 is given short shrift. The account of his activities in these last fifty-five years of his life occupies only about one twentieth of the text. But it is true, as the text tells us in this section, that the earl marshal granted him the town of Wantage in Oxfordshire and that on his death Fouke was buried in New Abbey at Alberbury, an abbey which he himself had founded.

Very little is known about the origins of the Fitz Waryn family. Even though the founder, Waryn de Metz, is said in the *Romance* to have arrived in England during the time of William the Conqueror, there is no record in the Domesday Book of a man of that name, or of his sons, holding lands in chief. The *Romance* states that William gave him the manor of Alberbury in Shropshire.[2] Meisel reports, however, that 'the very existence of Warin de Metz seems somewhat problematical' (p. 34). But she adds that 'it is possible that the "Warin" who occasionally appeared with the Peverel family in Henry I's reign was Warin de Metz'.[3] In the *Romance* Waryn de Metz marries William Peverel's niece, Melette. The first member of the

---

[2] 'Certainly the manor of Alberbury was never held in chief by the Fitz Warins, for it was one of Roger Corbet's manors (held of Earl Roger) during William's reign; and once the earls of Montgomery lost their lands, Alberbury was held by the Corbets in chief. The Fitz Warins did hold Alberbury in the twelfth and thirteenth centuries, but they held it of the Corbets' (Meisel, p. 172, n. 2). On Alberbury see *The Victoria History of the Counties of England, A History of Shropshire*, II, pp. 47–50, VIII, pp. 181–223, and D. George et al., *St Michael and All Angels Church, Alberbury: a 700th Celebration*.

[3] Meisel (p. 34) cites the *Antiquities of Shropshire* by R.W. Eyton, who, from the legendary material concerning Waryn de Metz of Lorrain, selects the following 'facts': (i) he lived in the time of Henry I, (ii) his marriage allied him with the Peverel family, then very powerful in Shropshire and the Marches, and (iii) he was related to the dukes of Brittany and consequently to the family of Lestrange, whose progenitor Guy is represented as having come to England and settled there on Waryn's suggestion (II, p. 3). Eyton also suggests that Waryn de Metz (or possibly his son William) acquired the lordship of Broseley (earlier Burwardsley) in the time of Henry I, 'perhaps by exchange, perhaps under a partial forfeiture of the previous Lord, perhaps by feoffment of the then Baron of Holgate' (pp. 3–4). He adds that in 1115 Waryn and Hamo Peverel were witnesses at the Archidiaconal Chapter, which sat at Castle Holgate under the presidency of Richard, Bishop of London. Eyton also states that it was presumably the same Waryn who attested with respect to the parochial jurisdiction of Wenlock Priory as Lord of Burwardsley (p. 4). Meisel gives the date of the death of Waryn de Metz as c. 1146 (p. 37).

family whose name appears in the documentary evidence is Waryn's son Roger. Some time between 1139 and 1144 a *Rogerius filius Warini* was a witness to a charter concerning an exchange of lands between the abbey of Shrewsbury and Walchelin Maminot, who was a nephew and one of the heirs of Hamo Peverel. The first mention of a family member by the name of Fulk/Fouke appears in a document dating from around 1145. Roger Fitz Waryn was again a witness to a charter of Walchelin Maminot, but on this occasion the charter was also witnessed by his brother *Fulco*.[4] Meisel thinks that, as his name precedes that of Fouke, Roger was the elder brother, and that he may well have died without heirs. For it was to Fouke I that Henry of Anjou, during his visit to England in 1149, gave the manor of Alveston in Gloucestershire.[5] Another early reference to Fouke Fitz

[4] For the first charter see *The Cartulary of Shrewsbury Abbey*, I, p. 26, item 28. In this charter, issued after the death of Hamo Peverel, Walchelin Maminot requires the monks of Shrewsbury Abbey to give him Crudgington in return for Uppington. Meisel, who cites only the manuscript (National Library of Wales, MS 7851 [Phillipps MS 3516]), gives the dates as 'between 1136 and 1141' (p. 34), but Hamo Peverel did not die until 1139. For the second charter, witnessed by both Roger Fitz Waryn and his brother Fouke, see *The Cartulary of Haughmond Abbey*, no. 39. In this charter Walchelin grants Bradford Mill to Haughmond Abbey. Walchelin Maminot was a cousin of William II Peverel, and when Hamo Peverel died he and William shared the inheritance (see John Hudson, *Land, Law, and Lordship in Anglo-Norman England*, p. 114). Walchelin was also Robert of Gloucester's castellan and a supporter of the Empress Matilda. In 1138 he held Dover Castle against Stephen (see J.H. Round, *Geoffrey de Mandeville*, p. 2, n. 2). For details concerning the Peverel family see Notes to the Translation, n. 9. There are also two other early references to members of the Fitz Waryn family. A William Fitz Waryn is mentioned in a charter dating from late 1139 confirming an earlier charter of Henry I (*Regesta regum anglo-normannorum: 1066–1154*, II, no. 1282) concerning the restoration of lands held by Bishop Roger of Salisbury and others (ibid., III, p. 69, no. 189) and a Geoffrey Fitz Waryn is mentioned in a charter from the Abbey of St Nicholas in Angers, dated between 1133 and 1139, in which the empress confirms the abbey's churches in England (ibid., p. 7, no. 20). Also in *The Cartulary of Shrewsbury Abbey*, Fouke Fitz Waryn I is a witness to a charter, dated 'c. 1144–1155', in which William Fitz Alan I grants the bank of the Severn and water for the Abbey's mill at Eyton (II, p. 287). See Eyton, *Antiquities of Shropshire*, II, p. 4.

[5] *Regesta regum anglo-normannorum: 1066–1154*, III, p. 121, no. 320. In this charter Alveston appears as Alceston. In 1156 Henry gave Fouke I the Leicestershire manor of Whadborough. Alveston seems to have been the first manor to be held in chief by the Fitz Waryns. Meisel comments that this gift 'seems to have been a reward for Fulk's loyalty to the cause of Matilda and her son' and that the 'substantial position' which the Fitz Waryn family obtained in England was acquired as a result of this support (p. 34). Fouke I's 'deep sense of gratitude' towards Henry is, in Meisel's view, confirmed by his gift of lands to the Augustinian canons of Launde in Leicestershire, gifts made, in Henry's own words, 'for the souls of my king, Henry, and his heirs and ancestors' (pp. 34–35). For Henry of Anjou's visit to England in 1149 see Round, *Geoffrey of Mandeville*, pp. 408–10.

Waryn, which is not mentioned by Meisel, occurs in the agreement between the earls of Gloucester and Hereford in 1148 or 1149. Here Fouke is
one of William of Gloucester's sureties and he appears as a tenant of his
honour, holding one knight's fee.[6]

Fouke I seems to have died in 1171. In the Pipe Roll *16 Henry II* (for
1170), he is shown to be in possession of Alveston, but in the Pipe Roll for
the following year this manor is in the hands of *Fulconis filii Fulconis filii
Warini*, i.e. in those of his son, Fouke II.[7] A notable event in the life of
Fouke I was the responsibility he was given by Henry II in 1160 for the
arming and provisioning of Dover Castle.[8] The fact that Henry bestowed
this important task upon him is clearly a mark of the esteem in which he
was held, esteem which may have had its roots in the support which he and
his family had given the Empress Matilda during the reign of King
Stephen. We have no firm evidence for Fouke I's support of Matilda,
except for the fact that it was before he became king that Henry bestowed
Alveston on Fouke I and that in June 1153 Fouke I is known to have been
present in Leicester when Henry confirmed his mother's gifts in Walcot.[9]
In general, it can be said that the relationship between Fouke I and Henry
II was one of mutual trust and respect.[10]

For reasons which are not clear, the warm relationship between Henry
II and the Fitz Waryn family did not survive the death of Fouke I. Fouke II,
writes Meisel, 'does not appear to have been a close associate of Henry II,
and it would seem that Fulk's relations with Richard I were equally distant'
(p. 35). There is certainly no sign in the records of any further gifts being
made to the family or even of the presence of Fouke II at court (except on

6 See R.H.C. Davis, 'Treaty between William Earl of Gloucester and Roger Earl of Hereford', p. 145, D. Crouch, 'The March and the Welsh Kings' (in E. King, *The Anarchy of
King Stephen's Reign*), pp. 281–83, and W.E. Wightman, *The Lacy Family in England and
Normandy 1066–1194*, p. 252. See also *The Red Book of the Exchequer*, I, p. 292.
7 'Et Fulconi filii Warini .x. li. bl. in Aloestan' ('And for Fouke Fitz Waryn, £10 in respect
of Alveston', Pipe Roll *16 Henry II*, p. 74); 'Et Fulchoni filio Fulconis filii Warini .x. li. bl.
in Aloestan' ('And for Fouke son of Fouke Fitz Waryn £10 in respect of Alveston', Pipe
Roll *17 Henry II*, p. 84).
8 'Et in munitione Castelli . de Doura . p. c. sumis frumti . et .x. sumis sal . et .xxx. bacon.
et .xi. pensis casei .xiii. li. et .v. s. et .viii. d. p. folc . fil . War.' ('And in the provisioning of
Dover Castle for a hundred loads of grain, ten of salt and thirty of hams and eleven
weys of cheese thirteen pounds five shillings and eight pence for Fouke Fitz Waryn'
(Pipe Roll *6 Henry II* (for 1160), p. 54).
9 *Regesta regum anglo-normannorum: 1066–1154*, III, p. 146, no. 379.
10 The Pipe Rolls indicate that Henry pardoned Fouke for small debts on three occasions
(1158, 1161 and 1163) and that in 1158 he gave him a gift of forty marks (Meisel, p. 35).

legal business).[11] When he succeeded his father, Fouke II had no difficulty in establishing his right to the lands which Fouke I had held in chief, but his attempts to get possession of the border castle of Whittington, which had seemingly been acquired at some stage from the Peverel family, were frustrated. During Henry's reign this castle was held by Roger de Powys and his heirs. In 1195 Fouke II's right to Whittington was recognized in the Curia Regis and it was confirmed in the following years. But at the time of his death in 1198 he had still not gained possession of this castle, which remained in the hands of the Powys family. As we shall see below, the struggle for the possession of Whittington is the central theme of *The Romance of Fouke Fitz Waryn*.

From the point of view of the land-holdings of the Fitz Waryn family, the most significant event in the life of Fouke II was his marriage to Hawyse, daughter of Joce (Joceas, Joyce) de Dynan. The date of the marriage is uncertain, but it probably took place before Joce's death in 1167. In order to explain the poor relationship between Fouke II and Henry II Meisel suggests that as a result of wealth acquired through this marriage Fouke II had no need to seek an extension of his possessions by means of royal service (p. 35). He did not, however, find it easy to enforce his claim to all his wife's considerable holdings. Hawyse was Joce's coheir, so he could only lay claim to half her lands. He certainly obtained possession of part of her inheritance, especially her lands in Berkshire, but as late as 1190, in the reign of Richard I, Fouke was still in conflict with Herbert Fitz Herbert over the Wiltshire manor of Stanton, along with Joce's other daughter, Sibyl, and her husband, Alan de Plugenai. It can be assumed, however, that his difficulties with respect to Hawyse's lands started a good deal earlier than this. The conflict concerning the manor of Stanton dragged on so long that it was not in fact settled until well after his death.[12]

The date of the birth of Fouke III, the hero of the *Romance*, is unknown. But we can note that the author of the *Romance* considers him to have been a virtual contemporary of King John, who was born in 1167. He was certainly an adult at the time of his father's death in 1198. Meisel places his date of birth 'no later than 1170' (p. 135). How important a person was he when he inherited his father's land? Sydney Painter expressed the view that

[11] Eyton states that in 1176 Fouke II was heavily fined by Henry II for forest-trespass, and he suggests that, because of the non-recognition of his claim to Whittington, Fouke had indulged in some rebellious act. Fines of this type, says Eyton, were 'probably levelled against persons whose disaffection during the late rebellion had developed itself in some overt and lawless act' (XI, pp. 37–38, see also VII, p. 69).

[12] See Meisel, pp. 36, 94–97 and 173 (n. 28).

in terms of land-holdings Fouke III was 'a very minor personage', who held merely two small mesne fiefs, £10 a year in the manor of Alveston and one or two knights' fees in chief (p. 49). However, as Meisel has shown in considerable detail (pp. 87–100), Fouke's lands, although not extraordinarily extensive, were very diverse. They included manors in Shropshire (Arlscot, Bradley, Broseley, Moston and Alderton), Staffordshire (Ashley upon Tern), Cambridgeshire (Tadlow) and Leicestershire (Whadborough). In addition, as we have seen, he had claim, through his mother, Hawyse, to half the lands which had belonged to Joce de Dynan. These included the important manor of Lambourn in Berkshire, which had been given to Joce by Henry II as compensation for the loss of his castle at Dynan (Ludlow). It was held in chief as a single knight's fee and measured at least fifteen square miles, perhaps double that amount.[13] In addition to lands in Berkshire, Hawyse owned lands in Wiltshire, Somerset, Devonshire and Hampshire.

Whittington Castle

Both within the *Romance* itself and in the real lives of Fouke III and his family, the territory which assumes the greatest importance is Whittington in Shropshire. In the *Romance*, Fouke's break with King John is stimulated by its disputed possession. The castle of Whittington was a great border castle and the original structure was probably erected by the Peverel family during the reign of Henry I. During Steven's reign it was held for the empress by the Peverels. In 1223 it was razed to the ground by Llywelyn ap Iorwerth, Prince of Wales, and in its place Fouke built a huge, moated castle with walls twelve to fifteen feet thick. The ruins of this castle can be seen to this day. R.W. Eyton in his *Antiquities of Shropshire* estimates that the manor of Whittington contained around eleven square miles (XI, p. 30). But Meisel points out that if one includes the surrounding woodland (now the area around Babbins Wood, Berrywood, Woodhouse and Hawkswood) it contained a minimum of seventeen and a half and a maximum of twenty-five square miles (p. 88). Painter states that Fouke III claimed Whittington 'on somewhat obscure grounds' (p. 49), but Meisel (p. 135) declares herself willing to accept the information which is provided by the *Romance* (in which the castle is called Blancheville). Here Whittington was first acquired by the Fitz Waryns as a gift of William

---

13 See Meisel, pp. 95–97.

Peverel. This William would be the nephew of William Peverel of Dover, to whom Henry I gave Whittington after it had devolved to his hands on the forfeiture of Earl Robert de Bellême. The elder William Peverel seems to have died childless and his nephew was certainly in possession of Whittington when the castle was fortified against Stephen in 1138. That William Peverel, the nephew, gave Whittington to the Fitz Waryns is for Meisel 'the only reasonable explanation' for their claim to this castle (p. 135). Whilst there is no clear-cut evidence for this particular gift, it is known that William Peverel did give Fulk I the manor of Tadlow in Cambridgeshire as a gift.[14]

If the Fitz Waryns did have possession of Whittington for a time, it is not known how or when they came to lose it. If the *Romance* is to believed, they lost it along with Maelor (the area around Wrexham, about twelve miles north of Whittington), when Iorwerth Drwyndwn conquered them as part of his rebellion against Henry II, who had refused to recognize him as Prince of North Wales. After a good deal of fighting, Henry and Iorwerth are said to have come to an agreement whereby Iorwerth restored Ellesmere to the king and returned to the barons of the March all the lands which had been taken from them. But Iorwerth refused to give back Whittington and Maelor to the Fitz Waryns. In their stead Henry is said to have bestowed Alveston on them. One problem with this account is that, when Iorwerth rebelled against Henry in 1175–77, the Fitz Waryns had already held Alveston for twenty-five years! Another problem is that, as we saw above, Whittington was held at that time by Roger de Powys, to whom it had been given by Henry II, who had resumed it in 1165.[15] The castle had also been resumed by Henry some time earlier as one of royal demesne, and on this occasion he had given it to Geoffrey de Vere, who became sheriff of Shropshire in 1164. It is not known when Geoffrey's investiture of Whittington took place and thus it is impossible to be certain of the length of his lordship of the castle.

Meisel is of the opinion that we can accept a good deal of what the

---

[14] On Tadlow see W. Farrer, *Feudal Cambridgeshire*, pp. 10–11. Painter thought that the Fitz Waryns' claim to Whittington had 'in some way' grown out of the gift of this Cambridgeshire fief, since William Peverel, Lord of Bourn, was also Lord of Whittington (p. 49). See Eyton, XI, 29–42. The Fitz Waryns maintained possession of Tadlow in spite of the fact that their right to it was called into question during the reign of King Richard (Meisel, p. 36, and p. 173, n. 30). See Notes to the Translation, n. 9.

[15] Eyton describes Roger de Powys as 'one of those Welshmen, whom Henry II thought it worth while to attach to the English cause by all manner of favour and patronage' (XI, p. 31).

Romance states about Whittington and Maelor, providing we accept that here, as elsewhere in the text, the author has been careless with names. The loss of Whittington and Maelor may in fact have occurred some time earlier than the *Romance* indicates, as early as the end of the reign of King Stephen. In 1149 Alveston was given to the Fitz Waryns by Henry of Anjou, and if Whittington and Maelor were lost around that time this would explain why Whittington never appears in Fouke's possession in the Pipe Rolls and 'why, once Whittington had reverted into the king's hands, Fulk II won his claim in the Curia Regis, for if a royal treaty had first deprived the Fitz Warins of this castle, then they would normally have first claim on it when it next became available' (Meisel, p. 136). If the Fitz Waryns did indeed have a claim over Maelor, which is entirely possible, then the hero of *The Romance of Fouke Fitz Waryn* 'may have had even greater justification for his rebellion than the surviving records would suggest' (Meisel, ibid.).

The hero of the *Romance*, Fouke III, succeeded his father on the latter's death in 1198. In 1195 Fouke II had fined forty marks 'for having the castle of Whittington as it was adjudged to him in the king's court', but the fine was not paid and it seems unlikely that the Fitz Waryn family took possession of the castle at that time.[16] Eyton states that in spite of the judicial decision in his favour Fouke II 'died while his efforts to make that decision effectual were still pending' (XI, p. 38). When Fouke III succeeded his father, Whittington was in the possession of Morys (Maurice, Meurich) de Powys, and the accession to the throne of King John in 1199 did not improve matters. In the year 1200 Fouke III fined £100 for the castle 'in an apparent attempt to resolve the question of Whittington once and for all' (Meisel, p. 36).[17] For his part, Morys de Powys fined the smaller sum of fifty marks.[18] It was Morys' offer which John accepted, and on 11 April 1200 he confirmed him in possession of Whittington. On Morys' death a few months later, John confirmed his sons, Werennoc and Wennoneo, in

---

16 'Fulco filius Warini debet xl m. pro habendo castello de Witinton' sicut ei adiudicatum fuit in curia regis.' (Pipe Roll *7 Richard I*, p. 246). See Painter, p. 49, and Eyton, XI, pp. 30–38.

17 'Fulco filius Warini debet c libras pro habendo juditio de castello de Witinton' cum pertinentiis . sicut jus suum quod ei adjudicatum est per considerationem curie regis' ('Fouke Fitz Waryn fines one hundred and fifty [marks] for having jurisdiction over the castle of Whittington with its appurtenances, as is his right according to the judgment of the king's court', Pipe Roll *2 John*, p. 175).

18 '[Meur]ich' Powis de Witinton' debet l m. pro habenda confirmatione regis' ('Morys Powys of Whittington fines fifty marks for having the king's confirmation', Pipe Roll *2 John*, p. 175). See also *Rotuli chartarum*, p. 43.

possession of the castle.[19] Fouke was furious that he had been denied justice in this matter and, according to the *Romance*, it was as a result of the grant of Whittington to Morys that he broke with the king. The *Romance* tells us that it was actually Fouke himself who killed Morys and Painter considers this story to be 'plausible' (p. 50). If Morys was killed by Fouke, his death must have taken place before 1 August 1200, the date on which his sons received possession of Whittington.

Outlawry

There is no reason to doubt that Fouke's period of outlawry began in the second half of the year 1200, even though the earliest documentary evidence for the rebellion dates from 9 April 1201. A Pipe Roll entry for that date indicates that all Fouke's Shropshire lands had reverted to the crown.[20] Roger de Hovedon tells us in his chronicle that when King John departed for Normandy in June 1201 he left Hubert de Burgh at the head of one hundred knights as custodian of the Welsh March, and the *Romance* may well contain a reminiscence of this when it states that John sent one hundred knights in pursuit of Fouke.[21] The first extant reference to the rebellion itself dates from 1202. On 30 April of that year King John pardoned a certain Eustace de Kivilly, who had spent some time as an outlaw in the company of Fouke.[22] Of greater interest is the evidence concerning a precise episode recounted in the *Romance*, the only episode in fact which enjoys such confirmation. The *Romance* tells us that at one stage during their period of outlawry Fouke and his companions took refuge in Stanley Abbey in Wiltshire, and the *Historia rerum anglicarum* of William of Newburgh confirms that in July 1202 men belonging to the sheriff of Wiltshire (William, Earl of Salisbury) besieged Fouke in the abbey for a period of two weeks.[23] Painter suggests that this siege was not pursued with the

---

[19] See Painter, p. 50, Meisel, p. 36, and *Rotuli chartarum*, p. 74.

[20] 'Fulconis filii Warini cum terra ipsius que sunt in manu nostra' ('With the lands of the said Fouke Fitz Waryn which are in our hands', *Memoranda Roll, 1 John*, p. 93).

[21] Roger de Hovedon, IV, p. 163. See the *Romance*, text p. 26, line 17, and translation, p. 152. See also Painter, pp. 48–49, Ellis, *Hubert de Burgh*, p. 13, and *Annales de Burton*, p. 208.

[22] *Rotuli litterarum patentium*, p. 10. This is fairly late into Fouke's period of outlawry and it may suggest that by that time one or two of his supporters were beginning to break away from him (see Thomas Wright, edition, pp. 222–23).

[23] 'Fulco filius Warini fugit ij Nonas Julii Abbatiam de Stanleye in Wiltescira, et ibi obsessus est cum sociis suis fere ab omni provincia et a multis aliis, qui illuc convenerant, xiiij. diebus. Sed in pace ecclesiae salvus exivit, et reconciliatus est in anno sequenti' ('On 6 July Fouke Fitz Waryn fled to Stanley Abbey in Wiltshire and here he was

greatest of vigour, as Fouke's maternal relatives had been generous bene-
factors of the abbey (p. 51). Indeed, when Fouke's pardon was later pro-
cured from the king, one of those who supported Fouke was Earl William
of Salisbury, who at the time of the siege had been away in Normandy with
the king.

Other evidence exists which indicates that Fouke was active in Shropshire during the period 1200 to 1201. In the *Romance* the author recounts
the origin of the Fitz Alan family. A number of Fouke's friends are presented as tenants of William Fitz Alan, the most important of the Shropshire barons. William Fitz Alan was sheriff of Shropshire, but in the spring
of 1201 he was removed from office and replaced by the Justiciar himself.[24]
Also in 1201 a certain Simon de Lenz received the sum of four marks in
order to support the bereaved son of Morys de Powys, whilst he was out
hunting outlaws.[25] Almost nothing is known of Fouke's activities in 1202
and 1203, except for the fact that there is evidence that a ship belonging to
Fouke, who like Eustace was well known as a ship's captain, was seized by
royal officials.[26] It is known, however, that in August, September and October of the year 1203 safe-conducts were issued to Fouke and his companions.[27] Also in 1203, in the Shropshire Assize Roll for that year, there is

besieged along with his companions by almost the entire province and by many others
who had gathered there, for fourteen days. But with the peace of the church he left in
safety and the following year he was reconciled', II, pp. 506–07). This entry actually
comes from the Continuation of William of Newburgh's *Historia* by a monk of Furness
Abbey, who at this point was copying the Stanley Abbey Chronicle (now Bodleian
Library, MS Digby 11).

24 Painter states that the Justiciar was 'undoubtedly acting through his sub-sheriff Henry
Furnel'. He adds that: 'As a goodly proportion of Fulk's friends mentioned in the
romance were Fitz Alan tenants, this change of sheriffs may well have been connected
with his activities' (p. 50).

25 'Et Simoni de Lenz iiij m. ad sustentationem suam ad querendos utlagatos homines'
('And for Simon de Lenz four marks to support him in the search for outlaws', Pipe Roll
3 John, p. 277).

26 *Rotuli litterarum clausarum*, I, p. 136, and Pipe Roll 6 John, p. 218 ('Et Willelmo capel-
lano . et Ricardo de Rishal' xl. s. ad reparationem longe nauis que fuit Fulconis f. Warini
per breue G. f. Petri'). Painter states that Fouke 'had a reputation as a ship-captain' and
thus that the *Romance* 'may well be on sound ground when it puts him afloat' (p. 51).
Painter also calls Fouke a 'bandit captain' (p. 53).

27 *Rotuli litterarum patentium*, pp. 33–34 (for the Latin text see also Wright, pp. 224–25).
The first safe-conduct (20 August) was granted to Fouke and his companions for a
fortnight to go to the king's court, which at that time was in Verneuil, Normandy.
Another safe-conduct, this time for a week, was granted on 12 September to Fouke,
Baldwin de Hodnet and their companions to go to the king in Herbetot. The third
safe-conduct, for a fortnight, was granted on 2 October to Fouke and the men he
wished to bring with him to visit the king at Montfort.

a reference to a certain Gilbert de Duure, 'who was outlawed as an associate of Fouke Fitz Waryn' and accused of 'carrying off hounds by force'.[28]
Moreover, in the same Assize Roll there is a passage which indicates that
Fouke's activities as a rebel 'were sufficiently large to provide cover for
illegal activities of unscrupulous men' (Meisel, p. 38). It appears that, in
order to gain possession of some land which William owned, the reeve of
High Ercall, a certain Richard Wigun, claimed that William had harboured
the outlaw Fouke Fitz Waryn and his companions. The jurors said that
William should be acquitted and that the claim should have been made
three years earlier, a statement which confirms that Fouke had become an
outlaw before the end of the year 1200.[29]

Fouke and his men were pardoned by the king on 15 November 1203.
The pardon was instigated at the behest of William of Salisbury and John
de Grey, Bishop of Norwich. On that date thirty-eight men who had
become outlawed because of their support for Fouke and fourteen men
who had joined Fouke's band as outlaws were also pardoned. Two of those
pardoned were Fouke's brothers and two were his cousins. The rest were
minor figures about whom nothing is known.[30] Just why John pardoned

---

[28] 'Moyses homo Hugonis appellauit Gillelbertum de Duure de eodem . qui utlagatus est
pro societate Folconis filii Warini' ('Moses, Hugh's [Hugh of Sidbury] man, appealed
Gilbert de Duure of the same, who was outlawed as an associate of Fulk Fitz Waryn',
Pleas before the King or his Justices, ed. D.M. Stenton, III, p. 78, item 723; the translation
is Stenton's).

[29] ibid., p. 82, item 740. I quote only the first sentence: 'Ricardus Wigun appellat
Willelmum prepositum de Ercalewe quod ipse recettauit utlagos Regis in domo sua .
scilicet Fulconem filium Warini et socios suos et hoc offert probare' ('Richard Wigun
appeals William the reeve of High Ercall that he received the king's outlaws in his house,
namely Fulk Fitz Waryn and his companions, and this he offers to prove'; Stenton's
translation).

[30] The full text of the pardon is contained in the *Rotuli litterarum patentium* (p. 36). It
reads as follows: 'Rex, etc., justiciariis, vicecomitibus, etc. Sciatis quod nos recepimus in
graciam et benivolentiam nostram Fulconem filium Guarini, ad peticionem venerabilis
patris nostri J. Norwicensis episcopi et comitis W. Saresberiensis, fratris nostri, remit-
tentes ei excessus quos fecit, eique perdonantes fugam et utlagariam in eum promul-
gatam. Ed ideo vobis mandamus et firmiter precipimus quod in firmam pacem
nostram habeat ubicumque venerit. Teste, etc.' ('The king, etc., to his justiciars, viscounts, etc. You are informed that we offer our grace and favour to Fouke Fitz Waryn,
according to the petition of our venerable father, J[ohn]., Bishop of Norwich, and
Count W[illiam] of Salisbury, forgiving him for the crimes which he has committed,
pardoning him for the flight and the accusation of outlawry promulgated against him.
And therefore I inform you and firmly instruct you that he should be admitted to our
firm peace wherever he may come. Witnessed by, etc.'). There follows a list of thirty-
eight names belonging to companions of Fouke who received their pardon at the same
time as Fouke himself: Baldwin de Hodnet, William Fitz Warin, John de Tracy, Roger de

Fouke is not clear, but Painter suggests that 'fierce and able soldiers were a valuable asset to a feudal monarch' and Fouke was 'too good to lose' (p. 52). In reality John cannot have been too preoccupied with Fouke's rebellion, as his mind was on other things. For most of the period of the rebellion he was in Normandy. Not long after his pardon Fouke offered the sum of two hundred marks for Whittington, a sum guaranteed by John de Grey. On this occasion Fouke's fine was accepted.[31] By the autumn of 1204 a certain amount of Fouke's lands had been returned to him and on 17 October King John gave instructions to the sheriff of Shropshire to restore to him the castle of Whittington, not just as a custodian but 'with all its pertinences as his right and inheritance'.[32]

The next event of great significance in Fouke's life occurred in 1207. In that year Matilda, the wealthy widow of Theobald Walter, chief vassal of William Marshal in Leinster and a powerful Lancashire baron, was given to him in marriage in return for a fine of one thousand two hundred marks and two palfreys.[33] This huge fine, originally made by Matilda's

Preston, Philip Fitz Warin, Ivo Fitz Warin, Ralph Gras, Stephen de Hodnet, Henry de Pontesbury, Herbert Branche, Henry le Norreis, William Malveisin, Ralph Malveisin, Abraham Passavant, Matthew de Dulvestir, Hugh Ruffus, William Gernus, Walter de Alveston, John de Preston, Richard de Preston, Philip de Hanwood, Hamo de Wikefield, Arfin Marnur, Adam de Carrickfergus, Walter Sumter, Gilbert de Dover, William de Eggemund, John de Lambourn, Henry Walenger, John Descunsit, William Fet, William Cook, his son Geoffrey Cook, Philip de Wem, Richard Scott, Thomas de Lideton and Henry Gloucester. This list is followed by one containing fourteen names belonging to men who had been outlawed for other reasons but who had afterwards joined forces with Fouke: Hugh Fressell, Oren de Postecotes, Roger de Walton, Reynald Fitz Reynald, William Fitz William, William Fitz Richard de Berton, Richard de Wakefield, Henry Fitz Robert the King de Uffington, John Fitz Toke, Henry the Frenchman, Walter Godric, his brother Thomas, Roger de Onderoude, Roger de la Hand and William Fitz John. Meisel thinks that, in view of allusions in the *Romance* to companions of Fouke not mentioned on this list, the list is 'probably incomplete' (p. 113). The pardon could not have been given at Westminster, as the *Romance* states, as John was in Normandy until 5 December 1203. On the date of the pardon, which seems to have been 15 November, he was in Caen. Meisel (p. 38) gives the date of the pardon as 11 November, on which date the king was in Rouen. On 11 November the king pardoned one of Fouke's companions, Vivian de Prestecotes, who had been outlawed for a crime against a certain Jorvet de Hulton (*Rotuli litterarum patentium*, p. 36, Wright, pp. 225–26). See ANTS edition, p. xxvii, Painter, *King John*, p. 51 (his figure for the outlaws who joined Fouke after they had been outlawed is seven) and Notes to the Translation, n. 44.

[31] *Rotuli de oblatis et finibus*, p. 224, and *Rotuli litterarum patentium*, p. 36.
[32] For the partial return of Fouke's lands see Pipe Roll *6 John*, p. 147, and for the gift of Whittington *Rotuli litterarum patentium*, p. 46. For references to Fouke in a Shropshire Feodary of 1211 and a writ of 1212 see Eyton, XI, p. 38.
[33] 'Fulco filius Warini debet m et cc m. (per plegios annotatos infra) et ij palefridos . pro

father, was taken over by Fouke, and the fact that he was thought able to pay such an amount 'suggests that the Fitz Warins were considered to be a family of considerable wealth and prominence' (Meisel, p. 39). But the payment of his marriage fine caused Fouke great difficulty and it seems to have dominated his life for a considerable period. He appears to have had no problem when it came to taking over Theobald Walter's own lands, but the acquisition of Matilda's dower lands from her father did lead to a dispute, which centred on the Yorkshire manor of Edlington. This matter dragged on interminably, and as late as 1223 three justices were appointed to hear the case.[34]

It is known that in the years following his pardon Fouke made an effort to improve his relationship with King John, whose loyal supporter he became. With an heiress as his wife and enjoying possession of his own lands and fortresses, he was in a position to be highly regarded by the king. In 1210 he accompanied John on his visit to Ireland and was with him at Allerton and Durham in September 1212.[35] In April 1213 the king gave Fouke a gift of twenty marks. At that time he was in Winchelsea, and he may well have gone overseas for a few weeks in the king's service.[36] In June 1213, in a letter which refers to Fouke's fidelity to him, the king ordered that a ship and the armaments from a Norwegian galley be given to Fouke by the constable of Bristol.[37] In May 1214 he sailed to France with King John and assisted him in his conflict with King Philip Augustus of France.

---

habenda in uxorem filia Roberti Vauasur . scilicet Matilde cum hereditate sua' ('Fouke Fitz Waryn fines one thousand two hundred marks (through the pledges mentioned below) and two palfreys to have the daughter of Robert le Vavasur as his wife, that is Matilda with her inheritance', Pipe Roll *9 John*, p. 110; for Robert's fine see, p. 71). See also *Rotuli de oblatis et finibus*, pp. 405–06. In the *Rotuli clausarum*, dated 1 October 1207, Matilda is referred to as Fouke's wife (I, p. 92). Meisel points out that this fine of twelve hundred marks (£800) was equivalent to nearly twenty per cent of the potential revenue from an average feudal levy (p. 39). See Notes to the Translation, n. 28.

34 The difficulties Fouke had in gaining possession of Matilda's lands may have been the reason why he did not pay his fine with any great speed. By 1214 he still owed £685.14s (Meisel, p. 39).

35 Eyton, VII, 7, p. 74, and *Rotuli chartarum*, pp. 187–88. Also in 1212 the king pardoned Fouke a debt of £20 and ordered the release of Fouke's men whom a certain Robert de Vieuxpont had taken prisoner (see Pipe Roll *14 John*, p. 17, and *Rotuli litterarum clausarum*, I, p. 126).

36 *Rotuli de liberate ac de misis*, p. 216.

37 *Rotuli litterarum clausarum*, I, p. 136. In his letter to the constable John referred to Fouke as 'our beloved and faithful one' ('dilecto et fideli nostro'). On 27 June Fouke witnessed a charter for John in Dorsetshire (*Rotuli chartarum*, p. 193, see Meisel, p. 40).

In July Fouke was in Anjou with John, and in September, when John wrote to Philip, Fouke was one of the witnesses.[38]

But a rapid turn of events soon occurred and Fouke was once more in opposition to John. By December 1214 Fouke was back in England, and he was still on good terms with John in early 1215. But in the spring of 1215 he joined forces with the barons opposed to the king and assembled with them at Stamford.[39] Later he defied the king at Brackley.[40] When John issued Magna Carta, Fouke was one of the barons for whom it was intended and he was one of those who were excommunicated by Innocent III's bull of 16 December 1215.[41]

It may be that Fouke III was a natural rebel or that his relationship with John, in spite of outward appearances, was never sufficiently solid for him to devote himself entirely to John's cause or to seek to maintain a tyrannical ruler in office. But it cannot be denied, as Meisel points out, that Fouke had a vested interest in John's defeat, for by the time of Magna Carta he was 'deeply in debt to the crown' (p. 41). At that time he owed a total of £1054 plus three war horses (including £685 for his marriage fine). His debts continued to mount and by 1219 he owed considerably more. Fouke may well have hoped that 'a new king would ignore the old debts of one of the barons who helped to put him on the throne' (Meisel, ibid.). All in all, Fouke seems to have been in two minds in respect of the rebel cause. In 1216 he signed a letter of truce with William Marshal, the royalist leader.[42] This was signed at Easter, but John seems not to have been unduly impressed by Fouke's temporary show of loyalty. At the end of June he ordered the seizure of the manor of Alveston in Gloucestershire.[43]

Fouke's vacillations are hard to explain, but Meisel suggests that, on the one hand, Fouke was alarmed that most of the Marcher barons were continuing to support the king and, on the other hand, he wished to maintain his alliance with Llywelyn ap Iorwerth, Prince of Wales, who was a leading supporter of the rebels (p. 175). However, Llywelyn seems to have let Fouke down in 1216, and this gave rise to a period of intense hostility between them, culminating in Llywelyn's capture of Whittington

---

[38] *Rotuli chartarum*, p. 199. See Eyton, VII, p. 74, and Meisel, p. 40.
[39] Roger of Wendover, *Flores historiarum*, II, p. 114, and Matthew Paris, *Chronica majora*, II, p. 585.
[40] The malcontent barons met at Brackley on 27 April 1215. See Eyton, VII, p. 74, and Matthew Paris, II, pp. 585–86.
[41] Roger of Wendover, *Flores historiarum*, II, p. 169, and T. Rymer, *Foedera*, I, p. 139.
[42] *Rotuli litterarum clausarum*, I, p. 270.
[43] ibid., p. 276.

in 1223. After John's death in 1217, and in spite of having been excommunicated by the pope, Fouke maintained his resistance to the crown. In September 1217 Henry III, acting through his regents, wrote to the sheriff of Leicestershire, ordering the seizure of all Fouke's lands in that county. In the letter he refers to Fouke as 'our manifest enemy' ('manifestus inimicus noster').[44] A few months later, however, in February 1218, Henry ordered the return of lands belonging to Fouke and Matilda, so a reconciliation between Fouke and the young king must have been effected by that date.[45] Indeed, Fouke, no doubt chastened by the failure of his second rebellion, seems to have tried hard to gain favour with Henry. He certainly succeeded in this aim to an extent, but the crown's wariness of him unfortunately led to the refusal to allow him to strengthen Whittington Castle, a fact which undoubtedly contributed to its fall in 1223.[46] However, the castle was not lost for long, as the sheriff of Shropshire was ordered in July of that year to give full possession of it to Fouke.[47]

The period of Fouke's life between 1223 and his death in 1258 was not without its problems and vicissitudes. But, as we saw earlier, it is dealt with so briefly in the *Romance* that we too can pass over it with similar brevity.[48] We can note that in the summer of 1228 Fouke made a truce with Llywelyn and that, although over the years he had reason to do so, he declined to oppose King Henry. He seems finally to have convinced the king of his trustworthiness. Between 1228 and his retirement from public life towards the middle of the century, Fouke received from Henry a number of relatively minor gifts, seemingly as marks of friendship, and also a good deal of help in paying off his debts to the crown, which remained with him after Henry's accession to the throne. In addition, during this period Fouke made more than one visit abroad in the king's service. Until Llywelyn's death in 1240 tension along the March remained high and in the 1230s Fouke and his younger brother William acted on Henry's behalf as standing arbitrators (*dictatores*). They had responsibility for the mainte-

---

[44] ibid., p. 321.
[45] ibid., p. 352.
[46] ibid., pp. 460, 520, annals of Dunstable, III, p. 82.
[47] In March 1223 the forester of the royal forest of Lyth was ordered to take care of Fouke's livestock, which had been removed from Whittington by Fouke's men before the arrival of Llywelyn (*Rotuli litterarum clausarum*, I, p. 537). The recapture of the castle must have taken place before July, as the order to the sheriff of Shropshire was given on 6 July. However, Fouke did not regain his second border castle at Alberbury until the summer of 1226 (*Rotuli litterarum clausarum*, II, 154).
[48] For a fuller account of these years see Meisel, pp. 42–51.

nance of the truce between Henry and Llywelyn, a position implying great trust on the king's part and requiring considerable diplomatic skill.[49] In 1245, Fouke was chosen by the barons assembled at Dunstable and Linton to act as their spokesman. He was to order the papal legate, Martin, to leave England. Matthew Paris reports that this action had the tacit assent of the king.[50]

It is difficult to know at what precise point Fouke III abandoned public life. His last public act seems to have been to serve as arbitrator for the king with respect to a dispute stemming from the Welsh truce. It was his responsibility to hear the respective claims and to make decisions according to justice.[51] Fouke did not die until around 1258, but he was apparently too old or too infirm to continue with any serious public duties. There is in fact no reason to doubt the statement made by the author of the *Romance* that in his last years he was blind. During the last few years of his life, it was his son, Fouke IV, who carried out his public duties and who held some of the lands which his father had held in chief or of other men. Fouke IV continued his father's support for Henry III, and on 14 May 1264 he was at Lewes with Henry, who was facing the army of Simon de Montfort. Fouke died that day, in a stream into which he fell or possibly was pushed.[52] On 20 December Simon de Montfort ordered Whittington Castle to be handed over to Peter de Montfort.[53] Fouke IV's son, Fouke V, was a minor at the time of his father's death and he fell into Peter's hands. He was only rescued in 1265 when Henry regained control of the kingdom. It was not until 1273 that Fouke V took over his father's lands. He continued to offer loyal service to the crown until his death in 1315. This section can be concluded with the remark of A.C. Reeves in his book *The Marcher Lords*: 'For nearly three hundred years there was a a Fulk fiz Warin as a Marcher lord, until the eleventh Fulk died in 1420 without a son to succeed him' (p. 145).

---

49 *Close Rolls of the Reign of Henry III, AD 1231–34*, pp. 369–70, *Calendar of Patent Rolls, AD 1232–47*, p. 200.

50 Matthew Paris, *Historia anglorum*, II, pp. 503–04, *Chronica majora*, IV, pp. 420–21, and Roger of Wendover, *Flores historiarum*, II, p. 228.

51 See *Calendar of Patent Rolls, AD 1232–47*, p. 466. Fouke was appointed arbitrator by Henry on 8 November 1245.

52 See William Rishanger, who in his *Chronica et annales*, states that Fouke was 'submersus in fluvio' ('drowned in the river', p. 28). For a more detailed account of the life of Fouke IV see Eyton, VII, pp. 66–97, and Meisel, pp. 50–54.

53 *Calendar of Patent Rolls, AD 1258–66*, p. 396.

3. *Fouke as a Hero of Romance: an Outline of the Story*

We have seen that the author of *The Romance of Eustace the Monk*, in the account of the life of his hero, concentrates in particular on his period of outlawry and that he delights in the description of the victories which his hero wins over his opponents. The author of *The Romance of Fouke Fitz Waryn* takes a similar view of his hero's activities, but in this case the account of the outlawry is more complex. It covers activities within England and in several locations overseas. In addition, a good deal of space is devoted to the life of the hero's ancestors and the text in fact takes on the role of a family history. The following is a summary, necessarily a lengthy one, of the essential characteristics of the story as it is told to us.

(i) Family history: the account of Fouke's ancestors

The early part of the text explains at great length the background to Fouke's birth, and it elucidates the territorial problems he will face when he reaches maturity. The story begins about a hundred years before his birth, at the time of the Conquest of England. After his coronation as King of England, William the Bastard granted lands to his supporters. Then he made his way to Shrewsbury in order to confront the Prince of Wales, Owain Gwynedd, who had laid waste the Welsh March and claimed it as his own. But Owain preferred to withdraw rather than to fight, and William was able to distribute lands in the March in such a way that they could be defended in the king's name. Roger de Bellême received the county of Shrewsbury and he began to build castles at Bridgnorth and Dynan. But Roger died before this work could be finished and the castles were completed by his sons. When Henry I came to the throne, he found Roger's sons to be treacherous, so he bestowed the castle of Dynan and the surrounding area on one of his own knights, Joce, who became known as Sir Joce de Dynan. (text pp. 3–4, translation pp. 132–33)

The text then relates the long and complex story of how the king's cousin, Payn Peverel, defeated the Devil at a place called Castle Bran. The Devil, who had entered the body of a giant by the name of Geomagog, was defeated by the power of the cross. The region occupied by the Devil and his companions was called Blanche Lande. Before the arrival of St Augustine, who built a chapel there in the name of Jesus, no one who had visited it had ever escaped. After this victory the king gave Blanche Lande to Payn Peverel, and the nearby town of Alberbury and all its fiefs were given to a knight from Metz. After Payn's death his lands were held by his sister's son, William Peverel, who extended Payn's territory, conquering the whole of the land of Morlas as far as Ellesmere, Maelor, Nanheudwy and the River Dee. William Peverel also built on Blanche Lande a tower called Blanchetour. The author tells us that the town which surrounds it is still called Blancheville, or Whittington in English. This is the first allusion to a location which will loom large within the text. (text pp. 4–8, translation pp. 133–36)

There follows a lengthy account of the way in which Melette, the niece of William Peverel, married Waryn de Metz, who thus became lord of Blancheville and all its fiefs. The marriage took place as result of a tournament, proclaimed because Melette knew of no one whom she would be willing to take as her husband. Waryn was the cousin of the Duke of Brittany and the latter provided him with all the support he needed in his quest, even to the extent of sending along his ten sons. Waryn was so successful at the tournament that all those present decided that he had held the field against all-comers. Melette, who had sent him her glove and asked him to defend her, was happy to marry him. In due course Melette had a son by Waryn and he was named Fouke. At the age of seven, Fouke was sent to be raised by Joce de Dynan, who brought him up along with his own children, one of whom was Hawyse, who was to become his wife and the mother of Fouke III, the hero of the *Romance*. Waryn's son, seemingly confused in the *Romance* with Fouke II, first came to prominence when he helped Joce de Dynan in his conflict with Walter (actually Gilbert) de Lacy. Joce's wife and daughters could see the danger he was facing in his fight, first with Walter then with Godard de Bruce and his two companions. Fouke, aged only eighteen, had been left behind in the castle, but his failure to participate in a rescue attempt aroused the contempt of the ladies. Spurred on by their criticisms, he grabbed an axe and an old rusty hauberk and set off on a packhorse to help his lord. He dealt quickly with Godard, then with the first of his two companions, Andrew de Preez. The second companion, Ernalt de Lyls, soon surrendered, as did Walter himself. (text pp. 8–12, translation pp. 136–40)

Thereupon Ernalt and Walter were imprisoned by Joce in his castle. Ernalt fell in love with Marion de la Bruere, the chief chambermaid of Joce's wife, and this was to lead to the escape of the prisoners and the loss of the castle. Marion agreed to assist in the escape on the understanding that Ernalt would marry her as soon as possible. But after the escape she was duped into providing information about the castle: the height of the

window used in the escape and the whereabouts of Joce and his household. During Joce's absence, Ernalt climbed up a carefully measured ladder
and entered the castle. Whilst he and Marion were in bed together, Ernalt's
company of men used the ladder to enter the castle, which was then taken,
with great slaughter of its occupants. Discovering what had happened,
Marion ran Ernalt through with his own sword whilst he lay in bed. She
then threw herself from a window, breaking her neck. This poignant story
is perhaps the highlight of the text until we reach the account of Fouke's
outlawry. (text pp. 12–18, translation pp. 140–45)

A force of seven thousand men was assembled in order to retake the
castle. But, although Joce, Waryn and Fouke inflicted considerable losses
on their enemies, they failed to recapture it, even after a lengthy siege. At
one point Waryn became ill and was forced to return to Alberbury, where
he died. Fouke, who was now married to Hawyse, then went to Alberbury
and accepted the homage and fealty of his father's tenants. Walter de Lacy
was still concerned that he might lose the castle of Dynan, so he made
contact with Iorwerth Droyndon, Prince of Wales. He told him to come
and take Maelor and Ellesmere, since William Peverel, who held them, was
dead. The lands would therefore fall to the king (now Henry II), who
would be hostile to him. Iorwerth raised twenty thousand men and attacked Joce and Fouke. After fierce fighting and a siege in Castle Key, a
league away from Dynan, Joce was captured and taken to Dynan, the castle
which was rightfully his. Fouke continued to fight, but, wounded in the pit
of the stomach by one of Iorwerth's knights, he was finally forced to take
flight and his lands were seized by his adversaries. (text pp. 18–20, translation pp. 145–47)

Faced with the loss of his lands, Fouke decided that the best course of
action was to consult the king, who was staying in Gloucester. Henry, we
are told (but there is no evidence for this), was related to Fouke by blood
and he welcomed him warmly. He had his wounds attended to and sent
for both his mother, Melette, and his wife, Hawyse. Hawyse became pregnant, and in due course she delivered a child, who was given the name
Fouke. It was this child who was to become the principal protagonist of
the *Romance* and its eponymous hero. The king ordered Walter de Lacy to
hand over Joce de Dynan and out of fear he did so. After staying with the
king for some time, Joce departed for Lambourn in Berkshire, where he
was soon to die. At that point the king placed Fouke in charge of his forces
and sent him to attack Iorwerth, who had captured the entire March from
Chester to Worcester. After fierce fighting and a war which lasted for four
years, the king and Iorwerth were reconciled. Iorwerth agreed to restore

Ellesmere to the king, and in addition he gave back to the barons in the area all the lands he had taken from them. But, significantly, he refused to give up Blancheville and Maelor. By way of compensation for their loss the king gave Fouke the town of Alveston and all the land belonging to it. Iorwerth gave Blancheville and Maelor to Roger de Powys and later he bestowed Maelor on his younger brother, Jonas. (text pp. 20–22, translation pp. 147–49)

(ii) Fouke III: the early years and the quarrel with Morys Fitz Roger

It is at this point that the story of Fouke III, the Fouke Fitz Waryn in the title of the *Romance*, really begins. The author, who has masterfully blended together the accounts of the important characters and issues in Fouke's background, now recapitulates for his public the territorial situation which affects Fouke's early years. He does so by drawing the audience directly into the narrative: 'Now you have heard how. . .'; 'You have also heard how. . .'. (text, p. 22, translation, p. 149). He goes on to relate an important event in the hero's childhood, one which he sees as being crucial to his later life. Henry II had Fouke brought up with his own four sons, Henry, Richard, John and Geoffrey. Fouke was on good terms with all the boys with the exception of John. One day he and John were sitting alone, playing chess, when John suddenly struck Fouke a great blow with the chessboard. Fouke retaliated by kicking John so hard in the chest that he went crashing against the wall and fainted. He helped John to regain consciousness, but John went to his father and complained. The king, however, supported Fouke and also had a beating administered to John for having complained. The author of the *Romance* considers this beating to be the source of John's later antagonism towards Fouke. (text pp. 22–23, translation p. 149)

Under King Richard, Fouke II and his son had enjoyed the king's favour. Fouke III and his brothers were knighted by Richard and they went overseas in search of fame and distinction. Fouke was especially successful, and everywhere he was praised for his strength, goodness and courage. He then learnt from Richard that his father was dead, and on his return to England he was invested with his father's lands. All went well until Richard died and John became king. John summoned Fouke to meet him in the Welsh March to discuss various matters, but before any meeting could take place, Morys, son of Roger de Powys, lord of Blancheville, heard of the king's visit and attempted to forestall the issue of the lordship of Blancheville. (text p. 23, translation pp. 149–50)

What happened next is so central to the story that the text is worth quoting in full:

When Morys, the son of Roger de Powys, lord of Blancheville, found out that King John was on his way to the March, he sent the king a fine, plump charger and a white moulted gerfalcon. The king thanked him very much for the presents. Then Morys came to speak with the king, who asked him to remain with him and be a member of his council. He made him warden of the entire March. When Morys saw the opportunity, he spoke to the king, begging him, if it were his pleasure, to confirm by his charter the right of himself and his heirs to the honour of Blancheville, as his father, King Henry, had formerly confirmed it for Roger de Powys, his father. The king well knew that Sir Fouke had full claim to Blancheville, but he recalled the blow which Fouke had once given him. Thinking he could avenge himself in this way, he agreed to put his seal to whatever Morys should put into writing. In respect of this Morys promised him a hundred pounds of silver. Nearby was a knight who had heard everything the king and Morys had said, and he hastened to Sir Fouke, telling him that the king was to confirm by his charter to Sir Morys the lands which belonged to him. Fouke and his four brothers came to the king and requested that they should have the benefit of common law and the lands which were theirs by right and reason as Fouke's inheritance. They asked the king to be good enough to accept from them the sum of one hundred pounds, on the understanding that he would be willing to grant them the decision of his court in respect of gain and loss. The king told them that whatever he had granted to Sir Morys he would maintain, whether anyone might be angry at this or not. Then Sir Morys spoke to Sir Fouke, saying: 'Lord knight, you are very foolish to claim my lands. If you say you have a right to Blancheville, you are lying, and but for the king's presence I should prove it to you on your body.' Without more ado Sir William, Fouke's brother, sprang forward and struck Sir Morys full in the face with his fist so that he was covered in blood. Knights intervened, so no further damage was done. Then Sir Fouke said to the king: 'Lord king, you are my liege lord, and I am bound by fealty to you whilst I am in your service and as long as I hold lands from you. You ought to maintain my rights, and yet you fail me both in rights and in common law. He was never a good king who denied justice to his free-born tenants in his court. For this reason I relinquish my homage.' So saying, he left the court and went to his lodgings. (text p. 23, lines 32–88 – p. 24, lines 1–33, translation pp. 150–51)

(iii) *Fouke as outlaw*

The consequences of this rupture between Fouke and King John occupy most of the remaining portion of the *Romance*. As we have seen, there is no clear-cut evidence for the circumstances surrounding this rupture, but the account contained in the *Romance* gives every impression of being broadly true. The text tells us that after Fouke has relinquished his homage he and his brothers left the king's presence. They dealt successfully with a company of twenty-five knights, who had been dispatched to bring them back. Twenty-four of the knights were either killed or wounded. Fouke then reported events to his mother in Alberbury and fled to Brittany, where he stayed for some time. In due course he, his brothers and their companions left Brittany and returned to England, making their way to Fouke's aunt in Higford (Shropshire). From there Fouke went alone to Alberbury, where he learned that his mother had died. Then, intent on ousting Morys Fitz Roger from Blancheville, he and his men went into nearby Babbins Wood in order to lie in wait for him. But Morys, informed of their presence by one of his men, set out with thirty knights and five hundred men on foot, and a battle ensued in which Morys was wounded in the shoulder and Fouke, in pursuit, was injured in the leg by a bolt from a crossbow fired from the castle. (text pp. 24–26, translation pp. 151–52)

Morys complained about Fouke's behaviour to King John, who dispatched a hundred knights throughout England to find him and bring him to justice. After a number of adventures in which he was often nearly captured, adventures which are at the very heart of this text, Fouke made his way back to Alberbury. His companion, John de Rampaigne, in an act of great daring, entered Blancheville, which was still in the hands of Morys Fitz Roger, and managed not only to discover that next day Morys and his men were going to Shrewsbury, but also to convince Morys that Fouke had been killed in Scotland. Whilst Morys was on his way to Shrewsbury, Fouke and his men launched an attack on him, and Morys and all his men were killed. Fouke immediately went to the king's brother-in-law, Llywelyn, Prince of Wales, in order to seek his peace. This was granted him and then all but destroyed at once, when Fouke confessed to having killed Morys, Llywelyn's cousin. However, any long-lasting antagonism between Fouke and Llywelyn was prevented by the latter's wife, Joan, and Fouke soon became involved in Llywelyn's conflict with Gwenwynwyn, who owned a large area of Powys and refused to submit to him. Llywelyn had already seized part of Gwenwynwyn's lands and these he gave to Fouke with the command that he should attack Gwenwynwyn and destroy all his lands. But Fouke, realizing that it was Llywelyn who was in the wrong, argued strongly for peace. Without further fighting a reconciliation was reached between Llywelyn and his enemy. (text pp. 26–34, translation pp. 152–59)

There was, however, no respite for Llywelyn or Fouke. The king had discovered that Fouke had killed Morys and that he was staying with Llywelyn. In order to take revenge against Fouke and the Prince, he summoned all his earls, barons and knights to meet him in Shrewsbury. But Fouke and Gwenwynwyn discovered the king's plans and made preparations to attack him at a ford which they knew he would have to cross. In the ensuing fight a large number of the king's men were wounded and he withdrew to Shrewsbury. Llywelyn and Fouke continued to anger the king by destroying the castle at Ruyton, which belonged to one of his faithful supporters, John le Estrange. In response to the latter's complaint the king ordered Sir Henry de Audley, lord of Redcastle, to take ten thousand knights and help him seek revenge. Llywelyn had restored Fouke's inheritance, so he was now in Blancheville, where he strengthened the castle. The forces of John le Estrange and Henry de Audley set off for Blancheville. Fouke armed his men, amongst whom were seven hundred knights from Wales, and made his way to the pass of Myddle. In the battle which was joined there Fouke and his companions killed many of their opponents and Fouke himself wounded John in the face, leaving him with a permanent scar. But seven hundred knights could not defeat ten thousand, so Fouke was forced to withdraw. In the fighting, two of Fouke's brothers, Alan and Philip, were wounded, and Audulf de Bracy, one of his staunchest supports (in real life perhaps his cousin), was captured and taken to Shrewsbury. A daring and ingenious rescue of Audulf was then effected by John de Rampaigne. So Fouke and his companions were gradually being forced into ever more serious conflict with the king, who in due course put pressure on Llywelyn to hand over Fouke to him, as a prelude to peace between himself and Llywelyn. Realizing what a dangerous situation he was in, Fouke decided to leave England and with his men he made his way to the court of Philip Augustus in France. (text pp. 34–40, translation pp. 159–65)

The period of time separating the initial rupture between Fouke and King John (p. 151 of the translation) and the final reconciliation (p. 181) lasted in reality about three years and it occupies around sixty per cent of the text. As we have seen, it begins with a series of battles which are interspersed with true outlaw-style behaviour. On the one hand, we encounter three battles against the forces of the king, two against those of

Morys Fitz Roger and one against those of John le Estrange and Henry de Audley. Much of this fighting is typical of contemporary border warfare and it corresponds to the author's earlier descriptions of struggles for the possession of land and power, which characterized the way of life of Fouke's ancestors. On the other hand, we are presented with behaviour by Fouke and his companions which is more typical of outlaw tactics: hiding in the forest to await an opportunity to attack the usurper of their lands, hi-jacking the king's cloth and other goods being transported through the forest by his merchants, escaping from the king's knights by the skin of their teeth in the forest of Kent. In addition, there is the rescue in Scotland of Robert Fitz Sampson and his wife, who had been captured and tied up in their own castle by a certain Peter de Brubille, whose habit it was to masquerade as Fouke Fitz Waryn whilst indulging in criminal activities. Also at this stage in the text we find John de Rampaigne disguising himself as a minstrel and entering Blancheville in order to obtain up-to-date information about what was going on there. The information acquired led to the fight in which Morys Fitz Roger was killed. This section of the text concludes with the daring rescue of the imprisoned Audulph de Bracy, again thanks to the resourcefulness of John de Rampaigne, who entered the castle in Shrewsbury disguised as a minstrel from Ethiopia. After John had drugged Henry de Audley and his companions, by placing a soporific powder in their drinks, he and Audulf escaped via a castle window, having knotted together a number of towels and sheets.

A third dimension to this early period of outlawry is the unexpected marriage of Fouke and Matilda de Caus. Fearing that this beautiful widow would succumb to King John's lust, Hubert le Botiler, Archbishop of Canterbury and brother to Matilda's first husband, summoned Fouke and asked him to take her as his wife. Persuaded by her beauty, nobility and wealth, Fouke agreed to do so, much to the merriment of his companions. Before recounting Fouke's departure for France, the author outlines the difficulties encountered by Matilda. Pregnant and still in fear of kidnap by the king, she was forced to take refuge in a church in Canterbury, where she gave birth to a daughter, Hawyse. Fouke then took her to Higford. Later she became pregnant again and stayed secretly in Alberbury. The king continued to keep her under observation, so she moved on and went to Shrewsbury. Still the king's attentions did not cease, but too heavily pregnant to travel she was forced to remain in Shrewsbury, where she gave birth to her second child, Joan, in the church of Our Lady. Things became even more difficult and she went on to have a son, who was born two months prematurely, on a mountain in Wales. Matilda and her lady, both weak, were taken to a grange at Carreg-y-nant. The child, originally baptized in a Welsh stream under the name John, was later confirmed by the bishop and called Fouke. As Fouke prepared for his hasty departure for France, he had Matilda taken to Canterbury, where she would be protected by the archbishop.

(iv) Fouke as Exile

Approximately half the account of Fouke's period as an outlaw depicts his experiences outside Britain. This period of his life began when he and his companions left the Prince of Wales and made their way to France. On arriving in Paris, they immediately found themselves involved in a tournament, which was being watched by Philip Augustus himself. Summoned to participate in the fighting by a certain Druz de Montbener, Fouke began by unhorsing Druz and another French knight. Then the king, impressed by Fouke's chivalric skills, interrupted the proceedings and asked him to remain at court for as long as he wished. Fouke was happy to do this, but he refused to provide his real name, preferring to be known by the pseudonym Amys del Boys. During his stay at the French court, Fouke was highly regarded. His chivalry and prowess were considered to be without equal. But his stay was brought to an abrupt end by the arrival of a letter from King John demanding that Philip should rid himself of Fouke Fitz Waryn. Although Philip was able to reply to John that no one of that name was at court, he soon realized that Fouke and Amys del Boys were one and the same. Although offered rich lands by King Philip, Fouke departed, making the important statement that 'he who cannot rightfully hold his own inheritance is not worthy to receive a gift of lands from another'. (text pp. 40–41, translation pp. 165–66)

But some time remained before Fouke could return to England to claim his lands. A number of adventures, many of an entirely new character, awaited him. It is at this point that he came into contact with a master mariner by the name of Mador de Mont de Russie. Mador built for Fouke a remarkable and well-equipped ship, in which he and his companions set sail for England. But their progress was thwarted when a knight in a passing ship recognized the quartered sail showing the arms of Fouke Fitz Waryn and claimed that he would deliver Fouke's body to King John that very day. Thanks to Mador's nautical skills, the knight's ship was cut down and Fouke's men overcame its occupants. Before it sank, a large amount of money and supplies were transferred to Fouke's ship. For the next year he and his companions sailed up and down the English coast, indulging in piratical attacks on property belonging to King John. (text pp. 41–43, translation pp. 166–67)

Then a new adventure befell Fouke and his companions. They were blown off course and carried to an island three days journey north of Scotland. In need of food, they approached a young shepherd, who offered to provide them with such food as he possessed. But soon they were in the hands of six tall and fierce peasants, whose hospitality appeared distinctly suspect. Having challenged Fouke's companions to a game of chess and defeated them all in turn, Fouke was called upon to play a game or alternatively to wrestle with the fiercest of the peasants. Fouke responded by striking off the head of the peasant with his sword and soon all six peasants had been dealt with. Thereupon Fouke discovered an old woman, who was struggling to blow a horn in order to summon help. With her were seven beautiful girls, who had been held captive by the peasants. Taking the girls to the boat, along with what treasure and supplies he could find, Fouke blew the peasants' horn, and he and his companions proceeded to kill two hundred of the inhabitants of the islands, all of whom were robbers and thieves. (text pp. 43–45, translation pp. 167–69)

Fouke had Mador take him to Orkney, as one of the captives was the daughter of Aunflor, lord of Orkney. Having handed over his daughter and the maidens to Aunflor and received rich gifts in return, Fouke spent some time sailing in the seas around Britain, especially in the northern seas beyond Orkney. In Sweden he encountered serpents and foul beasts. One of the serpents attacked him and pierced the centre of his shield, but he succeeded in stabbing it through the heart. Trying at one stage to get back to England, he was blown off course by a terrible storm, which blew him towards the kingdom of Iberia. Landing near a beautiful castle, he was surprised to find it unoccupied. He learnt from a peasant that he had landed at Carthage (presumably Carthagena on the south-east coast of Spain) and that the place was unoccupied because it had been terrorized by a dragon, which had abducted the daughter of the Duke of Carthage and carried her away to a high mountain at sea. Fouke returned to his boat and sailed on until he saw a mountain in the sea. He and Audulf de Bracy climbed slowly up the mountain and on the summit they saw the bones and weapons of the dragon's victims. In a cave Fouke came across the duke's daughter and after a fierce fight with the dragon he rescued her. Taking with him the gold on which the dragon had slept to cool itself down, Fouke restored the maiden to her father, who offered him as a reward the whole of Carthage and the hand of his daughter in marriage. Unable to accept this offer, in view of his marriage to Matilda, Fouke left the duke, who gave him a gift of fine jewels and swift horses, and sailed towards England. (text pp. 45–48, translation pp. 169–72)

Fouke's aim now was to take revenge on King John or to challenge him directly for his inheritance. Discovering that the king was at Windsor, Fouke and his men made their way to the Forest of Windsor, which they knew well. One day, when the king went hunting, Fouke disguised himself as a charcoal-burner, in the manner of Eustace the Monk, and managed to lead the king to a spot where his companions could capture him. Unfortunately, however, although he extracted from the king an oath that he would restore all his lands to him, the king later refused to keep the oath on the grounds that it had been made under duress. There follows an interesting passage in which James of Normandy, the king's cousin, claims that the English nobles were traitors to the king, because they refused to capture Fouke on account of their kinship with him. This is vigorously denied by Ranulf, Earl of Chester. James and his companions set off in pursuit of Fouke and his men, but James was captured and his men either killed or injured. At this point Fouke played a trick on the king, exchanging armour with James and taking him back to the king. Thinking he was James, the king gave Fouke his own horse to continue the pursuit of Fouke's men and ordered the hanging of Sir Fouke. Once the mistake had been discovered, the king himself, with his earls and barons, set off after Fouke, who was mourning the serious injury which his brother William had sustained in the battle. In spite of the pleas of the Earl of Chester, Fouke would not surrender. So a further battle ensued in which Fouke and his men were successful. They managed to defend themselves well and finally to take flight. But Fouke himself was severely wounded, and he did not regain consciousness until his company had got back to the coast, where Mador was waiting. William, who had been left behind, was at first taken to an abbey by the Earl of Chester and then transferred to the king's dungeon. (text pp. 48–52, translation pp. 172–76)

This outlaw-style episode is followed by another remarkable adventure at sea. Sailing near to Spain, Fouke and his companions arrived at an island called Beteloye, which was completely devoid of any inhabitants, man or beast. Fouke's companions went ashore, leaving him to enjoy a long sleep on the ship. But a severe gale broke the ship's ropes, and Fouke, in the manner of a true romance hero, was transported to the land of Barbary, which was ruled over by King Messobryn. Fouke defended himself stoutly against the king's men, but finally he agreed to come before the king, who had him well cared for. Again he used a pseudonym, Maryn le Perdu de France. His stay in the land of Barbary was enlivened by the presence of the king's beautiful sister, Isorie. Learning that Isorie's brother had been seeking the hand of the daughter of the Duke of Carthage, whom Fouke had rescued from the dragon, and that her refusal had led to war, Fouke was finally persuaded by Isorie to undertake a single combat. If he lost, the King of Barbary would make good the maiden's losses, and if he won, the maiden would marry the king. Fouke agreed on the understanding that the king would become a Christian. The battle was fierce and it was only concluded on the discovery that Fouke was fighting his own brother, Philip, whom the maiden had earlier rescued from the island of Beteloye along with his brothers. The maiden's father had died and she had even been to England in search of military assistance from Fouke and his brothers. The battle was then abandoned and the maiden married the king with great honour. (text pp. 53–56, translation pp. 176–79)

We are now not far from the reconciliation between Fouke and King John. After their stay in Barbary, Fouke and his companions returned to England. Their first task was to discover whether or not Fouke's brother, William, was still alive. Again John de Rampaigne came into his own. Disguised as a merchant, he managed, by making contact with the mayor of London, to get himself introduced to the king at Westminster, where he gained the king's permission to bring his merchandise and his companions ashore. He also found out that William, although in a sorry state, was still alive and being held in the palace. In due course Fouke and his men rescued William, whilst he was being taken to prison by his guards, and they all left England and sailed to Brittany. After spending a few months there, Fouke made up his mind to confront the king and to reclaim his inheritance. Again he and his men succeeded in capturing King John, this time in the New Forest. But on this occasion, the king was persuaded to grant Fouke his peace and this was duly concluded at Westminster. Fouke and his men surrendered to the king, and all Fouke's land holdings in England were restored to him. Hugh, the earl marshal, granted him authority over Ashdown, Wantage and other lands. He and his men created at Wantage a fair and a market town, which, the author claims, were still in existence when the *Romance* was being written. (text pp. 56–58, translation pp. 179–81)

(v) *After the pardon*

The author tells us very little about Fouke's activities after his reconciliation with King John. We learn of one heroic act and then the text moves swiftly to its end. After staying for a time with the earl marshal, Fouke joined forces with Earl Ranulf of Chester, who needed to defend his lands in Ireland. There they encountered a huge assembly of their enemies, but the battle turned out to be unusual and short-lived. The earl was immediately challenged to send out his most valiant knight in single combat against a hideous, black giant. Three young brothers made the attempt, but they were easily killed by the giant's axe. Then Fouke tried his hand, and although the giant struck him and almost killed him he managed to run the giant through with his lance and then remove his head. The earl proceeded to bring order to his Irish lands without further difficulty. Fouke took the giant's axe back to Blancheville, where he built a new castle. (text p. 58, translation p. 181)

Now back at Blancheville, Fouke was surrounded by his family and able to demonstrate his abilities as a lord. He distributed gifts liberally and maintained his land in peace. He was at all times a good and generous host. As a penance for what he felt was a life of sin, he founded a priory called the New Abbey, near Alberbury. His wife was soon to be buried there. Later Fouke married Lady Clarice d'Auberville by whom he had further children. His daughter Eve was sought by and given to Llywelyn, Prince of Wales, who died a year and a half after the marriage. Afterwards Eve became the wife of the Lord of Blancminster. Only one further event in Fouke's life is recounted. Some time later he became blind, after seeing a bright light in his bedroom and hearing a voice proclaiming that God had granted him penance. We are told that Fouke remained blind for seven years before his death. His wife, Lady Clarice, died a year before him. Both Fouke and Clarice were buried at the New Abbey. In his life he had fulfilled the prophecy of Merlin, which stated that a wolf would come from the Blanche Lande and chase away the leopard. The wolf was Fouke Fitz Waryn, the leopard King John. (text pp. 58–61, translation pp. 181–83)

4. *The Structure and Themes of the* Romance

As we saw earlier, the text of the *Romance* falls easily into three parts of unequal length: (1) the history of the hero's family, (2) the account of his period of outlawry, (3) the brief account of the final years after his pardon. The second section can be further divided into two parts: (i) Fouke's rebellion against King John and its immediate aftermath, (ii) his marvellous adventures at sea and his eventual pardon. This division into either three or four uneven parts is reminiscent of the structure of *The Romance of Eustace the Monk* (see above, pp. 45–49). Moreover, the episodic nature of the account of Fouke's victories over his principal opponent, King John, recalls, sometimes in points of detail, Eustace's victories over the Count of Boulogne. But, as the summaries of the two texts indicate, the account of Fouke's life and adventures possesses a greater density and a more complex structure than those we find in the story of Eustace. The focus for all the activities of Fouke III is not merely vengeance or self-aggrandizement, but the struggle for the possession of Whittington Castle. Nor is the story simply an account of the deeds of one man. The hero's activities fit into a wider context, and the text can therefore be described as a family or ancestral romance.[54]

The appearance of the hero, Fouke III, is delayed until about a third of the way through the text. It is important to note that the author places the account of the hero's birth in the context of a territorial crisis facing both his own father and his mother's father, Joce de Dynan (text p. 22, translation p. 149). We have seen above (p. 111) that just as he informs us of the birth of Fouke III the author speaks directly to his public and recalls the territorial crisis into which the baby has been born: his father has lost Blancheville and Maelor and Joce has lost the castle and honour of Dynan to Walter de Lacy. Thus it will come as no surprise to the reader of the *Romance* that the issue of land and its possession comes to dominate the hero's life. It will be his task to recover his father's lands. Whether he is fighting King John or a dragon, his mind is on the lands which Payn Peverel received from William the Conqueror. But, from the point of view of the structure of the text, it is noticeable that the author does more than recount the story of Whittington and the Fitz Waryn family. He has an eye for a good yarn and does not hesitate to slow down the account of events

---

[54] In her *Anglo-Norman Literature and its Background* M. Dominica Legge places her study of *Fouke le Fitz Waryn* within a section entitled 'The "Ancestral Romance"' (pp. 139–75). The other texts placed by Legge in this category are *Guillaume d'Angleterre*, *Waldef*, *Boeve de Haumtone*, *Fergus* and *Gui de Warewic*. The section ends with a summary of the main themes of the ancestral romance. They lent prestige to a family regarded as *parvenu*. They present a hero who is a founder of a family (he is a king or becomes one). There is a period of exile, 'if possible involving wanderings over sea, with mention of exotic places, their fauna, and other details'. Whether derived from truth or fiction, the tale is ornamented with signs and wonders (with at least one fight with a dragon). The burial of the hero in a monastery is a standard feature. Fighting and marriage are important, *courtoisie* has little place. Nearly all the ancestral romances were written by members of the regular clergy (pp. 174–75). See also S. Dannenbaum, 'Anglo-Norman Romances of English Heroes: "Ancestral Romance"?', and B.J. Levy, 'The Ancestral Romance in Mediaeval French with Special Reference to Anglo-Norman Literature'.

to relate the unusual and exciting circumstances. From Payn Peverel's victory over the Devil and the loss of Dynan Castle through the ill-advised actions of Marion de la Bruere to descriptions of the rescue of a series of damsels in distress, the text moves with stunning effect from dry historical detail to cameo scenes worthy of any courtly romance.

But, in addition to the account of the struggle for Whittington, it is possible to detect in *The Romance of Fouke Fitz Waryn* a broader theme: the abuse of authority. Like the author of *The Romance of Eustace the Monk*, the man who chronicled the adventures of Fouke III was at pains to describe the conflict between his hero and a man with considerable political power, in this case no less a figure than King John himself. This allows the author to treat the account of the hero's period of outlawry, situated in the early years of John's reign, as at once an account of the misuse of royal power. The ANTS editors express the view that the *Romance* presents a 'bitterly satirical and disdainful portrayal of King John as lustful, vindictive, faithless to his sworn word, and finally craven and grovelling in the face of the just indignation of his vassals' (p. xxix). Elizabeth A. Francis, in her article 'The Background to *Fulk FitzWarin*', describes the *Romance* as 'essentially a moral demonstration of royal delinquency' (p. 322). This deliquency is manifested not only in feudal matters, such as disinheritance and a desire for vengeance, but also in the domain of sexuality. For the author of the *Romance* states that John was hated above all for his lechery: 'If he ever heard of any beautiful maiden or lady, wife of an earl or a baron or anyone else, he wanted to have his way with her, either by tricking her with promises or gifts or by taking her by force. For this he was most hated, and this is why so many great English lords renounced their homage' (translation p. 161). It was because she was coveted by King John and thus in great danger that Hubert le Botiler wanted Fouke to marry Matilda de Caus. The archbishop tells Fouke that 'King John desires her so much because of her beauty that she can scarcely protect herself' (p. 156). Even after the marriage he still desired her and 'wanted to carry her away by force' (p. 163). John's spitefulness and vindictiveness are adumbrated in the first episode in which he is mentioned. Apparently losing at chess, he struck Fouke with the chessboard, and when Fouke retaliated he ran to his father to complain, only to find that his complaint fell on deaf ears and to receive a beating for having made the complaint.

John's inability to capture Fouke and have him punished for thwarting him becomes a leitmotif of the text, and whenever he is unsuccessful in catching him, his frustration manifests itself in anger and pettiness. We are told that when he learned that Fouke had married Matilda de Caus, he inflicted great losses on the archbishop and on her (p. 163). He hated the idea of anyone harbouring Fouke, as happens in the case of both Llywelyn, Prince of Wales (p. 160), and King Philip Augustus of France (p. 166). He was even angry with one of his staunchest supporters, Ranulf, Earl of Chester, when he learned that he had been concealing Fouke's brother, William (p. 176). Of great importance is the fact that, according to the author, Fouke was not the only land-owner to be disinherited by John. When Fouke, disguised as a charcoal-burner, captured John, he told him that he would die 'because of the way he had damaged and disinherited him and many worthy men in England' (p. 173). In the author's opinion John lacked above all that commitment to 'dreit heritage', something by which the magnates of the time set such store. The author makes two general statements concerning John and both are wholly negative: 'All his life he was evil, quarrelsome and resentful' (p. 123); 'He was a man without a conscience, wicked, quarrelsome, hated by all good people and lecherous' (p. 161). Moreover, on one occasion Fouke says to Llywelyn that John is 'incapable of having peace with you or me or anyone else' (p. 159). We must not fail to notice, however, that like Renaud de Boulogne in *The Romance of Eustace the Monk*, John is, in the way that he is so easily tricked or captured, a figure of fun, someone who is constantly vulnerable and subject to outbursts of frustration. As such he is reminiscent of a host of heroes in comedy or farce.[55]

5. *The* Romance *as Family History*

It will be recalled that we are dealing with a fourteenth-century prose romance which is clearly adapted from a verse text.[56] The latter seems to have been composed in the second half of the thirteenth century. Where did the original author obtain his material, much of which, in spite of the occasional sortie into the worlds of demons and dragons, is extraordinar-

[55] The author's picture of John conforms to that painted by a number of chroniclers especially Roger of Wendover and Matthew Paris. See W.L. Warren, *King John*, pp. 8–16. For a recent interpretation of the character of King John see Ralph V. Turner, *King John*, Chapter 1.

[56] For passages which remain in verse see the ANTS edition, pp. 6, 60–61. On a number of occasions the verse passage underlying the prose account can be reconstructed. See the notes to the ANTS edition, pp. 62, 70–71, 73–74, 78–80, etc. See also A.C. Wood, edition pp. 62–63, Brandin, 'Nouvelles Recherches sur *Fouke Fitz Waryn*', pp. 24–25, M.D. Legge, p. 172, and Wright, edition pp. vi–vii.

ily accurate? The answer given to this question by the earlier editors, Thomas Wright and Louis Brandin, was that the author was writing for a member of the Fitz Waryn family (Wright, pp. xix–xv, Brandin, p. iv). However, in his article 'The Sources of Fouke fitz Warin', Sydney Painter expresses the view that this is unlikely. He points out that between 1256 and 1264 the Fitz Waryn house was headed by Fouke IV and from 1264 to 1314 by Fouke V. The *Romance* contains a number of factual errors and both Fouke IV and Fouke V were too knowledgeable about the history of the family to have allowed this to happen. For example, the author tells us that Fouke III acquired the manor of Wantage from an earl marshal by the name of Hugh. But in reality there was never an earl marshal of this name. From 1246 to 1306 the office was held by two Roger Bigods, uncle and nephew. The father of the elder Roger Bigod was indeed called Hugh, but in point of fact it was not the earl marshal but William Marshal the younger who made the grant of Wantage to Fouke III.[57] In addition, the *Romance* states that Sybil, sister of Fouke's mother, married Payn Fitz John. In reality, Payn Fitz John preceded her father, Joce, as constable of Ludlow Castle. Sybil's husband was actually Hugh de Plugenai (or Plucknet).

Janet Meisel finds Painter's argument convincing, and she adds that 'no commissioned work could possibly have combined Fulk I and Fulk II into a single character or could have stated that the wife of Fulk III was Maud de Caus instead of Matilda le Vavasur' (p. 133). Nevertheless, Meisel thinks that the author's 'precise and detailed knowledge of certain aspects of the Fitz Warins' history' would suggest that he had 'some connection with the family' (pp. 133–34). He knew, for example, that the Fitz Waryns originally acquired Whittington from the Peverels and he was correct in stating that Fulk's III's first fine for Whittington was £100.

Painter concluded that the principal source of the material used by the author of the *Romance* was a series of legends concerning Fouke III, which 'were current in his native district, Shropshire' (p. 15). He adds that, by the end of the thirteenth century, Fouke III had clearly become 'a popular romantic figure' (ibid.). From this point of view, *The Romance of Fouke Fitz Waryn* would have been composed in order to respond to public demand for an account of Fouke's adventures and for an audience which would have welcomed an account of the victory of justice over oppression

---

[57] See Notes to the Translation, n. 45.

rather than for a limited audience requiring an account of the legendary deeds of earlier family members.

Be that as it may, the facts which are incorporated into the *Romance* must at some stage have been transmitted to the author by someone who was closely connected with Fouke III. The ANTS editors think that an important role must have been played by Fouke's mother, Hawyse. They are of the opinion that Hawyse possessed a 'dominating personality' and that she would have been able to 'pass on to the children of Fouke and Matilda the oft-told tale of the years of exile, which gained fresh topicality with Fouke's renewed opposition in the decade of Stamford and Magna Carta' (p. xxxii). The importance of Fouke's mother within the *Romance* had already been stressed by Elizabeth Francis, who pointed out that she had, whilst still a girl, stung her future husband into performing his first deeds of bravery at the siege of Ludlow. Hawyse was later to become, says Francis, 'the inspiring mother of the brave sons who risk all to save their heritage' (p. 323). The *Romance* indicates that on several occasions during his outlawry Fouke sought refuge with Hawyse at Alberbury or with relatives at Higford (text pp. 25, 30–33, 38, translation pp. 151–52, 156–58, 164).

However, if Hawyse was the principal source of information, it is odd that she is said in the *Romance* to have died during Fouke's period of outlawry (text p. 25, translation p. 152). In reality, she lived on well beyond that period. Meisel (p. 112) gives her death as 1218, but in fact she may not have died until the 1230s when she would have been in her eighties or nineties (ANTS edition, p. xxxii). It may be that Hawyse's memories were indeed one of the sources of the author's account of the activities of Fouke III, but the precise way in which she contributed to their transformation into *The Romance of Fouke Fitz Waryn* remains a mystery. Moreover, Meisel points out that some of the author's errors are not of the kind which Hawyse could have made. In addition, she would not have known the details of the marriages of the children of Fouke III, as they took place after her death (p. 207). We can conclude that the author of the text, an extremely accomplished writer, drew on a number of sources for his story, but he failed to discover or to record with complete accuracy all the details relating to the family history.

6. *The Topography of the* Romance

Like *The Romance of Eustace the Monk, The Romance of Fouke Fitz Waryn* contains a large number of references to precise geographical locations. The author is clearly keen for his public to follow with great precision the course of the exploits and adventures of Fouke and his ancestors. In all we find around a hundred allusions to toponyms within Great Britain, especially to Shropshire and the surrounding area. Throughout the text there are references to Whittington (Blancheville) and other locations connected with the Fitz Waryn family: Alberbury, Babbins Wood, Ellesmere, Maelor (now Maelor Saesneg, east of Offa's Dyke), etc. Alveston in Gloucestershire, given to the real Fouke I by Henry of Anjou in 1149, is mentioned twice (text pp. 22, 59, translation pp. 149, 182). The ANTS editors point to the fact that in addition to topographical terms which occur throughout the text there is an interesting density of terms in one particular section of the text (text pp. 25–38, translation pp. 152–64). These pages offer 'a chain of toponyms stretching from the fringes of Staffordshire through northern Shropshire and the Oswestry "salient" into the most northerly commotes of southern Powys and across the Berwyns to Bala in Penllyn' (p. xxx). They add that this is a 'surprisingly dense assemblage of toponyms from a relatively small area of Britain lying athwart Offa's Dyke (towns and castles on the English side, administrative regions on the Welsh)' (p. xxxi). The toponyms are of two types, those referring to places visited by Fouke after his break with King John (Higford, Myddle, Great Ness, Ruyton, Babbins Wood, Ystrad Marchell, Llannerch, Mechain, Mochnant, Bala and Ffordd Gam Elen) and six designating the provenance or possessions of personages within the story: Audley (Henry de Audley), Hodnet (from Baldwin de Hodnet), Redcastle (Henry de Audley, owner of Redcastle), Wem (Hawyse, lady of Wem), Meole Brace (Audulf de Bracy) and Knockin (John le Estrange, lord of Knockin and Ryton).

Before the reader encounters the dense pages of topography relating especially to northern Shropshire, an important part of the text is taken up with the account of the upbringing of the hero's father in Ludlow (Dynan) and loss of Ludlow Castle to Walter de Lacy (text pp. 10–19, translation pp. 139–47). There are references in this section not only to Ludlow Castle but also to the Rivers Corve and Teme and to surrounding locations, Caynham, Linney and Whitcliffe. Later in the text, once Fouke has entered upon his period of rebellion, the geographical allusions broaden to include not only the locations in northern Shropshire and adjacent parts of Powys already mentioned but also a wide variety of places in other parts of Britain. In typical outlaw fashion, he spends time in various forests of England: his home forest of Babbins Wood, the Forest of Braydon, the Forest of Kent, the Forest of Windsor and the New Forest. One adventure takes him to Scotland and others to places such as Carthage (probably Cartagena in Spain), the islands of Orkney and the countries of Scandinavia. His last foreign adventure before his pardon finds him in the kingdom of Barbary and in the final adventure recounted in the *Romance* he is with the Earl of Chester's army in Ireland.

7. *Date and Place of Composition of the* Romance

It is generally agreed that the verse text of the *Romance* was composed in the second half of the thirteenth century and the prose version towards the beginning of the fourteenth century. As the death of Fouke III, which occurred around 1258, is recorded at the end of the text, the *Romance* in its completed form cannot pre-date that year. Elizabeth Francis (pp. 322–23) quotes approvingly the conclusion reached by G.G. Stephenson in his unpublished dissertation that the verse text was composed during the period 1260–67. The earlier editors, Wright and Brandin, had accepted a date of composition between the death of Fouke III and that of Fouke IV, who died at the battle of Lewes in 1264 (Wright, pp. ix–x, Brandin, p. vii). Meisel also points out that the *Romance* makes no mention of the death of Fouke IV and it is her opinion that the author would certainly have alluded to the fact that he died a hero's death in support of his king (p. 133). The ANTS editors, however, are concerned about the missing last fifty years of Fouke's career and they consider it unlikely that a poet writing in the period of Fouke IV would have passed over these years so swiftly (p. xxxv). They are not convinced by the argument of Elizabeth Francis that Fouke IV's royalist sympathies would have led to Fouke III's opposition to Henry III being ignored for political reasons (pp. 326–27). It is the editors' view that, if one takes into consideration the reservations expressed by Sydney Painter concerning the link with Fouke's descendants (see above, p. 124) and the observations made by G.G. Stephenson with respect to the elaborate descriptions in the text of coat devices, a late thirteenth-century date for the verse original is more likely (p. xxxv, n. 31b).

In the sixteenth century a copy of the now lost verse text came into the hands of the antiquary John Leland. Under the title 'Thinges excerptid owte of an old Englisch boke yn Ryme of the Gestes of Guarine, and his

Sunnes', Leland analysed an English poem and then, because the English book lacked a 'Quayre or ii', he proceeded to translate 'owte of an olde French Historie yn Rime of the Actes of the Guarines onto the Death of Fulco the 2'. Wright (edition p. viii) thought that Leland's French poem and the verse text from which the extant prose *remaniement* was made were one and the same. But L. Brandin has shown convincingly that the two poems were not identical ('Nouvelles Recherches', pp. 32–38).[58]

Do the geographical references studied above (section 6) suggest where the author of the verse text might have lived, either before or during the period in which he wrote his story? Earlier editors associated the composition of the verse text with Whittington and Alberbury. But, from the very outset the town of Ludlow (Dynan) has an important role to play in the text and it is likely that the author of the verse romance came either from Ludlow or lived there for some time. Although the story is fundamentally about Fouke III and his adventures, the history of Dynan and Joce occupy the author for a considerable time. The author clearly possessed a profound knowledge of the castle and town of Ludlow, and the editors of the ANTS edition, who think that the author belonged to the Ludlow of Geoffrey and Piers de Geneville, comment that: 'He knew every inch of the grand fortress in the north-west of the town, on the natural eminence towering above the valley of the Teme, the biggest, perhaps of the Lacy castles: its early Norman inner bailey and chapel, the Mortimer Tower in the western wall of the outer bailey, and behind the hall and the domestic buildings on the northern side the sheer drop to the district of Linney' (p. xxxvi).[59] Whitcliffe, the hill close to the castle, and the nearby village of Caynham are also mentioned in the text. The ANTS editors conclude that the author must have been a native of Ludlow (p. xxxv).

[58] For comparisons of points of detail in Leland's account and in the prose version translated in this volume see also the notes to Wright's edition and the ANTS edition, Introduction, pp. xxi–xxvi, and Notes, *passim.*

[59] Derek Renn comments that 'the author clearly knew his Ludlow, mentioning the three baileys and two ditches, and the highest tower within the third bailey' (' "Chastel de Dynan" ': the First Phases of Ludlow', p. 56). Renn is impressed by the *Romance* author's 'spirited account' of the early history of Ludlow Castle and he thinks that it is by no means impossible that, as the author states, the castle was begun by Roger de Bellême (i.e. Roger de Montgomery) (ibid., pp. 56–57). Roger came to England in 1067 and the county of Shropshire was given to him in 1071. Renn suggests that he, or perhaps his son Robert, could have been Lord of Ludlow and founded the castle in spite of the fact that this remains unrecorded (ibid., p. 57). Eyton (V, pp. 233–35) rejects the account in the *Romance*, as does the *Victoria History of Shropshire*, I, pp. 288–90. See Notes to the Translation, n. 4.

However, Meisel is possibly closer to the truth when she asserts that the author is more likely to have been 'a native of northwestern Shropshire who lived for a time in Ludlow', as his knowledge of Whittington, the Fitz Waryn family and the northern Shropshire March would have been difficult to acquire unless he had lived in that area (p. 134). A native of the area around Whittington, who had gone to live in Ludlow, would therefore have been ideally placed to compose *The Romance of Fouke Fitz Waryn*. In the later years of the thirteenth century Ludlow was in the hands of the Geneville lords, who had inherited it through a Lacy coheiress. In the telling of his story the author was able to create a clear association between his hero and the history of Ludlow. Meisel suggests plausibly that the author was 'a promising local lad whom Fulk III sent to his Lacy friends and who later honored his first patron by composing a romance about him' (p. 134).

8. *The Manuscript*

Fouke le Fitz Waryn is extant in one manuscript only: British Library, Royal 12. C. xii (early fourteenth century). The manuscript contains a miscellany of items (thirty-six in all), many in Latin, but some in French and one in English (a unique version of the *Short English Metrical Chronicle*). In addition to *Fouke le Fitz Waryn* (ff. 33r–60v) the manuscript also contains the Anglo-Norman version of *Ami et Amile*, source of the Middle English *Amis and Amiloun*. The scribe who compiled the manuscript could well be the person who put the thirteenth-century poem into prose (ANTS edition, p. xxxvii). M. Dominica Legge dates the prose version 'before 1314' and the manuscript 'soon after 1322' (*Anglo-Norman Language and Literature*, p. 171). The ANTS editors date the copy of the prose reworking of the original verse text to the period 'c. 1325–40' (p. xxxvii).[60]

The name of the copyist of the Royal manuscript is not known, but he was certainly a priest and 'probably a canon of Hereford and a follower of Adam de Orleton, bishop of Hereford from 1317 to 1327' (ANTS edition, p. xxxviii). It seems likely that he accompanied Adam when he left Hereford to become bishop of Worcester in 1327. The same scribe was also

---

60 These remarks and those which follow rely heavily on the section entitled 'The Manuscript' in the ANTS edition (pp. xxxvii–liii), which the reader of the present volume is urged to consult for further details. See also H.L.D. Ward, *A Catalogue of Romances in the British Museum*, I, pp. 501–08.

responsible for folios 49–140 of MS Harley 2253, a well-known anthology of Anglo-Norman and Middle-English literature (plus some Latin items).[61] He also contributed some additions to a collection of devotional and ascetic texts in MS Harley 273. On folio 6v of the Royal manuscript, which contains *Fouke le Fitz Waryn*, there is a link with the bishops of Hereford in the verses containing seal-mottoes. In addition, the binding leaves of MS Harley 2253 indicate a connection with the bishop and chapter of Hereford.

MS Harley 2253 has its origin in Ludlow,[62] so it is interesting to recall the knowledge of Ludlow displayed by the author of the original version of *Fouke le Fitz Waryn*. The Ludlow connection was no doubt one of the factors which sparked the enthusiasm of the *remanieur / copyist* of the extant romance. Although they describe him as the Hereford scribe, as he seems to have been a canon of Hereford, the ANTS editors ask us to think of the scribe who copied *Fouke le Fitz Waryn* 'as born and bred in Ludlow, where his father or some older relative might have been in the service of Geoffrey de Geneville[63] or his successors' (p. xli). They add that 'he seems to have been an idealistic young man, a medieval "high churchman", with a firm conviction of the need for resistance, exile and martyrdom in the ecclesiastical cause' (ibid.). Judging from the other texts in his compilations, he was committed to serious and semi-scientific material, but he also clearly loved history, politics, legend and humour (he was not averse to including ribald fabliaux in his collections). If he inherited a verse romance about Fouke, he may have remodelled it for his own purposes or specifically to please Adam de Orleton, who was a very political bishop.[64] The story of Fouke Fitz Waryn III's struggle against King John was ideally

---

[61] See Carter Revard, 'Richard Hurd and MS. Harley 2253', *Notes and Queries*, 224 (1979), 199–202.

[62] Revard concludes that 'the scribe of MS. Harley 2253 actually worked in and around Ludlow during the years 1314–1349' (p. 200), but he adds that 'MS. Harley 2253 was not begun before 1330' and not finished before c. 1347 (p. 202, n. 8).

[63] Geoffrey de Geneville (or Joinville) had literary connections in that his eldest brother, Jean de Joinville, was the author of the *Vie de saint Louis*, a biography of Louis IX. Geoffrey inherited Ludlow Castle and half of the manor of Ludlow through his marriage in 1252 to Matilda (Maud) de Braose, granddaughter and coheiress of Walter de Lacy. Matilda died in 1304 and Geoffrey himself in 1314. His son Piers, to whom in 1283 he left his Lacy Land in England and Wales, predeceased him in 1292. His heiress was his granddaughter Joan and she married Roger Mortimer. Like Fouke III in his later years, Geoffrey de Geneville was a trusted diplomat. In 1267 he took part in negotiations with Llywelyn ap Gruffydd and he was involved in Anglo-French peace negotiations in 1298–99.

[64] There are certainly elements in Orleton's career which suggest that he would have been

suited to appeal to anyone who had fought or was likely to fight for what he believed in, or to someone who had known what it was like to be in conflict with his king.

9. A Note on the Translation

The present translation is based on the edition of the text by E.J. Hathaway, P.T. Ricketts, C.A. Robson and A.D. Wiltshire (Oxford: Blackwell, Anglo-Norman Text Society, 1976). This excellent edition is accompanied by a substantial introduction and very helpful notes. As in the case of *The Romance of Eustace the Monk*, sudden changes of tense in the text have been avoided in the translation. The story has been told here in the past tense. One particular problem encountered by the translator of this text is the task of finding an appropriate form in English for the large number of toponyms and personal names. Readers are urged to consult both the indexes of proper names in the present volume, in which the forms found in the text are provided alongside the English form used in the translation, and the equivalent indexes in the ANTS edition. The paragraphs in the translation relate largely to the divisions found in the ANTS edition, which on the whole are not those of the manuscript (see edition pp. cxxiv–cxxv). But from time to time a particularly long section has been further subdivided. Some of the sentences in the original text are also rather long, as the author frequently makes use of the conjunction *e* 'and' to add clauses which would render the sentence somewhat awkward in English. These long sentences, and also some very short ones, have been modified, where appropriate, in order to improve the flow of the English text.

---

interested in the story of Fouke Fitz Waryn. G.A. Usher, in 'The Career of a Political Bishop: Adam de Orleton', points out that Orleton had a 'capacity for survival despite the hostility of the powerful' (p. 33). Orleton was accused of various crimes including treason and organizing the escape of Roger Mortimer from the Tower in 1323. He also seems to have had an 'excessive devotion to revenge' (p. 47). The ANTS editors suggest that the brief alliance between Adam Orleton and Roger Mortimer was no doubt seen by the compiler as 'a blow struck in defence of a righteous cause' (p. xliii). Revard, however, points out that the compiler of MS Harley 2253 cannot have been in Bishop Adam Orleton's *familia* itself (p. 202, n. 9). He adds that it is doubtful that Roger Mortimer of Wigmore was his employer, but he could have been in the service of (or lived very close to) the lesser barons of Richard Hurd's castle (three miles south of Ludlow), and certainly he could have had access to the great barons of Wigmore and Ludlow, the Mortimers.

The Romance of Fouke Fitz Waryn

In the months of April and May, when the meadows and the grass are green once more and every living thing recovers its strength, beauty and power, the hills and the valleys resound to the sweet song of the birds, and each person's heart is uplifted and full of joy at the beauty of the time and the season. At this time one should recollect the adventures and the brave deeds of our ancestors, who strove to seek honour in loyalty, and one should speak of such things as could be profitable for many people. (3, 1–8)

Lords, you have heard before now that William the Bastard, Duke of Normandy, came to England with a great army and a host of men and conquered the entire land by force. He killed King Harold, had himself crowned in London and established peace and laws according to his will, bestowing lands on the various individuals who came with him. At that time Owain Gwynedd, a brave and valiant warrior, was Prince of Wales, and the king was afraid of him most of all. This Owain had laid waste the entire March and everything from Chester to The Wrekin was devastated.[1] The king equipped himself very richly and came with a great army to the county of Shrewsbury, where he found all the towns from Chester to Shrewsbury burnt, for the Prince claimed the entire March as his own and as belonging to Powys.[2] (3, 9–21)

The Prince withdrew, for he did not dare wait for the king. The king was very wise and thought that he would give the lands in the March to the most valiant knights in the entire army, so that they could defend the Prince's March for their own benefit and for the honour of their lord, the king. The king called Roger de Bellême and gave him quite freely the entire county of Shrewsbury, and he was called earl palatine. Outside the town of Shrewsbury, Roger founded an abbey dedicated to St Peter and he endowed it very richly. He retained the earldom all his life. Then he began a castle at Bridgnorth and another at Dynan, but he did not complete them. (3, 22–31)

After Roger's death, his son, Robert, possessed the entire earldom of

Shrewsbury, and Arnulf, his younger son, had Pembroke. They were extremely unruly and treacherous men, who committed grievous crimes against their lord, King Henry, son of William the Bastard and brother to King William Rufus. They completed the castle of Bridgnorth in defiance of King Henry, and because of this the king disinherited them and banished them for good, giving their lands to his own knights.[3] The castle of Dynan and the surrounding area towards the River Corve, along with all its fiefs, he gave to Sir Joce, his knight, who thereafter took the surname of Dynan and was everywhere called Joce de Dynan. This Joce finished the castle which Roger de Bellême had begun in his day and he was a strong and valiant knight. For a long time the town was called Dynan and now it is called Ludlow. Beneath the town of Dynan Joce built a bridge of stone and lime over the River Teme, on the highway which runs through the March, from Chester to Bristol. Joce constructed his castle at Dynan with three bailey-walls and surrounded it with a double moat, one inside and one outside.[4] (3, 32–34; 4, 1–16)

King William the Bastard approached the mountains and the valleys of Wales and he saw a very large town, formerly enclosed within high walls, which was completely gutted and laid waste. He set up his tents on a plain beneath the town, saying that he would remain there that night. Then the king enquired of a Briton what the town was called and how it had come to be laid waste. 'Lord,' said the Briton, 'I shall tell you. The castle was formerly called Castle Bran, but now it is called the Old Border. Once upon a time, Brutus, a very valiant knight, came to this country, as did Corineus, from whom Cornwall gets its name, and many others originating from the lineage of Troy. No one lived in these parts except for a vile race of people, great giants, whose king was called Geomagog. They heard of the arrival of Brutus and set out to confront him. In the end all the giants were killed except for Geomagog, who was astonishingly tall. Corineus, the valiant, said he would gladly do combat with Geomagog in order to test the latter's strength. At the first onset the giant grasped Corineus so tightly that he broke three of his ribs. Corineus became angry and gave Geomagog such a hard kick that he fell into the sea from a great rock. Thus Geomagog was drowned. An evil spirit immediately entered Geomagog's body and he came to these parts and defended the area for a long time, so that no Briton dared live there. Long afterwards, King Bran, son of Donwal, had the city rebuilt, the walls repaired and the great moats strengthened. He turned it into a borough and a great market-place. The Devil came one night and carried off everything inside. Since then no one has ever lived there.'[5] (4, 17–38; 5, 1–4)

The king was astonished at this. The king's cousin, Payn Peverel, a fierce and bold knight, heard everything and said he would put the marvel to the test that very night.[6] Payn Peverel armed himself very richly and took his shield of shining gold with a cross indented azure, together with fifteen knights and other men-at-arms. He went to the highest palace and encamped there. When night fell, the weather became so foul, dark and black, and there arose such a storm, with thunder and lightning, that all those present became so terrified that they could move neither hand nor foot because of fear. They just lay flat on the ground like dead men. Payn, the fierce, was very much afraid, but he put his trust in God, for whom he carried the sign of the cross, and he saw that his only source of help was God. He lay down on the ground and with true devotion prayed to God and his mother Mary, asking them to defend him that night from the power of the Devil. Scarcely was his prayer finished when the Devil arrived in the likeness of Geomagog. He carried a huge club in his hand, and from his mouth spewed fire and flame which lit up the whole of the town. Payn had placed his entire trust in God and, crossing himself, he attacked the Devil boldly. The Devil raised his club and aimed a blow at Payn, but he avoided it. The Devil, through the power of the cross, became frightened and lost his strength, for he could not approach the cross. Payn pursued him, striking him with his sword in such a way that he began to cry out and fell flat on the ground in surrender. 'Knight,' he said, 'you have conquered me, not by your own force, but by the power of the cross which you are carrying.' 'Vile creature that you are,' said Payn, 'tell me who you are and what you are doing in this town. I call upon you in the name of God and the Holy Cross.' The Devil began to tell the story in the very same words that the Briton had used previously, telling him that, when Geomagog was dead he surrendered his soul immediately to Beelzebub, their prince, and he had entered Geomagog's body and come to these parts in his likeness, in order to guard the great treasure which Geomagog had amassed and placed in a house which he had built underground in the town. Payn asked him what sort of creature he was and he replied that he used to be an angel, but now because of his offence he was the spirit of the Devil. (5, 5–39)

'What treasure did Geomagog have?' said Payn. 'Oxen, cows, swans, peacocks, horses and all other beasts, wrought in pure gold. He also had a golden bull which, thanks to me, was his oracle, in which he placed his entire belief. It told him what was to happen. Twice a year the giants were accustomed to honour their god, the golden bull which contained such a remarkable amount of gold. Later it came about that this whole region was called Blanche Lande, and I and my companions enclosed the plain with a high wall and a deep ditch so that there was no way in except through this town, which was full of evil spirits. On the plain we held jousts and tournaments, and many people came to see these spectacles, but no one ever escaped. Finally there came a disciple of Jesus, named Augustine, and by his preaching, he robbed us of many of our people. He baptized them and built a chapel in his name, which caused us great misfortune.' 'Now,' said Payn, 'you will tell me where the treasure is of which you have spoken.' 'Vassal,' he said, 'say no more about this, for it is destined for others. But you will be lord of this entire domain, and those who come after you will hold it with great strife and war.' (5, 39; 6, 1–18)

'From your sleeve will issue the wolf who will do wonders, who will have sharp teeth and be known by all. He will be so strong and fierce that he will drive the boar out of Blanche Lande, so great will be his power. The leopard will chase the wolf and threaten it with its tail. The wolf will leave the woods and the hills and dwell in the water with the fish. He will cross the sea and circle this entire island. Finally he will overcome the leopard with his cunning and his skill. Then he will come to this plain and make his home in the water.'[7] (6, 19–36)

When the spirit had said this, he departed from the body, and Payn was so terrified that he almost died. When it was all over, the night cleared and the weather became fine. The knights and the others, who had been frightened, recovered their wits, and they were astonished at what had happened. Next day the events were recounted to the king and the whole army, and the king had the body of Geomagog carried away and thrown into a deep pit outside the town. He preserved the club and displayed it to many people for a long time because of its remarkable size. (6, 37–38; 7, 1–7)

The king left there and entered a region next to Blanche Lande, which once belonged to a Briton named Meredith ap Bleddyn. On its border stood a small castle called Croes Oswallt, but now called Oswestry. The king summoned a knight, Alan Fitz Flaald, and gave him the castle with all the fiefs belonging to it. From this Alan are descended all the great lords of England who have the surname Fitz Alan. Later this Alan had the castle greatly enlarged.[8] (7, 8–15)

The king crossed the River Severn and saw that the region all around was good and fair. He summoned a knight, who was born in Lorraine, in the city of Metz, and who was renowned for his strength, beauty and courtliness. His banner was of red samite with two golden peacocks. The king gave him Alberbury and all the fiefs belonging to it. Thus the king gave his best and most loyal knights all the lands, chases and fiefs from Chester to Bristol. (7, 16–22)

The king called Payn Peverel and gave him Blanche Lande with its forest, wastes, chases and the entire region. There was a mound surrounded by marshland and water, and on it Payn built a fine, strong tower. The mound was called The Berth, and a river runs alongside it which, taking its name from Payn Peverel, was called Peverel. But later it was called Pevereye. When the king had made arrangements for these lands, he returned to London and from there he went to Normandy, where he died. Then William Rufus, his son, reigned in England, and after him came Henry, his younger brother, who later detained his elder brother, Robert Curthose, in prison for his entire life. I shall not explain the reason for this here. (7, 23–33)

Then it came about that Payn Peverel died in his castle in the Peak, and William Peverel, his sister's son, received and held Payn's entire inheritance.[9] Then this William conquered by force of arms the whole of the land of Morlas as far as the River Dee, Ellesmere, Maelor and Nanheudwy. This William built a tower on Blanche Lande and called it Blanchetour, and the town which surrounds it is still called Blancheville or Whittington in English. In Ellesmere he built another tower and another on the River Ceiriog. William had two beautiful nieces, Helen, the elder, and Melette, the younger. He married Helen to Fitz Alan and along with her in marriage he gave the entire land of Morlas as far as the River Ceiriog. Melette was by far the more beautiful and because of her beauty she was highly desired. But no one found favour with her. William discussed this with her and asked her to let him know whether there was any knight in the land whom she was willing to take as her husband. If there was no one, he would help her as best he could. 'Certainly, lord,' she said, 'there is no knight in the whole world whom I would take for his wealth or the lands he holds. But, if ever I had any man, he would be handsome, courtly, well-educated and the most valiant man in all Christendom. I set no store by wealth, for I can truly say that he is rich who has what his heart desires.' William, on hearing this, smiled and said: 'Fair niece, you have spoken well and I shall do my best to help you find such a husband. I shall give you Blanchetour and all that belongs to it, with all its fiefs, for a woman who has land as her fief will be all the more sought after.' Then William sent out a proclamation in many lands and many cities: 'That any valiant knight who wants to joust for love should come at the feast of Michaelmas to Peverel Castle in the Peak, and the knight who is most successful and who wins the tournament will have the love of Melette de la Blanchetour and he will be lord of Blancheville and all its fiefs.' This proclamation was soon made known in many lands. Waryn de Metz, the valiant, had neither wife nor child, but he informed John, Duke of Brittany, about the nature of this proclamation and asked for his help and assistance in this matter. The Duke was very valiant. He had ten sons who were knights, the most handsome and valiant in the whole of Brittany: Roger, the eldest, Howel, Audwyn, Urien, Theobald, Bertrem, Amys, Guichard, Girard and Guy. The duke dispatched to his cousin, Waryn de Metz, his ten sons and a hundred knights with them, each provided with good mounts and costly equipment. He received them with great honour. Eneas, the son of the King of Scotland, came with the Earl of Murray, the Bruces, Dunbars, Umfrevilles and two hundred knights. Owain, the Prince of Wales, came with two hundred shields, and the Duke of Burgundy with three hundred knights. Ydromor, the son of the King of Galloway, came with a hundred and fifty knights. The English knights numbered three hundred. Waryn de Metz and his company camped in tents erected in the forest close to where the tournament was to be held, all dressed just as they pleased in red samite. In warlike fashion their chargers were covered completely right down to the ground. Waryn himself, so as not to be recognized, wore a golden crest. Then the tabors sounded, as did the trumpets, bugles and Saracen horns, so that the valleys echoed to the sound. Then the tournament began, hard and fierce. There one could see knights unhorsed and many a harsh blow delivered on body and neck. (7, 34–39; 8, 1–39; 9, 1–11)

The maiden and a number of ladies had gone up into a tower and they saw the fine assembly of knights and how each one conducted himself. I do not intend to describe the blows and the general conduct, but Waryn de Metz and his company proved to be the most successful that day, as well as the most handsome and valiant. Of all those present Waryn was the most highly esteemed on all counts. Evening came and the tournament could not proceed any longer because of the dark. The knights returned to their lodgings. Waryn and his company went back secretly to their tents in the forest and, after removing their armour, rejoiced greatly. None of the other great lords knew what had become of them or who they were, so secretively did they conduct themselves. Everyone failed to recognize them. (9, 12–23)

The next day a joust was proclaimed everywhere. Then Waryn, entirely unrecognized and as if there by chance, went to the joust, dressed in green ivy leaves fresh from the forest. When the Duke of Burgundy saw him, he immediately rushed towards him and struck him a great blow with a lance. Waryn struck him back so that he was unhorsed in the middle of the lists.

Then he did the same with another, then a third. Melette of the Blanche-tour sent him her glove and asked him to defend her. He said he would do so to the best of his ability, and then he went back into the forest where he armed himself with his red armour and came with his companions on to the field. He was the victor in the tournament and held the field against all-comers. Then it was decided by all the great lords, heralds and judges that Waryn, the knight who seemed to be there by chance, had deserved to win the prize for the tournament and also Melette of the Blanchetour. He took her with great joy and the maiden took him. So they summoned the bishop of the region and, in sight of everyone, he married them. William Peverel held a sumptuous celebration for the marriage, and when the celebrations were over Waryn took his wife and his company and they went to Blancheville, where they remained for forty days in great joy. Then the ten brothers with their hundred knights went back to Brittany. But Guy, the youngest brother, remained in England and conquered many fine lands by the sword. He was called Guy le Estrange and from him are descended all the great lords of England who have the surname Estrange.[10] (9, 24–39; 10, 1–8)

Waryn de Metz held the lordship of Blancheville for a long time in great honour, but Iorwerth, the son of Owain, Prince of Wales, did him a great deal of harm, killing his men and destroying his lands.[11] Then they fixed a date for a battle in which many a brave man perished. Finally Iorwerth had the worst of it, for he lost a good number of his men. Abandoning the field, he fled in dishonour. Then Waryn appointed a very brave and valiant knight, Guy Fitz Candelou de Porkington, to guard the honour of Blancheville and his other lands. (10, 9–17)

It so happened that the lady became pregnant. When she had delivered the child, at the time which God had ordained, they called him Fouke. When the boy was seven years old, they sent him to Joce de Dynan to be educated and brought up, for Joce was a knight of great experience. He received him with great honour and great affection and brought him up with his children in his own chambers. For he had two daughters, the younger of whom was the same age as Fouke, and she was called Hawyse. The elder daughter was called Sybille. At that time there was great discord and war between Sir Joce de Dynan and Sir Walter de Lacy, who used to spend a good deal of time at Ewyas. Because of this discord many fine knights and many valiant men lost their lives, for each one launched an attack on the other, setting fire to the other's lands, plundering and rob-bing their people and causing all kinds of other damage. When Fouke was eighteen years of age, he was very handsome, strong and tall. (10, 18–31)

One summer day, Sir Joce rose early and climbed up one of the towers in the middle of his castle to survey the countryside. He looked out towards the mountain called Whitcliffe and saw the fields covered in knights, squires, men-at-arms and valets, some armed and on horseback and some on foot. He heard the horses neighing and saw the glittering helmets. Amongst them he caught sight of Sir Walter de Lacy's banner, shining with its fresh gold with a fess gules. Then he shouted to his knights, ordering them to arm themselves, mount their chargers and take their crossbowmen and archers. They should make their way to the bridge beneath the town of Dynan and hold the bridge and the ford, letting no one cross. Sir Walter and his men expected to be able to cross safely, but Sir Joce's men drove them back, and many on both sides were wounded and killed. Then Sir Joce arrived with his banner argent with three lions passant azure, crowned or. With him he had five hundred knights and men-at-arms, on horse and on foot, in addition to burgesses and their men, who were good fighters. Then with a great show of force Joce crossed the bridge and the two sides joined battle hand to hand. Godebrand, who carried Lacy's banner, was pierced through the body by Joce with a lance. So Lacy lost his banner. Then a general battle ensued and many men on both sides were killed. But Lacy had the worst of it, for he was discomfited and took flight, making his way along the River Teme. (10, 32–39; 11, 1–14)

The lady with her daughters and her other maidens had gone up into the tower, from which they saw the entire battle. They prayed devoutly to God that he would protect their lord and his men from harm and damage. Joce de Dynan recognized Walter de Lacy by his arms and saw him fleeing alone, for he was terrified of losing his life. He spurred his horse and crossing hills and valleys in a short while caught up with Lacy in a valley beneath the wood, over towards Bromfield. He ordered him to turn round. Lacy could see no one other than Sir Joce, so he turned round very boldly and they exchanged blows with each other forcibly, for neither had any thought of sparing the other. They dealt each other great and fierce blows. Thinking that the combat was lasting too long, Joce raised his sword angrily and struck Lacy on his shield, splitting it in two and wounding him seriously in his left arm. Joce attacked him keenly and was close to capturing him when Sir Godard de Bruce, accompanied by two knights, came to his aid. Sir Godard and his companions attacked Sir Joce very boldly on all sides and he defended himself against them like a lion. (11, 14–32)

The lady and her daughters in the tower saw their lord so hard pressed that they could scarcely endure it. They cried out, fainted and lamented greatly, for they did not expect to see their lord alive again. Fouke Fitz

Waryn had been left in the castle, for he was only eighteen years old. Hearing the cry from the tower, he went up quickly and saw his lady and all the others in tears. He went to Hawyse and asked her what the matter was and why she appeared so unhappy. 'Hold your tongue,' she said, 'you are not much like your father, who is so bold and so strong. You are a coward and always will be. Do you not see my lord there, who has cared for you greatly and brought you up lovingly? His life is in danger for want of help, whilst you, wretch, run up and down in safety, without giving him a thought.' The young man, as a result of the reproof she had uttered, became flushed with anger and distress. Then he climbed down the tower and found in the hall an old, rusty hauberk, which he donned as best he could. He grabbed hold of a large Danish axe and went to a stable beside the postern leading to the river. There he found a packhorse, which he mounted, and going out through the postern he soon crossed the river and reached the field, where his lord had been unhorsed and was on the point of being killed if he had not suddenly come up. Fouke had a wretched helmet, which scarcely protected his shoulders, and at his first attempt he struck Godard de Bruce, who had seized his lord, with his axe, slicing right down the middle of his spine. He put his lord back on his horse, turned towards Sir Andrew de Preez and with his axe dealt him such a blow on his helmet of white steel that he cleaved right through it, down to his teeth. Sir Ernalt de Lyls saw that he had no chance of escaping, for he was seriously wounded. So he surrendered to Sir Joce. Lacy defended himself, but he was soon captured.[12] (11, 33–39; 12, 1–23)

Now Sir Walter de Lacy and Sir Ernalt de Lyls were captured and taken over the river to the castle of Dynan. Then Sir Joce spoke: 'Friend burgess, you are very strong and valiant. If you had not been there, I should soon have been dead. I am very much beholden to you and shall be for ever more. You will remain with me and I shall never let you down.' Joce thought he was a burgess, for burgesses have rarely worn armour and those worn by the young man were rusty and wretched. Then the young man replied, saying: 'Lord, I am not a burgess; do you not recognize me? I am Fouke, your ward.' 'My dear son,' he said, 'blessed be the time I have spent bringing you up, for effort expended on a worthy man is never wasted.' Then they took Walter and Sir Ernalt to the tower called Pendover where they attended to their wounds, looking after them with great honour. The lady and her daughters and their maidens brought comfort and solace each day to Sir Walter and Ernalt de Lyls. (12, 24–39)

Sir Ernalt was a handsome young man and he fell deeply in love with Marion de la Bruere, a very noble maiden, who was chief chambermaid to the lady of the castle of Dynan. Sir Ernalt and the maiden spoke to each other frequently, for each day she was accustomed to come to the tower with her lady in order to bring comfort to Sir Walter de Lacy and Sir Ernalt. It so happened that when Sir Ernalt saw the opportunity he spoke to the maiden and told her that she was the one he loved most and that he was so deeply in love with her that he could get no rest day or night unless she would yield to him, for she could provide him with relief for all his misery. If she were willing to do this, he would give her assurance of his own free will that he would never love any other woman but her, and as soon as he was free he would take her as his wife. The maiden heard this fine promise and agreed to do his bidding in all things. She received his pledge that he would keep his promise. The maiden promised that secretly and in every possible way she would help them to be released from prison. Taking towels and sheets, she brought them to the tower and sewed them together. Using them, she let Sir Walter and Sir Ernalt down from the tower. She asked them to keep their faith and the promise which they had made to her. They told her that they would behave loyally towards her and not break any agreement, and they entrusted her to God. (13, 1–22)

All alone, Sir Walter and Sir Ernalt made their way on foot and at day break they reached Ewyas, Sir Walter de Lacy's castle. When the people saw that their lord had returned hail and hearty, there is no need to ask if they were pleased. For they thought they had lost him for good. (13, 23–27)

Joce de Dynan rose early and went to the chapel in his castle, which was built and dedicated in honour of St Mary Magdalene, whose dedication feast is St Cyriac's Day, with seventy days of pardon. He then attended divine service, after which he climbed up the highest tower in the castle's third bailey, which by many is now called Mortimer. It is called Mortimer because one of the Mortimers had been imprisoned in it for a long time. Joce surveyed the countryside, and seeing nothing untoward he came down and sounded the horn for washing. Then he sent for his prisoner, Sir Walter, for he honoured him so greatly that he never wished to wash or eat before him. The prisoners were sought in vain throughout the castle, for they had escaped. Sir Joce showed no sign of regret that they had gone and he paid no attention to the matter. (13, 28–39; 14, 1–2)

Sir Walter decided that he would avenge himself or die. He summoned his men from Ireland and hired mercenaries, knights and others, so that violent hostility and fierce fighting developed between Sir Walter and Sir Joce. The earls and barons of England saw the great carnage and the harm which had been done and was still being done daily between them. They arranged a love-day between Sir Walter and Joce, and on that occasion all grievances were redressed and the parties reconciled. They embraced each other before the great lords. (14, 3–10)

Joce de Dynan sent a letter to Waryn de Metz, the father of the young man, Fouke, and to Melette, his good wife. Fouke was somewhat dark-skinned and for this reason he was later called by many Fouke le Brun. Waryn, Melette and their great retinue went to the castle of Dynan, where they were received with great honour and joy. They spent a pleasant week there. Joce spoke to Waryn in very courtly fashion, saying: 'Lord, you have here a son whom I have brought up on your behalf. I hope he will be valiant and worthy. He will be your heir if he survives you, and I have two daughters who are my heirs. If it pleased you, I should like us to be allied through marriage. Then we shall scarcely fear any great lord in England or be afraid that our cause would fail to be maintained with justice and reason. If you agree, I should like Fouke le Brun to marry Hawyse, my younger daughter, and for him to be heir to half my land.' Waryn thanked him warmly for his fine offer, saying that he would agree to it with all his will. The next day they sent to Hereford for the bishop, Robert de . . .[13] The bishop came and married them with great honour. Joce held a great festival which lasted for a fortnight. (14, 11–29)

When the celebrations were over, Sir Joce, Sir Waryn and their house-holds left for Hartland, for they wished to spend some time there. Marion de la Bruere feigned illness and retired to her bed, saying that she was so sick that she could not move except with the greatest difficulty. So she stayed at the castle of Dynan. Joce ordered her to be well looked after, and for fear of Lacy and others he hired thirty knights and six hundred men-at arms and valets and put them in charge of his castle until his return to that region. When Joce had departed, the next day Marion sent her mes-senger to Sir Ernalt de Lyls, asking him through the great friendship be-tween them not to forget the agreements which had been reached between them and to come with all haste to speak to her at the castle of Dynan, for the lord and lady, together with the majority of the household, had de-parted for Hartland. He should come to the very same place where he had previously escaped from the castle. When Sir Ernalt heard his beloved's message, he immediately sent the messenger back, asking her out of love for him to measure the height of the window by which he had previously escaped from the castle and to tell him what kind of people, how many and which members of his household their lord had left behind. She should let him know this through the same messenger. The maiden, who did not suspect any treason, took a silken thread and let it down to the ground through the window. She gave Sir Ernalt all the information concerning the castle. Then Sir Ernalt sent a message back to his beloved, saying that on the fourth day he would be with her before midnight, by means of the very window through which he had left. He asked her to wait for him there. (14, 30–38; 15, 1–17)

Sir Ernalt de Lyls had a ladder made out of leather, the same length as the silk thread which his beloved had sent him. Then Sir Ernalt went to his lord, Walter de Lacy, and told him that Fouke, son of Waryn de Metz, had married Hawyse, daughter of Sir Joce de Dynan and that Waryn and Sir Joce had left a garrison in the castle of Dynan and gone to Hartland in search of mercenaries, to gather their men together there and assemble an army of countless men. 'When the entire army is assembled, they will immediately come to Ewyas and burn and capture your lands. If they capture you, you will be cut into small pieces and you and your people will be disinherited for ever. The maiden whom you know well has sent me word of this, for she knows and has heard the truth.' When Sir Walter heard this news, he turned pale with anguish and said: 'Certainly, I cannot believe that Sir Joce would be so deceitful towards me, seeing that we have been reconciled and kissed each other before many witnesses. I should hate our peers to say that the agreement had been broken on my side and that Sir Joce should be the one regarded as the loyal knight.' 'Lord,' said Sir Ernalt, 'you are my lord. I am warning you of danger, for I know the truth from the maiden who has heard the matter discussed. So do not say on some other occasion that I knew something to your detriment and did not attempt to warn you of it, or that I have ever broken faith with you.' Sir Walter became very thoughtful, not knowing what to do for the best in this emergency. Then he said: 'Sir Ernalt, what do you advise me to do?' 'Lord,' he said, 'you will do well to heed my advice. I shall go with my company and take the castle of Dynan by trickery, and when Sir Joce has left his stronghold he will be less able to trouble you and will abandon his plans. Consequently, you will be avenged on him for the shame he has often inflicted on us. You must remember, lord, that rightly or wrongly a man must avenge himself on his enemy.' Sir Walter followed Sir Ernalt's advice completely, believing that everything he had said was the truth. But he was lying like a false knight. (15, 18–39; 16, 1–11)

Sir Ernalt prepared his company of men, which was large, for he had in it more than a thousand knights, squires and men-at-arms. He came to the castle of Dynan at night and had one part of his company remain in the wood near Whitcliffe and the other part lie in wait in the grounds beneath the castle. The night was very dark, so they were not spotted by a sentry or anyone else. Sir Ernalt took a squire, who carried the leather ladder, and then approached the window, where Marion was waiting for them. When she saw them, she had never been so happy. She lowered a rope and drew up the leather ladder, securing it to a battlement in the wall. Ernalt climbed up the tower easily and nimbly and took his beloved in his arms. He kissed her and they were full of joy. They went into another chamber, where they supped and went to bed, leaving the ladder hanging there. The squire who had carried it went to fetch the knights and the great company of men, who were hidden in the lord's garden and elsewhere, and brought them to the ladder. A hundred, well-armed men climbed up the leather ladder. Descending Pendover Tower, they went along by the wall behind the chapel, where they found the guard asleep, as he had become heavy-headed as death approached. They captured him immediately, intending to throw him down from his tower into the deep moat. But he begged for mercy, requesting that he be allowed to whistle a tune before he died. They granted him this. He did so in order that the knights of the household should be warned, but it was all in vain. As he was whistling, most of the knights and men-at-arms were cut down. In their beds they screamed and yelled out for God to take pity on them, but Sir Ernalt's companions were without pity. Everyone inside met a cruel death. Many a bed sheet which was white in the evening became all red with blood. Finally, they did throw the guard down into the deep moat, where his neck was broken.[14] (16, 12–39; 17, 1–3)

Marion de la Bruere lay beside her beloved, Sir Ernalt, completely unaware of his treachery. Hearing a great uproar in the castle, she got up and looked down into the castle. She heard the clamour and the cries of the wounded and saw armed knights with shining helmets and hauberks. Immediately she realized that Sir Ernalt had deceived and betrayed her, and she began to cry tenderly, saying piteously: 'Alas, why was I ever born? For because of my misdeeds my master, Sir Joce, who brought me up lovingly, has lost his castle and his fine men. Had it not been for me, nothing would have been lost! Alas that I ever trusted this knight, for by his flattery he has deceived me, and my lord as well, which means even more to me!' Sobbing, Marion drew forth Sir Ernalt's sword, saying: 'Lord knight, wake up, for without permission you have brought a band of strangers into my lord's castle. Although you, lord, and your squire were given hospitality by me, the others, who are here because of you, were not. Since you have deceived me, you cannot reasonably blame me if I offer you a service in accordance with your deserts. You will never boast to any future beloved that through deceiving me you conquered the castle of Dynan and the region.' The knight sat up. With the drawn sword which she held in her hand Marion ran him through the body and he died instantly. Marion knew that if she were captured she would be subjected to a cruel death. She did not know where to turn, so she threw herself from a window, which looked out towards Linney, and broke her neck. (17, 4–28)

The knights who were in the castle unlocked the gates and went into the town. They opened the gates of Dynan over towards the river and let in all their men. Then they stationed a large number of men at the end of each street in the town. They set fire to the town and made two fires in each street. On seeing the fire, the burgesses and the men-at-arms rose from their beds, some naked, some dressed. They did not know what to do, for they were all beside themselves. Lacy's knights and the squires fell upon them, massacring and killing them in great numbers. The burgesses could not and did not know how to defend themselves, so that all those who were found were cut down or burnt in the fire. The maidens made their way along the alleyways and saw their fathers and brothers lying there in the streets, cut to pieces. They went down on their knees, begging for mercy and for their lives to be spared. This was to no avail, as the story informs us: men, women and children, young and old, were all killed by weapons or by fire. Then day broke and they sent word to their lord that he should come to the castle of Dynan with all his forces, and so he did. He placed his banner on Pendover Tower as a sign of victory, because he had conquered a place where he had formerly been imprisoned. But the town and everything within it had been burnt to ashes. (17, 29–39; 18, 1–10)

When the news reached Sir Joce and Waryn de Metz, they were sorrowful, sad and grief-stricken. They sent messages far and wide, summoning their relatives, friends and their own people, with the result that in a month they had seven thousand good, well-armed men. They came to Castle Key, which is built on a hill one league away from Dynan. But at that time Castle Key was old and its gates were rotten, for no one had lived there previously for a hundred years. For Key, seneschal to my lord King Arthur, had built it. The whole area belonged to him and the name still remains, for people call it Keyenhom. Next day Joce, Waryn and Fouke le Brun went with their men to the castle of Dynan and attacked it very fiercely on all sides. Sir Walter and his knights defended the battlements and the walls with great boldness. Then Sir Walter and his Irishmen emerged from the castle and launched a great onslaught on those outside. Joce, Waryn and Fouke attacked them from all sides and killed large numbers of them. The Irishmen lay all over the meadows and the gardens, cut to pieces, with the result that Sir Walter and his men had the worst of it. He and his men retreated. They went back inside the castle and defended the walls. If they had stayed outside any longer, they would soon have heard very bad news. Sir Joce and Sir Waryn returned to their lodgings and removed their armour. When they had eaten, they made merry. Next day they attacked the castle very keenly on all sides. They could not capture it, but whatever forces they encountered outside they cut to pieces. The siege lasted for a long time. But later it so happened, with the agreement of a king of England, that the gates of the castle, which were treble, were burnt and destroyed by fire kindled by hams and grease. The tower over the gate was burnt from within and the high tower in the castle's third bailey, which was so strong and well built that no one at that time knew of one better or stronger, was in great part knocked down. The bailey was almost entirely destroyed. (18, 11–38; 19, 1–4)

Sir Waryn became ill. He took his leave of Sir Joce and went with just one squire to Alberbury, where he died. When his father was dead, Fouke le Brun went to Alberbury and took the homage and fealty of all his father's tenants. He took leave of Melette, his mother, and Hawyse, his wife, and returning to Sir Joce told him what had happened to his father. Joce was greatly saddened by this news. (19, 5–11)

Sir Walter was upset and distressed that he had lost his men. He was very much afraid of being defeated and overcome. He thought for a long time and then sent a letter to Iorwerth Drwyndwyn, Prince of Wales, as his lord, friend and relative, saying in the letter 'that Sir William Peverel, who held Maelor and Ellesmere, was dead'. He also told him that 'those lands were in his lordship, belonging to Powys, and Sir William held them wrongly by the gift of the King of England, and the king would take them into his own hands. If this happens, he will be a very bad neighbour for you, for he has no love for you. For this reason, lord, come and claim your right, and, if it pleases you, may you be willing to come and bring me aid, for I am grievously besieged in the castle of Dynan.' (19, 12–23)

When Iorwerth heard the news, he assembled more than twenty thousand men, from Wales, Scotland and Ireland, and made his way swiftly towards the March, burning the towns and robbing the people. He had such a large force of men that the countryside could not withstand them. Joce was wary, and realizing that Iorwerth was coming he, his men and Fouke armed themselves and boldly attacked Roger de Powys and his brother Jonas, who came in the vanguard of Iorwerth's army.[15] They killed many of their men, and unable to sustain the battle Roger and Jonas fell back. Then came the forces of Iorwerth, whose arms were or and gules quarterly and in each quarter a leopard. He attacked Sir Joce and Fouke, who defended themselves for a long time, killing many of their men. But they had such large forces that Sir Joce could not sustain the battle. He returned to Castle Key, a league away from Dynan. But things had gone badly wrong for him, as he had lost many of his men. Iorwerth and Lacy, who was then very happy, pursued Sir Joce and Fouke and besieged them in the castle. He attacked them fiercely, and for three days Joce, Fouke and their knights, without food or drink, defended their frail and ancient fortress against the entire army. On the fourth day Sir Joce said that honour would be better served if they left the castle and died honourably on the battlefield rather than dying dishonourably of hunger in the castle. Immediately they entered the field, and at their first encounter they killed more than three hundred knights, squires and men-at-arms. Iorwerth Drwyndwyn, Lacy and their men attacked Sir Joce and his men, who defended themselves like lions. But so many men pressed them that they could not hold out any longer, for Sir Joce's horse had been killed and he himself seriously wounded. Some of his knights had been captured, others killed. Then they took Sir Joce and his knights and sent them to prison in the castle of Dynan, where he used to be lord and master. (19, 24–38; 20, 1–16)

When Fouke saw Sir Joce captured and taken away, he almost went out of his mind with grief and anger. He spurred his horse and with his lance struck a knight, who was taking him away, right through his body. Then Owain Cyfeiliog, a bold and fierce knight, arrived, and with a lance of ash he struck Fouke in the pit of the stomach and the lance broke. The stump remained in his body, but his bowels were not damaged. Fouke realized that he was grievously wounded and no longer able to defend himself. So he took flight, and the others chased him for two leagues and more. When they could not catch up with him, they returned and took possession of all the lands which Fouke had held. They captured Guy Fitz Candelou de Porkington, who was Fouke's constable, taking him to prison in Rhuddlan along with his seven sons. (20, 17–29)

Fouke was deeply upset at what had happened to his lord. Having heard that King Henry was staying in Gloucester, he made his way there. As he approached the town, the king was on his way to take his ease in a meadow after dinner. He saw Fouke arriving on horseback, fully armed and riding very fearfully, for he was weak and his charger weary. 'Let us wait,' said the king, 'we shall soon hear some news.' Fouke came up to the king on horseback, for he was unable to dismount. He told the whole story to the king, who rolled his eyes fiercely and said he would avenge himself on such criminals within his kingdom. He asked him who he was and where he was born. Fouke told the king where he was born and of what people. He told him he was the son of Waryn de Metz. 'Fair son,' said the king, 'you are welcome to me, for you are of my blood and I shall help you.' The king had his wounds attended to and sent for his mother Melette, his wife Hawyse and the rest of his household. He retained them and had Hawyse and Melette reside in the queen's chambers. Hawyse was pregnant, and when her time came she was delivered of a child whom they named Fouke. In his time he was very famous, and rightly so, for he had no equal in strength, boldness and excellence. (20, 30–38; 21, 1–11)

When Fouke le Brun's wound had healed, King Henry sent a letter to Sir Walter de Lacy, ordering him on pain of life and limb to hand Joce de Dynan, his knight, over to him along with those knights who were wrongfully imprisoned. If he did not do so, he would come for them himself and punish him in such a way that the whole of England would speak of it. When Walter de Lacy had heard the message, he was very frightened by it. He handed over Sir Joce and his knights, providing them with equipment and horses honourably and taking them through the postern towards the River Teme, across the Teme's ford and beyond Whitcliffe, until they reached the high road to Gloucester.[16] When Sir Joce arrived in Gloucester, the king received him with great joy, promising him the support of law and reason. Joce stayed with the king as long as he wished. Then he took his leave and went to Lambourn, where he spent some time. But soon afterwards he died and was buried there. May God have mercy on his soul! (21, 12–26)

King Henry summoned Fouke and made him constable of his entire army.[17] He put him in command of all the forces in his land, telling him to take a large number of men and make his way to the March, from which he should drive out Iorwerth Drwyndwyn and his army. Thus Fouke was made master over everyone, for he was strong and courageous. The king remained in Gloucester, for he was ill and could scarcely travel. Iorwerth had captured the entire March, from Chester to Worcester, and dispossessed all the barons in the March. Sir Fouke launched many a fierce assault on Iorwerth with the king's army, and in a battle in Wormsley, near Hereford, caused him to take flight and abandon the field. But before this happened, many men had been killed on both sides. The fierce and arduous war between Sir Fouke and the Prince lasted for four years until, at the request of the King of France, a love-day was arranged at Shrewsbury, between the king and Prince Iorwerth. They embraced each other and were reconciled, and the prince restored to the barons of the area all the lands he had taken from them. He gave Ellesmere back to the king, but he would not give up Blancheville and Maelor for any amount of money.

'Fouke,' said the king, 'since you have lost Blancheville and Maelor, instead I grant Alveston to you in perpetuity with all the land belonging to it.' Fouke thanked him sincerely. King Henry gave his daughter Joan to Llywelyn Fitz Iorwerth, a seven-year-old child, and as a marriage gift he gave them Ellesmere and many other lands.[18] He took Llywelyn with him to London. Prince Iorwerth along with his household took leave of the king and he made his way towards Wales. He gave Blancheville and Maelor to Roger de Powys. Roger later gave Maelor to Jonas, his younger brother. (21, 27–39; 22, 1–14)

Now you have heard how Sir Joce de Dynan and his daughters, Sybille, the elder and Hawyse, the younger, were dispossessed of the castle and the honour of Dynan, which Walter de Lacy held wrongfully. The town of Dynan was later restored and rebuilt and called Ludlow. You have also heard how Sir Fouke Fitz Waryn de Metz was dispossessed of Blancheville and Maelor. Sybille, his elder sister, was afterwards married to Payn Fitz John, a very valiant knight.[19] (22, 15–22)

Fouke and Hawyse had remained so long with the king that he had five sons, Fouke, William, Philip the Red, John and Alan.[20] King Henry had four sons, Henry, Richard the Lionheart, John and Geoffrey, who later became Count of Brittany. Henry was crowned during his father's lifetime, but he died before his father. After his father's death came Richard, and after Richard his brother John, who all his life was evil, quarrelsome and resentful. Fouke, the younger, was brought up with King Henry's four sons and was greatly loved by all of them except John, with whom he often fell out. It happened that John and Fouke were sitting all alone in a chamber playing chess when John took the chessboard and struck Fouke a mighty blow with it. Realizing he was injured, Fouke raised his foot and kicked John in the chest so hard that his head went crashing against the wall, with the result that he became giddy and fainted. Fouke was dismayed, but glad that there was no one in the room apart from the two of them. He rubbed John's ears and he regained consciousness. He went to his father, the king, and complained bitterly. 'Hold your tongue, wretch,' said the king, 'you are always trying to pick a quarrel. If Fouke did anything to you which was harmful, it was just what you deserved.' He summoned John's master and had him well and truly beaten because he had complained. John was very angry with Fouke, so that afterwards he could never feel any true love towards him.[21] (22, 23–29; 23, 1–5)

When King Henry, his father, was dead, King Richard reigned. Because of his loyalty, he cherished Fouke le Brun Fitz Waryn, and he summoned before him in Winchester Fouke le Brun's five sons, young Fouke, Philip the Red, William, John and Alan, and also their cousin Baldwin de Hod-net.[22] He equipped them all very richly and dubbed them knights. Young Sir Fouke and his brothers crossed the sea with their companions in search of fame and distinction, and they did not hear of any tournament or joust without him wanting to be there. Everywhere he was praised so much that people said with one voice that he had no equal in strength, goodness and courage, for he possessed such grace that he never attended any combat without being considered and held to be the best. It so happened that their father, Fouke le Brun, died. King Richard sent a letter to Sir Fouke, telling him to come to England to receive his lands, for his father was dead. Fouke and his brothers were grief-stricken at the death of Fouke le Brun, their good father. They returned to London, to King Richard, who was very glad to see them. He restored to them all the lands in the possession of Fouke le Brun on his death. The king made preparations for his journey to the Holy Land and entrusted the entire March to the protection of Sir Fouke. The king loved him dearly and cherished him for his loyalty and great renown, and as long as King Richard lived Fouke enjoyed the king's favour. (23, 6–27)

After Richard's death, John, King Richard's brother, was crowned King of England. Then he summoned Sir Fouke to come and speak with him about a number of matters relating to the March. He said he would go and visit the March, and he went to Castle Baldwin, which is now called Montgomery,[23] and when Morys, the son of Roger de Powys, lord of Blancheville, found out that King John was on his way to the March, he sent the king a fine, plump charger and a white moulted gerfalcon. The king thanked him very much for the presents. Then Morys came to speak with the king, who asked him to remain with him and be a member of his council. He made him warden of the entire March. When Morys saw the opportunity, he spoke to the king, begging him, if it were his pleasure, to confirm by his charter the right of himself and his heirs to the honour of Blancheville, as his father, King Henry, had formerly confirmed it for Roger de Powys, his father. The king well knew that Sir Fouke had full claim to Blancheville, but he recalled the blow which Fouke had once given him. Thinking he could avenge himself in this way, he agreed to put his seal to whatever Morys should put into writing. In respect of this Morys promised him a hundred pounds of silver. (23, 28–38; 24, 1–8)

Nearby was a knight, who had heard everything the king and Morys had said, and he hastened to Sir Fouke, telling him that the king was to confirm by his charter to Sir Morys the lands which belonged to him. Fouke and his four brothers came to the king and requested that they should have the benefit of common law and the lands which were theirs by right and reason, as Fouke's inheritance. They asked the king to be good enough to accept from them the sum of one hundred pounds, on the understanding that he would be willing to grant them the decision of his court in respect of gain and loss. The king told them that whatever he had granted to Sir Morys he would maintain, whether anyone might be angry at this or not. Then Sir Morys spoke to Sir Fouke, saying: 'Lord knight, you are very foolish to claim my lands. If you say you have a right to Blancheville, you are lying, and but for the king's presence I would prove it to you on your body.' Without more ado Sir William, Fouke's brother, sprang forward and struck Sir Morys full in the face with his fist, so that he was covered in blood. Knights intervened, so no further damage was done. Then Sir Fouke said to the king: 'Lord king, you are my liege lord, and I am bound by fealty to you whilst I am in your service and as long as I hold lands from you. You ought to maintain my rights, and yet you fail me both in rights and in common law. He was never a good king who denied justice to his free-born tenants in his court. For this reason I relinquish my homage.' So saying, he left the court and went to his lodgings. (24, 9–33)

Fouke and his brothers armed themselves forthwith, as did Baldwin de Hodnet, and when they had gone half a league from the city twenty-five knights came after them, well mounted and fully armed, the strongest and most valiant in the king's entire household. They commanded them to turn back, saying that they had promised the king their heads. Sir Fouke turned round and said: 'Fair lords, you were very foolish when you promised to give what you cannot have.' Then they joined battle with lance and sword in such a way that four of the king's most valiant men were killed immediately and all the others wounded to the point of death, apart from one who, seeing the danger, took flight. This man came to the city and the king asked him if Waryn had been captured. 'No,' he said, 'he was not even harmed. He and all his companions have gone and we were all killed, apart from myself who escaped with great difficulty.' The king said: 'Where is Girard de France, Peter de Avignon and Sir Amys le Marquis?' 'They were killed, lord.' Then ten knights came on foot, for Sir Fouke had taken their horses. Some of them had lost their noses, others their chins, and they were all discomfited. The king swore a great oath that he would take vengeance on them and all their lineage. (24, 34–38; 25, 1–14)

Fouke came to Alberbury and told Lady Hawyse, his mother, how they had fared in Winchester.[24] He took a large sum of money from his mother and went with his brothers and his cousins to Brittany, where he stayed as long as he pleased. King John took into his own hands all the lands which Fouke held in England and inflicted great damage on his entire family. (25, 16–21)

Fouke, his four brothers and his cousins Audulf de Bracy and Baldwin de Hodnet took leave of their friends and cousins in Brittany and came to England.[25] They rested in woods and on moorland by day and travelled by night, for they did not dare await the king, as they lacked the forces to withstand him. Then they came to Higford, to Sir Walter de Higford, who had married Lady Vyleyne, daughter of Waryn de Metz, but her real name was Emmeline and she was Sir Fouke's aunt.[26] Then Fouke went to Alberbury, and on his arrival he was told by the local inhabitants that his mother had been buried. Fouke mourned her deeply and prayed most devoutly for her soul. (25, 22–33)

That night Sir Fouke and his men went into a forest called Babbins Wood, close to Blancheville, to keep a look out for Morys Fitz Roger. Then a young man from Morys' household came along and spotted them. He went back and told Morys what he had seen. Morys armed himself splendidly and took his shield, green with two boars of beaten gold. Its border was argent charged with fleurs-de-lys azure. In his company he had the nine sons of Guy de la Montagne and the three sons of Aaron de Clerfountaygne, so that there were thirty men, well mounted, accompanying them and five hundred men on foot. When Fouke saw Morys, he came swiftly out of the forest and a fierce battle began between them, in which Morys was wounded in the shoulder and a number of his knights and foot soldiers were killed. In the end Morys fled towards his castle with Fouke pursuing him. Fouke tried to strike him on the helmet as he fled, but the blow landed on the crupper of his horse. Then Morgan Fitz Aaron arrived and, shooting from the castle, he struck Fouke in the leg with a bolt from a crossbow. Fouke was very distressed that he could not avenge himself on Sir Morys as he wished, and he paid no heed to the wound to his leg. Sir Morys complained to the king that Fouke had returned to England and wounded him in the shoulder. The king became extraordinarily angry and he ordered a hundred knights with their followers to travel all over England to seek out Fouke, capture him and hand him over to the king, dead or alive. All their expenses would be paid by the king, and if they could capture him he would give them lands and rich fiefs. The knights covered the whole of England in their search for Fouke, but whenever they heard that Sir Fouke was in a certain place they refused to go there at any price. For they feared him beyond measure, some because of their love for him and others because they were afraid of his strength and his noble chivalry and that they would be harmed or killed as a result of his strength and courage. (25, 34–38; 26, 1–26)

Sir Fouke and his company came to the Forest of Braydon and remained there in secret, for they did not dare do so openly because of the king. Then there came from abroad ten merchants who had purchased with the King of England's money the most magnificent cloths, furs, spices and gloves for the persons of the King and the Queen of England. They were taking all this through the forest to the king and twenty-four men-at-arms were in attendance in order to guard the king's treasure. When Fouke caught sight of the merchants, he summoned his brother John and told him to go and speak with these people and find out where they hailed from. John spurred his horse and coming to the merchants asked them who they were and where they were from. An arrogant and haughty spokesman sprang forward and asked him what business it was of his to enquire who they were. John asked them kindly to come and speak with his lord in the forest or, if they refused, they would do so in spite of themselves. Then one of the men sprang forward and gave John a great blow with his sword. John struck him back on the head and he fell to the ground in a faint. (26, 27–38; 27, 1–6)

Then Sir Fouke and his company came up and attacked the merchants, who defended themselves with great vigour. In the end they surrendered, for they were forced to do so. Fouke took them into the forest and they told him that they were the king's merchants. When Fouke heard this, he was delighted. He said: 'Lord merchants, if you lost these goods, who would suffer the loss? Tell me the truth.' 'Lord,' they said, 'if we lost them through our cowardice or through want of proper care, we would suffer the loss, and if we lost them in any other way, through peril at sea or by force, the loss would be the king's.' 'Are you telling the truth?' 'Yes, lord,' they said. When Sir Fouke heard that the loss would be the king's, he used his lance to measure the rich cloth and the costly furs, and he clothed in this rich cloth all those who were with him, great or small, and gave to each according to his rank. But each man had a liberal allowance. Each one took what he wanted from the rest of the goods. (27, 7–22)

When evening came and the merchants had eaten well, he entrusted them to God and asked them to greet the king on behalf of Fouke Fitz Waryn, who thanked him warmly for his fine robes. During the whole period of his exile, neither Fouke nor any of his men ever attempted to harm anyone other than the king and his knights. When the merchants and their men came before the king, wounded and maimed, and recounted to him what Fouke had charged them with and how he had taken his property, the king almost went mad with rage and he set up a hue and cry throughout the realm: to the person who brought him Fouke, dead or alive, he would give a thousand pounds in silver and in addition all the lands in England belonging to Fouke. (27, 23–34)

Fouke departed and came to the Forest of Kent, where he left his knights in the thick of the forest. He himself rode off alone along the highway and met a messenger who had garlanded his head with a chaplet of red roses and was singing merrily. Fouke begged him to be kind enough to give him the chaplet; if he were willing to do business with him, he would pay him double its value. 'Lord,' said the messenger, 'a man is very mean with his possessions if he refuses to give a chaplet of roses at the request of a knight.' He gave the chaplet to Fouke, who gave him twenty sous for it in return. The messenger knew him well, for he had often seen him. The messenger came to Canterbury, where he met the hundred knights who had been searching for Fouke throughout the whole of England. He said to them: 'Lords, where have you come from? Have you found what you have been looking for, by the command of our lord, the king, and for your own advancement?' 'No,' they said. 'What will you give me?' he said. 'I shall take you to the place where I saw him today and spoke with him.' They gave and promised the messenger so much that he told them where he had seen him and how he had given him twenty sous for the chaplet which he had been pleased to give him. (27, 35–39; 28, 1–14)

The hundred knights hastily summoned knights, squires and men-at-arms throughout the region. They surrounded the entire forest and placed beaters and receivers there, as if they were hunters, and they positioned old folk and others throughout the fields with horns to raise the cry when they saw Fouke and his companions coming out of the forest. Fouke was in the forest and knew nothing of what was happening. When he heard a knight blowing a great bugle, he became suspicious and ordered his brothers, William, Philip, John and Alan, to mount their horses, and they did so at once. Audulf de Bracy, Baldwin de Hodnet and John Malveysin did the same.[27] The three brothers of Cosham, Thomas, Peter and William, were good crossbowmen and all Fouke's other followers were ready for the assault. (28, 15–27)

Fouke and his companions emerged from the forest and saw in front of all the others the hundred knights who had been looking for them throughout England. Blows were exchanged, and they killed Gilbert de Montferrant and Jordan de Colchester and many other knights in their company. They passed right through the hundred knights and then came back amongst them, unhorsing them in large numbers. At length there arrived so many knights, squires, burgesses, men-at-arms and other people without number that Fouke realized that the battle could not continue. So he went back into the forest. But John, his brother, was wounded in the head, through his helmet. But, before they returned to the forest, many good knights, squires and men-at-arms had been cut down. Fouke and his companions spurred their horses and fled. The people raised the cry on all sides and pursued them everywhere to the cry of the horn. Finally, they went down a path and encountered only one man raising the cry with a horn. One of their company struck him in the body with the bolt from a crossbow. He ceased raising the cry. (28, 28–39; 29, 1–5)

Fouke and his companions left their horses and fled on foot to an abbey close by. When the porter saw them, he ran to close the gates. Alan was very tall. He quickly climbed over the walls and the porter began to run away. 'Wait!' said Alan. He ran after him and took the keys from him. With the staff from which the keys hung he struck him a blow which would rightly make him suffer for having fled. Alan let all his brothers in. Fouke took the habit of an old monk, and donning it immediately took a great crutch in his hand and went out of the gate. He shut the gate after him and set off, limping along on one foot and supporting his whole body on the great crutch. Then up came knights and men-at-arms with a large number of others, and a knight said to him: 'Old sir monk, have you seen any armed knights passing this way?' 'Yes, lord, may God repay them for the damage they have done.' 'What have they done to you?' 'Lord,' he said, 'I am old and so infirm that I cannot help myself. Seven of them came on horseback and about fifteen on foot, and because I could not get out of their way quickly enough they did not spare me at all, but let their horses run against me. This was a sin from which they gained little.' 'Say no more,' he replied, 'you will be well avenged this very day.' The knights and all the others passed quickly on in pursuit of Fouke and they were soon a league away from the abbey. Sir Fouke stood upright in order to be able to see more. (29, 6–28)

Then Sir Girard de Malfee arrived with ten companions, all well mounted knights. They had come from abroad and had brought with them some excellent horses. Then Girard said mockingly: 'Here's a big, fat monk with a belly large enough to hold two gallons of wine.' Fouke's brothers were inside the gate, and they had heard and seen how Fouke had conducted himself. Without more ado, Fouke raised the great crutch and struck Sir Girard beneath the ear so that he fell to the ground quite stunned. Seeing this, Fouke's brothers rushed out and captured the ten knights along with Sir Girard and all their equipment. They bound the men tightly in the porter's lodge, took all their equipment and their good horses and rode away without stopping until they came to Higford, where John was healed of his wound. (29, 29–38; 30, 1–4)

When they had been there for a while, there came a messenger who had been looking for Sir Fouke for a very long time. He greeted him on behalf of Hubert, Archbishop of Canterbury, and asked him to come quickly and speak with him at once. Fouke took his men and came to the forest next to Canterbury, where he had been before. He left his whole company there, except for his brother William. Fouke and William dressed as merchants and came to Bishop Hubert in Canterbury. The archbishop, Hubert le Botiler, said to them: 'Fair sons, you are very welcome to me. You well know that Theobald le Botiler, my brother, has been called to God and that he had married Lady Matilda de Caus, a very rich woman and the most beautiful in the whole of England. King John desires her so much because of her beauty that she can scarcely protect herself from him. I have her here and you will see her. I beg you, dear friend Fouke, and command with my blessing, to take her for your wife.' Fouke saw her and knew very well that she was beautiful, good and of high reputation and that in Ireland she had strong castles, cities, lands, rents and great homages. With the agreement of his brother William, and on the advice of Archbishop Hubert, he married Lady Matilda de Caus. Fouke stayed there for two days and then took his leave of the bishop, leaving his wife there. He returned to his companions in the wood and told them everything he had done. They poked fun at him, laughing and calling him 'husband', and asking him where he would take the beautiful woman, whether to some castle or to a wood. They all made merry together. But everywhere they did a great deal of damage to the king, but to no one other than those who were openly their enemies.[28] (30, 6–31)

A knight called Robert Fitz Sampson dwelt in the March of Scotland and he had frequently received Sir Fouke and his followers, and entertained them with great honour. He was a man of great wealth and his wife, whose name was Lady Anabel, was a very courtly lady. At that time there was a knight in that country called Peter de Brubille. This Peter was in the habit of assembling all the sons of noblemen in the area, some of whom were dissipated and others ribalds, and they roamed around the country killing and robbing law-abiding people, merchants and others.[29] This Peter, when he went robbing people with his company, called himself Fouke Fitz Waryn. For this reason Fouke and his companions were wrongly accused of something for which they were not to blame. Fouke, who for fear of King John did not stay very long in one place, came one night to the

March of Scotland and arrived very close to the court of Sir Robert Fitz Sampson. He saw a great light in the court and heard voices within and his name often mentioned. He made his companions wait outside whilst he himself went boldly into the court and then into the hall. He saw Peter de Brubille and other knights sitting at supper, and Robert Fitz Sampson and his good lady and their household had been bound and cast to one side of the hall. Sir Peter and his companions were all masked, and all those serving there were kneeling before Sir Peter and calling him their lord Sir Fouke. The lady, who lay bound beside her husband in the hall, said most piteously: 'Oh, Sir Fouke, have mercy in God's name! I have never done you any wrong, but have loved you as best I could.' Sir Fouke stood up, having heard everything that they had said. But when he had heard the words of the lady who had been so kind to him, he could not contain himself for anything on earth. Unaccompanied, he moved forward, and with his drawn sword in his hand said: 'Silence now. I order all those of you I can see here to remain absolutely motionless.' He swore a great oath that anyone bold enough to move would be cut into small pieces. Peter and his companions considered themselves trapped. 'Now,' said Fouke, 'which of you has himself called Fouke?' 'Lord,' said Peter, 'I am a knight and my name is Fouke.' 'In God's name,' he said, 'Sir Fouke, rise immediately and bind all your companions firmly, or else you will be the first to lose your head.' Peter was terrified by this threat, and he got up and freed the lord and lady and all the rest of the household, and he bound all his companions well and firmly. When they were all bound, Fouke made him cut off the heads of all those he had bound, and when he had beheaded all his companions, Fouke said: 'You craven knight, who call yourself Fouke, you are lying. I am Fouke and this you will soon know well. I shall pay you back for having me falsely accused of theft.' At once he cut off his head, and when he had done this he summoned his companions. They dined there and made merry. In this way Sir Fouke rescued Sir Robert and all his wealth so that he lost nothing. (30, 32–39; 31, 1–38; 32, 1–3)

The king regularly inflicted great damage on Sir Fouke. But Fouke was as wise and cunning as he was strong and bold, so that very often the king and his men pursued him by following his horses' hoofprints and Fouke frequently had the horses shod and the shoes reversed. In this way the king was deceived and tricked in his pursuit. Sir Fouke underwent many harsh battles before he won his inheritance. (32, 4–10)

Sir Fouke took leave of Sir Robert Fitz Sampson and came to Alberbury. He took up residence in a nearby forest on the river. Fouke called John de Rampaigne, saying: 'You are very skilled in minstrelsy and the jongleur's

157

art. Are you brave enough to go to Blancheville and play before Morys Fitz Roger and find out what is happening there?' 'Yes,' said John. He crushed a herb and placed it in his mouth. His face began to swell and to become grossly puffed up. It became so colourless that his own companions scarcely knew him. He dressed in very poor garments, took his pouch and jongleur's instruments, and with a large staff in his hand he went to Blancheville, where he told the porter he was a jongleur. The porter took him to Sir Morys Fitz Roger, who asked him where he was born. 'Lord,' he replied, 'in the March of Scotland.' 'What news do you have?' 'Lord, I have none, except about Sir Fouke Fitz Waryn, who has been killed in a robbery which he committed in the house of Sir Robert Fitz Sampson.' 'Are you telling the truth?' 'Yes indeed,' he said, 'everyone in the region says so.' 'Minstrel,' said Morys, 'for your piece of news I shall give you this pure silver cup.' The minstrel took the cup and thanked his good lord very much. John de Rampaigne was very ugly in face and body, so the scoundrels there made fun of him, ill-treated him and pulled him about by the hair and the feet. John raised his staff and gave one of the scoundrels such a blow on the head that his brains flew into the middle of the floor. 'Wretched scoundrel,' said the lord, 'what have you done?' 'Lord,' he said, 'have mercy in God's name! I cannot help it. I have an illness, which is very serious. You can see this by my face, which is so swollen. This illness takes away all my sense at certain times in the day, so that I cannot control myself.' Morys swore a great oath that, had it not been for the piece of news he had brought, he would have had his head cut off at once. The jongleur quickly withdrew, for he thought he had stayed there for a very long time. He returned to Fouke and told him word for word how he had got on and that he had heard in the court that Sir Morys, his fifteen knights and his household were going the next day to the castle in Shrewsbury, for he was the warden of the whole March. When Sir Fouke knew this, he was very happy and so were his companions. (32, 11–38; 33, 1–9)

The next day Fouke rose early and donned all the armour he required, as did his companions. Morys came towards Shrewsbury, along with fifteen knights and the four sons of Guy Fitz Candelou de Porkington and the rest of his household. When Fouke saw him, he was very pleased, but also very angry with him because he was keeping his inheritance from him by force. Morys looked towards the Pass of Ness[30] and saw a shield quarterly gules and per fess indented argent, and by his arms he knew it was Fouke. 'Now I know well,' said Morys, 'that jongleurs are liars, for there I can see Fouke.' Morys and his knights were very bold and they attacked Fouke and his companions boldly, calling them thieves and saying that

before evening their heads would be placed on the high tower in Shrewsbury. Fouke and his brothers defended themselves most vigorously and Sir
Morys, his fifteen knights and the four sons of Guy Fitz Candelou de
Porkington were killed there. So Fouke now had that many less enemies.
(33, 10–25)

Fouke and his companions went from there towards Rhuddlan to talk
to Sir Llywelyn, the prince whom Joan, daughter of King Henry and sister
of King John, had married, for the prince, Sir Fouke and his brothers had
been brought up together at King Henry's court. The prince was very glad
that Sir Fouke had come, and he asked him what sort of agreement there
had been between himself and the king. 'Lord,' said Fouke, 'none, for I am
unable to gain peace under any circumstances. For this reason, lord, I have
come to you and my good lady in order to have your peace.' 'Certainly,'
said the prince. 'I grant and give you my peace and you will receive a good
welcome from me. The King of England is incapable of having peace with
you or me or anyone else.' 'Lord,' said Fouke, 'many thanks, for I put my
trust in you greatly and in your great loyalty, and since you have granted
me your peace, I shall tell you something else. Certainly, lord, Morys Fitz
Roger is dead, for I have killed him.' When the prince knew that Morys
was dead, he was very angry, and he said that, if he had not granted him his
peace, he would have had him drawn and hanged, because Morys was his
cousin. Then the good lady arrived, and made peace between the prince
and Sir Fouke, in such a way that they embraced each other and put aside
all their anger. (33, 26–39; 34, 1–5)

At that time there was great discord between Prince Llywelyn and
Gwenwynwyn, son of Owain Cyfeiliog. A large part of the territory of
Powys belonged to this Gwenwynwyn and he was very arrogant, haughty
and proud. He was not willing to submit in any way to the prince, rather
did he cause a great deal of destruction in his land. The prince had destroyed Mechain castle by force and he had captured Mochnant, Llannerch
and other lands which belonged to Gwenwynwyn. The prince assigned the
ownership of all his land to Fouke and commanded him to attack
Gwenwynwyn and destroy all his lands. Fouke was wise and very wary,
knowing full well that it was the prince who was in the wrong. He spoke to
him in these fine words: 'Lord, in God's name, have mercy! If you do what
you have decided, you will be greatly blamed by everyone in foreign king-
doms. Lord, please, may my words not anger you. Everyone says that you
have sinned against him and for that reason, in God's name, have mercy
on him. He will return to you and, if you so wish, serve you willingly, and
you do not know when you may need your barons.' Fouke spoke so ear-

nestly to the prince that he and Gwenwynwyn were reconciled, and the prince gave him back all his lands, which had previously been taken from him.[31] (34, 6–25)

King John was in Winchester. Then news came to him that Fouke had killed Morys Fitz Roger and that he was staying with Llywelyn, the prince who had married his sister Joan.[32] He became very thoughtful and for a long time said nothing. Then he said: 'Ah, Virgin Mary! I am king and I govern England. I am Duke of Anjou and of Normandy and all Ireland is in my power. Yet I cannot find or get in all my domain, whatever I may give, anyone who is willing to avenge me for the damage and shame which Fouke has inflicted on me. But I shall not fail to avenge myself against the prince.' (34, 26–35)

The king summoned all his earls, his barons and his other knights to Shrewsbury, ordering them to be present on a certain day in Shrewsbury with all their men.[33] And when they had come to Shrewsbury, Llywelyn was warned by his friends that King John would wage a great war against him. He called Fouke and told him the whole story. Fouke assembled at the castle of Bala in Penllyn thirty thousand fine men, and Gwenwynwyn, son of Owain, came with his men, who were strong and bold. Fouke was very skilled in war, and he knew all the defiles through which John would have to pass. The pass was very narrow and surrounded by woods and marshes so that he could pass only by the highway. This pass is called the Ffordd Gam Elen.[34] Fouke and Gwenwynwyn came to that pass with their men, and beyond the highway they dug a ditch, long, deep and broad, and they filled the ditch with water so that no one could pass, either because of the marsh or because of the ditch. Beyond the ditch they constructed a very well-fortified palisade and the ditch can still be seen to this day. (34, 36–38; 35, 1–14)

King John came to the ford with all his army and thought he could get across it in safety. On the other side he saw more than ten thousand armed knights, who were guarding the pass. Fouke and his companions had crossed the ford by a private road, which they had built, and they were on the same side as the king. Gwenwynwyn and many other knights were with them. The king called out at the sight of Fouke and the king's knights attacked him on all sides. But it was very unfortunate for them that they could only approach Fouke head on, along the causeway. Fouke and his companions defended themselves like lions. They were often unhorsed, but they remounted just as often, and many of the king's knights were killed. Gwenwynwyn was severely wounded in the head through his helmet. When Fouke saw that neither he nor his men could hold their ground

for long outside their ditch, they returned by their private road and defended their palisade and the ditch. They hurled and cast quarrels and
other darts at the king's men, killing many of them and wounding a huge
number. This fierce and arduous struggle lasted until evening. When the
king saw so many of his men killed and wounded, he was so grieved that
he did not know what to do. So he went back towards Shrewsbury. (35,
15–33)

King John was a man without a conscience, wicked, quarrelsome, hated
by all good people and lecherous. If he ever heard of any beautiful maiden
or lady, wife or daughter of an earl or a baron or anyone else, he wanted to
have his way with her, either by tricking her with promises or gifts or by
taking her by force. For this he was hated the most, and this is why many
great English lords had renounced their homage to the king. As a result,
the king was far less feared. (35, 34–38; 36, 1–3)

John le Estrange, lord of Knockin and Ruyton, stayed permanently on
the king's side, and he inflicted losses on the prince's men.[35] For this
reason, the prince had his castle at Ruyton destroyed and his men captured
and imprisoned. This distressed John greatly. The prince went to Bala
castle and summoned Fouke. He gave and restored to him all of
Blancheville, his inheritance, as well as Ystrad Marchell and Dinorben.
Fouke thanked him profusely and taking the men of his choice went to
Blancheville, where he had the castle strengthened and repaired throughout. (36, 4–11)

John le Estrange came to the king and told him that Fouke and his men
had inflicted great losses on his men and destroyed the castle of Ruyton.
He begged the king, for he was on good terms with him, to help him as
best he could and thus he would be taking vengeance on Sir Fouke and his
men. The king summoned Sir Henry de Audley, who was lord and first
owner of Redcastle and its fiefs.[36] He ordered him to take ten thousand of
the most valiant knights in England, saying that he and his knights should
be obedient to Sir John le Estrange. Sir Henry and Sir John and their
knights made preparations to leave for Blancheville, and on their way,
whatever they encountered, men or woman, they killed, and they pillaged
the land. A hue and cry rose everywhere. (36, 4–23)

Fouke was in Blancheville, and with him there he had a fine company of
men, because he had recently regained possession of these lands. Seven
hundred knights from Wales and a large number of men-at-arms were
there. When the news reached Fouke that Sir John and Sir Henry were on
their way towards their region, they armed themselves at once and went
secretly to the pass of Myddle. When Sir John saw Sir Fouke, he spurred his

horse and gave Sir Fouke such a blow with his lance that it flew into small pieces. Sir Fouke struck him back in the face through his helmet and the blow was visible for the rest of his life. Sir John fell flat on the ground. He was very valiant and leaped to his feet at once, yelling out: 'Now lords, everyone against Fouke!' Fouke replied like a proud man: 'Certainly,' he said, 'and Fouke against everyone!' Then the knights on both sides came to blows. Fouke and Sir Thomas Corbet[37] and his other companions killed many men, and Alan Fitz Waryn and Philip, his brother, were wounded. When Fouke saw his brothers wounded, he nearly went out of his mind with rage. Sir Fouke went into the thick of the fray and anyone he reached had no escape from death. That day Sir Fouke had only seven hundred knights and his opponents ten thousand or more. For this reason Fouke could not win the battle. So he went back towards Blancheville. Sir Audulf de Bracy was unhorsed in the thick of the battle and he defended himself very bravely. In the end he was captured and taken to Shrewsbury. (36, 24–39; 37, 1–7)

Sir Henry and Sir John were very pleased to have captured him. They came to the king in Shrewsbury and handed Sir Audulf over to him. The king spoke most fiercely to him and swore a great oath that he would have him drawn and hanged, as he was a traitor to him and a thief. He had killed his knights, burnt his cities and demolished his castles. Audulf answered him boldly, saying that he had never been a traitor, nor had any of his family. Fouke was in Blancheville, and he had the wounds of his brothers and the other men washed and dressed. Then he remembered Sir Audulf and searched for him everywhere. When he could not be found, he thought he would never see him again. No one could have displayed greater grief. Then John de Rampaigne came and saw Fouke in such distress. 'Lord,' he said, 'cease this show of grief. If it pleases God, before prime tomorrow, you will have good news of Sir Audulf de Bracy, for I myself shall go and speak to the king.' (37, 8–22)

John de Rampaigne was skilled in the use of the tabor, the harp, the viol and the citole and in the jongleur's art. He attired himself very richly, just like any earl or baron, and dyed his hair and his whole body as black as jet, so that the only thing which was white was his teeth. He hung round his neck a very fine tabor, then he mounted a fine palfrey and rode through the town of Shrewsbury right up to the castle gate, with many people staring at him. John came before the king and, kneeling down, greeted him in very courtly fashion. The king returned his greetings and asked him where he was from. 'Lord,' he said, 'I am an Ethiopian minstrel; I was born in Ethiopia.' The king replied: 'Are all the people in your land your colour?'

'Yes, lord, men and women.' 'What do they say about me in foreign realms?' 'Lord,' he said, 'you are the most renowned king in all Christendom, and it is because of your renown that I have come to see you.' 'Fair lord,' said the king, 'welcome.' 'Sire, my lord, I thank you.' John said that he was famous more for his wickedness than for his goodness, but the king did not hear him. That day John performed on the tabor and other instruments a great deal of minstrelsy. (37, 23–39; 38, 1–2)

When the king had gone to bed, Sir Henry de Audelee sent for the black minstrel and took him to his chamber. There they played many songs, and when Sir Henry had had his fill of drink, he said to a servant: 'Go and get Sir Audulf de Bracy, whom the king intends to put to death tomorrow. Before he dies, he will have a good night.' The servant soon brought Sir Audulf into the room and then they talked and amused themselves. John began a song which Sir Audulf used to sing. Sir Audulf raised his head and looking at his face recognized him with great difficulty. Sir Henry asked for something to drink and John was most helpful. He jumped nimbly to his feet and served him from the goblet in full view of everyone. John was clever. He threw some powder into the goblet without anyone noticing, for he was a good juggler. Everyone who drank became so drowsy that very soon after drinking they lay down to sleep. When they were all asleep, John took one of the king's fools and placed him between the two knights whose task it was to guard Sir Audulf. John and Sir Audulf took the towels and sheets which were in the room and escaped through a window overlooking the River Severn, and they made their way to Blancheville, which was twelve leagues from Shrewsbury. It was not possible to hide what had happened for long, for the next day the king was told the truth of the matter and he was very angry at this escape. (38, 2–1–23)

Fouke had risen early the next day, for he had slept little that night. He looked towards Shrewsbury and saw Sir Audulf and John coming. There is no need to ask if he was happy when he saw them, and he ran to embrace and kiss them. He asked for their news and Sir Audulf told him how John had acted and how they had escaped. At this, Fouke, who had been distressed, was happy and joyful. (38, 24–30)

Let us now leave Fouke and speak of Lady Matilda de Caus. When the king, who had desired her so much, learned in truth that she was married to Sir Fouke, his enemy, on the advice of Archbishop Hubert, he inflicted great losses on the archbishop and on the lady, for he wanted to carry her away by force. She fled to the church, where she was delivered of a daughter. The archbishop baptized her Hawyse and she later became the Lady of Wem.[38] (38, 31–37)

Fouke and his companions came one night to Canterbury, and from there they took the lady to Higford, where she remained for some time. Then it happened that the lady became pregnant and she stayed secretly in Alberbury. The king had her spied upon and she went secretly from there to Shrewsbury. She was spied upon there too and was so heavily pregnant that she could not travel. She fled to the church of Our Lady in Shrewsbury, where she was delivered of a daughter, who was baptized Joan and later married to Sir Henry de Pembridge.[39] Then Matilda had a son, who was born on a mountain in Wales and baptized John, in a stream which comes from the Fountain of Maidens.[40] The lady and the child were very weak, for the child was born two months prematurely, and when the child was confirmed by the bishop he was called Fouke. The lady and the child, who were weak, were taken from the mountain to a grange, which was at Carreg-y-nant. (38, 38–39; 39, 1–14)

Since the king could not in any way avenge himself on Fouke, nor dishonour and capture the lady, he sent a letter to Llywelyn, who had married his sister Joan, asking him out of love for him to rid his household of his mortal enemy and traitor, Fouke. He would give him back all the lands which his ancestors had ever taken from his lordship, on the understanding that he would let him have Fouke's body. (39, 15–21)

The prince summoned his wife Joan to his room and showed her the letter from her brother, the king, When she had heard the contents of the letter, she let Fouke know secretly what it contained and that the king wanted to make peace with her husband. When Fouke heard this news, he was grief-stricken and feared treason. Through Baldwin de Hodnet, he secretly sent Lady Matilda to the archbishop in Canterbury and instructed Baldwin to come to him in Dover. Fouke, his four brothers, Audulf and John de Rampaigne put on the armour they desired and with their other men they came to Castle Bala to meet the prince. 'Lord,' said Fouke, 'I have served you loyally to the best of my ability. But now, lord, one does not know whom to trust. For you are willing to give me up because of the king's great promise. The king has sent you a letter which, lord, you have concealed from me. So, lord, I am all the more afraid.' 'Fouke,' said the prince, 'stay with me, for I certainly did not intend any treachery towards you.' 'Certainly, lord,' said Fouke, 'I believe it fully, but, lord, I shall not remain on any account.' He took leave of the prince and all his companions, and from there he travelled night and day, until he arrived in Dover, where he met Baldwin who had taken the lady to the archbishop. They set sail and arrived at Wissant. (39, 22–39; 40, 1–3)

When Fouke, his brothers and his other companions came to Paris, they saw King Philip of France, who had come into the fields to see his French knights joust. Fouke remained silent, as did his companions, when they saw such a fine assembly. They remained to watch the jousts, and when the French saw the English knights they made a much greater effort to perform well. Then Sir Druz de Montbener, a very arrogant Frenchman, summoned Sir Fouke and asked to joust with him. Fouke immediately granted his request, and he and his brothers armed themselves and mounted their good horses. John de Rampaigne was very richly attired and well-mounted, and he had a magnificent tabor, which he struck as he entered the lists. The hills and the valleys resounded and the horses capered. When the king saw Sir Fouke armed, he said to Sir Druz de Montbener: 'Take great care, for it is clear that this English knight is very brave and valiant.' 'Lord,' he said, 'there is no knight on earth whom I would not dare to encounter on horseback or on foot, hand to hand.' 'May God be with you,' said the king. Fouke and Druz spurred their horses and struck each other. Fouke struck him with his lance in the middle of his shield and pierced his fine hauberk. The blow went right through his shoulder so that Fouke's lance flew into pieces and Sir Druz fell flat on the ground. Fouke captured Sir Druz' horse, and leading it away he offered it to him as a present, for Sir Fouke had no desire to hold on to the horse. Then a French knight came up, who intended at his pleasure to avenge Sir Druz. With his lance he struck Fouke in the centre of his shield so that he broke his lance into pieces. Fouke struck him back in the centre of his helmet so that he splintered his lance. Whether he liked it or not, the knight was unhorsed. Fouke's brothers and his companions were ready to joust, but the king refused to allow it. The king came spurring up to Fouke, saying: 'English knight, God bless you, for you have done very well.' He begged him to remain with him, and Fouke thanked the king very much and agreed to stay as long as he wished. Everywhere that day Fouke was well regarded, praised and esteemed by many people. Fouke had such grace that he never went anywhere where boldness, chivalry, prowess and excellence were to be found without being considered the finest man there and without peer. (40, 4–38; 41, 1–2)

Fouke stayed with King Philip of France and he was loved and honoured by the king, the queen and all good men. The king asked him what his name was and Fouke told him he was called Amys del Bois. 'Sir Amys,' said the king, 'do you know Fouke Fitz Waryn, who is greatly praised everywhere?' 'Yes, lord,' he said, 'I have often seen him.' 'How tall is he?' 'Lord,' he said, 'as I understand it, he is the same size as myself.' The king replied: 'He may well be, for you are both valiant.' Fouke never heard of any tournament or joust throughout the whole of France without wanting to be there. He was praised everywhere and loved and honoured for his prowess and his largesse. (41, 3–13)

When the King of England knew that Fouke was staying with King Philip of France, he sent word to the king, asking him, if it pleased him, to be willing to banish from his household and his retainers Fouke Fitz Waryn, his mortal enemy. When the King of France had heard the contents of the letter, he declared by St Denis that no knight of that name was amongst his retainers and he sent such a reply to the King of England. When Sir Fouke heard this news, he came to the King of France and asked leave to depart. The king said: 'Tell me if you need anything and I shall make ample amends for what is causing you to want to leave me.' 'Lord,' he said, 'I have heard such news that I am forced to leave.' By these words the king realized that he was Fouke. The king said: 'Sir Amys del Bois, I think you are Fouke Fitz Waryn.' 'In truth, lord, I am.' The king replied: 'You will stay with me and I shall give you richer lands than you have ever had in England.' 'Certainly, lord,' he said, 'he who cannot rightfully hold his own inheritance is not worthy to receive a gift of lands from another.' (41, 14–31)

Fouke took leave of the king and came to the sea, where he saw the ships afloat on the sea. There was no wind in the direction of England and the weather was very fair. Fouke saw a mariner, who seemed bold and fierce, and he called to him, saying: 'Fair lord, is this ship yours?' 'Lord,' he said, 'it is.' 'What is your name?' 'Lord,' he said, 'Mador del Mont de Russie, where I was born.' 'Mador,' said Fouke, 'are you well acquainted with this profession and with how to carry people to various regions by sea?' 'Certainly, lord, there is no land of any repute in the whole of Christendom, to which I could not take a ship in perfect safety.' 'Certainly,' said Fouke, 'you have a very perilous profession. Tell me, Mador, fair, sweet friend, how did your father die?' Mador replied that he was drowned at sea. 'How did your grandfather die?' 'In the same way.' 'What about your great-grandfather?' 'In the same way, and all my relatives, as far as I know, to the fourth degree.' 'Certainly,' said Fouke, 'you are very foolhardy to risk putting to sea.' 'Lord,' he said, 'why? Each creature will have the death which is destined for him. Lord,' said Mador, 'if you please, answer my question. Where did your father die?' 'Certainly, in his bed.' 'And your grandfather?' 'The same.' 'What about your great-grandfather?' 'Certainly, all those I know about in my family died in their beds.' 'Certainly, lord,' said Mador, 'since all your family died in bed, I am astonished that you risk going to bed.' Then Fouke realized that the mariner had spoken the truth and that

166

each man will have the death which is destined for him, and he does not know which, whether on land or at sea. (41, 32–38; 42, 1–18)

Fouke spoke to Mador, who understood how to handle ships, and asked him for love of him and for his own financial advantage to design and fit out a ship. He would cover the outlay. Mador agreed, and the ship was built in a forest beside the sea, following at all points Mador's design. All its rigging and whatever fittings pertained to it were remarkably fine and splendid and it was remarkably well provided with supplies. Fouke, his brothers and his companions set sail and drew near to England. Then Mador saw a well-armed ship coming towards them, and when the ships came close to each other a knight spoke to Mador, saying: 'Lord mariner, whose ship is this which you are steering and where is it from? For no such ship is accustomed to pass this way?' 'Lord,' said Mador, 'it is mine.' 'Upon my word,' said the knight, 'it is not. You are thieves. I recognize it clearly from the quartered sail which is of the arms of Fouke Fitz Waryn. He is in the ship, and this very day I shall deliver his body to King John.' 'Upon my word,' said Fouke, 'you will not. But if you desire anything from us, you will have it willingly.' 'I shall have all of you and whatever you have, in spite of yourselves.' 'Upon my word,' said Fouke, 'you are lying.' Mador, who was a good and bold mariner, allowed his ship to sail on. It cut the other ship down the middle, so that the sea entered it and the ship was lost. But before that happened, many harsh blows were administered. When the ship had been overcome, Fouke and his companions took a great deal of money and supplies and brought them to their ship. Then the other ship perished and sank. (42, 19–38; 43, 1–5)

Fouke spent that whole year sailing along the English coast. He had no wish to harm anyone other than King John. He often took property from him and whatever else he could. Fouke set sail towards Scotland, and then a west wind got up which drove them three days away from Scotland. Then they caught sight of what appeared to them to be a beautiful and very delightful island. They made their way over to it and found a good harbour. Fouke, his four brothers, Audulf and Baldwin went ashore in order to visit the island and get supplies for their ship. Then they saw a young man guarding sheep, and when he saw the knights he went towards them and greeted them in an uncouth jargon. Fouke asked him if he knew of any food for sale in the country. 'Certainly, lord,' he said, 'none at all, for this is an island inhabited by only a few people and they live off their beasts. But if you wish to come with me, you will willingly have such food as I possess.' Fouke thanked him and went with him. The youth led them into an underground cavern, which was very fine, and had them sit down and treated them very kindly. 'Lord,' said the youth, 'I have a servant in the hills. May it not displease you if I blow my horn to summon him and we shall soon dine.' 'Do so in God's name,' said Fouke. The youth left the cavern, gave six blasts on his horn and came back to the cavern. (43, 6–26)

Soon six large, tall and fierce-looking peasants arrived, dressed in coarse and wretched tabards. Each one had a large club in his hand, hard and strong, and when Fouke saw them he suspected evil intent. The six peasants went into a chamber, took off their tabards and dressed themselves in a fine green cloth and shoes of orphrey. In all these garments they were as richly attired as any king could be, and returning to the hall they greeted Sir Fouke and his companions. They asked for the chessmen and a magnificent chessboard was brought to them with pieces of pure gold and silver. Sir William sat down to play a game, but he soon lost. Sir John played another and also lost immediately. Philip, Alan, Baldwin, Audulf, one after the other, played a game and each one lost his. Then one of the fiercest of the shepherds said to Fouke: 'Will you play?' 'No,' he said. 'Upon my word,' said the shepherd, 'you will play or wrestle, whether you like it or not.' 'Upon my word,' said Fouke, 'wretched, villainous shepherd, you are lying. Since I must wrestle or play, whether I like it or not, I shall play with you in the way I have learnt.' He leaped up, raised his sword and gave him such a blow that his head flew off into the middle of the place, then another, then a third. In that way Fouke and his companions killed all the villainous rascals. (43, 27–39; 44, 1–8)

Fouke went into a chamber and found a old woman sitting there. She had a horn in her hand and kept putting it to her mouth, but she could not make a sound with it. When she saw Fouke, she begged him for mercy, and he asked her what use the horn would be if she could blow it. The old woman told him that if the horn were blown help would arrive in abundance. Fouke took the horn and entered another chamber, where he saw seven maidens who were remarkably beautiful and splendidly attired. They were working on magnificent cloth, and when they saw Fouke they fell to their knees and begged for mercy. Fouke asked them where they were from, and one of them said: 'Lord, I am the daughter of Aunflor, King of Orkney, and my lord was resident in a castle of his in Orkney, called Castle Bagot, which is on the sea, beside a very fine forest. It happened that I and these maidens with four knights and others set sail in a boat. We had gone out to enjoy ourselves. Then suddenly the seven sons of the old woman in this place arrived in a ship with their company. They killed all our companions and brought us here. They have abused our bodies, against our will, God knows. So we beg you in the name of God, in whom you trust, to help us in our captivity, if you can escape from here, for I can see from your appearance that you are not resident in this land.' Fouke comforted the maidens, saying that he would help them as best he could. Fouke and his companions found great riches, provisions and armour, and Fouke found there the haubergeon which he considered to be so splendid and which he loved so much that he used it in secret. All his life he refused to sell it or give it away at any price. (44, 9–34)

Fouke provisioned his ship richly and took the maidens to it, looking after them as best he could. Then he ordered all his men to arm themselves speedily, and when they were all armed to their satisfaction he raised the hue and cry with the little horn he had taken from the old woman. Then more than two hundred of the thieves from the region came running through the fields. Fouke and his company set on them and they defended themselves vigorously. More than two hundred of the robbers and thieves were killed there, for there was no one on the entire island except for robbers and thieves, who were accustomed to kill any one they could get hold of and capture at sea. Fouke asked Mador if he knew how to take him by sea to the kingdom known as Orkney. 'Yes, certainly,' he said, 'it is just an island and Castle Bagot is very near the harbour.' Fouke said: 'That is the castle where I should like to be.' 'Lord, you will be there this very day.' When Fouke had arrived, he asked the maidens whether they were acquainted with that country. 'Certainly, lord,' said one of them, 'it is the kingdom of Aunflor, my father.' Fouke came to the castle and gave his daughter and the maidens back to the king. He received Fouke with great honour and gave him rich gifts. (44, 35–38; 45, 1–15)

Fouke had sailed so far to see marvels and adventures that he had circled the seven islands of the ocean, Brittany, Ireland, Gothland, Norway, Denmark, Orkney and Sweden. No one lives in Sweden apart from serpents and other foul beasts. There Fouke saw horned serpents. Their horns were very sharp and they had four feet and flew like birds. One such serpent attacked Fouke and struck him with its horn, piercing the centre of his helmet. Fouke marvelled at the blow, and he quickly realized that, when the serpent struck him on the shield, it could not quickly withdraw its horn. Fouke stabbed it through the heart with his sword. There Fouke saw a dragon-like beast, which had the head of a dog, a beard, feet like a goat and ears like a hare, and many other beasts which St Patrick drove out of Ireland and shut up there through the power of God.[41] For the worthy St Patrick was in favour with him. To this day no dragon-like beasts inhabit the land of Ireland, except for tailless lizards. (45, 16–32)

Fouke went sailing over the ocean towards the north, beyond Orkney.

There he found so much cold and ice that no one could endure the cold. Because of the ice the ship could make no progress in the sea. Fouke turned back towards England, and then a most terrible storm arose. They all thought they would die because of this storm and prayed devoutly to God and to St Clement that he would deliver them from the storm. This storm lasted a fortnight, whereupon they saw land, but did not know which one. Fouke went ashore and saw a very beautiful castle. He entered the castle, for the gate was open, but he found no living creature, man or beast, either inside the castle or in the entire country. He was astonished that such a beautiful place was unoccupied. He returned to his ship and told his men the story. 'Lord,' said Mador, 'let us leave the ship and go ashore, except for those who will guard our food. Perhaps we shall soon hear from someone what sort of country this is.' (45, 33–39; 46, 1–8)

When they came ashore, they met a peasant. Mador asked him what land this was, what it was called and why it was uninhabited. The peasant said to them: 'This is the kingdom of Iberia and this region is called Carthage. This castle belongs to the Duke of Carthage, who holds it from the King of Iberia. This duke had a daughter, the most beautiful maiden known in the kingdom of Iberia. One day this maiden climbed up the chief tower of this castle. Then a flying dragon came and took the maiden. It carried her to a high mountain at sea and ate her there. This dragon has killed and destroyed everything in the country. That is why no one dares live in this land, and the duke does not dare enter the castle, so terrible is the dragon.' (46, 9–20)

Fouke returned to his galley and they sailed on until they saw a great mountain at sea. 'Lord,' said Mador, 'that is the mountain where the dragon lives. Now we are all in danger.' 'Hold your tongue,' said Fouke, 'as yet you see nothing untoward. Lord Mador, do you intend to die of fright? We have seen many a dragon, and God has delivered us from many a danger. So far we have never been in danger from which, through God's mercy, we have not escaped. Your cold comfort would put cowards to death.' (46, 21–28)

Fouke took Audulf de Bracy with him, and step by step he went up the mountain, which was very high. When they reached the summit of the mountain, they saw lying there many good hauberks, helmets, spears and other weapons, and beside the weapons they saw nothing other than the bones of men. They also saw a large and beautiful tree with a spring beneath it with fine and clear running water. Fouke looked around him and saw a hollow rock. He raised his right hand and crossed himself in the name of the Father, the Son and the Holy Ghost. He drew his sword and

170

went in boldly, as one who had put his entire trust in God. He saw a very fair maiden weeping and displaying great grief. Fouke asked her where she was from. 'Lord,' she said, 'I am daughter of the Duke of Carthage, and I have been here for seven years without seeing a single Christian, unless he came here against his will, and if you are able to do so, in God's name go away, for if the dragon comes back in here you will never escape.' 'Certainly,' said Fouke, 'I have no intention of going, but I shall hear and see more. Maiden,' said Fouke, 'what does the dragon do to you? Does it do you any harm?' 'Lord,' she said, 'the dragon is strong and fierce, and it could carry an armed knight into these mountains, if it could get him in its talons. It has brought and eaten many people, whose bones you can see outside. It prefers human flesh to any other. When its hideous face and beard are smeared with blood, it comes to me and has me wash its face, beard and breast in clear water. When it wants to go to sleep, it goes to its bed, which is made of pure gold, for its nature is such that it gets exceptionally hot, and gold by its nature is very cold. To cool itself, it sleeps on gold, and when it goes to bed it takes a large stone, as you can see there, and places it in front of the door for fear of me, so that I cannot kill it whilst it is asleep. For it has human intelligence and is very much afraid of me. In the end I know it will kill me.' 'In God's name,' said Fouke, 'it will not, if it pleases God.' (46, 29–39; 47, 1–21)

Fouke took the maiden and passed her into the safe-keeping of Sir Audulf. They left the rock and had only just come out when they saw the dragon come flying through the air towards them. From its mouth, which was hot, it spewed forth horrible smoke and flames. It was a very foul beast with a huge head, square teeth, cruel talons and a long tail. When the dragon saw Fouke, it struck out at him, and with its talon, as it flew, it gave him such a blow on the shield that it rent it in two. Fouke raised his sword and struck the dragon on the head as hard as he could. The blow caused it no harm whatsoever, nor did it flinch at all under it, so hard were its scales and its horny skin. The dragon began its flight from afar in order to strike violently, and Fouke, who could not withstand the blow, dodged behind the tree which stood beyond the spring. Fouke realized that he could not harm the dragon from in front. So he took care, when the dragon turned to attack, to strike it in the body on its tail, cutting it in two. The dragon began to yell and roar. It sprang towards the maiden, trying to catch her and take her away. But Sir Audulf defended her. The dragon grasped Sir Audulf in its talon so tightly that, if Fouke had not arrived with all haste, it would have crushed him. Fouke then came and cut off its talon, and with great difficulty he freed Sir Audulf, for it had clawed him with its talon through his hauberk. Fouke struck the dragon right in the mouth with his sword and in that way he killed it. (47, 22–38; 48, 1–6)

Fouke was very weary and he rested for a time. Then he went to the dragon's bed and carried whatever gold he found there to his galley. John de Rampaigne examined Sir Audulf's wound and tended to it, for he was skilled in medicines. Mador turned his ship back towards Carthage, and they reached that country and returned his daughter to the duke, who was full of joy when he saw her. The maiden told her lord what sort of life she had been living and how Fouke had killed the dragon. The duke fell at Fouke's feet and thanked him for his daughter, begging him, if he pleased him, to remain in that land. He would give him the whole of Carthage and also his daughter in marriage. Fouke thanked him with all his heart for his generous offer and said that he would willingly take his daughter if his Christian faith could allow it, but he already had a wife. Having said this, Fouke remained there until Audulf was cured of his wound and then he took leave of the duke, who was very distressed at his departure. The duke gave them many fine and beautiful jewels and handsome, swift horses. To each of them he gave rich gifts. (48, 7–23)

Fouke and his companions sailed towards England. When they reached Dover, they went ashore, leaving Mador with the ship in a certain place, where they could find him when they wanted to. Fouke and his companions had discovered from the peasants that the king was at Windsor and they set out secretly along the road towards Windsor. During the day they slept and rested. At night they travelled until they came to the forest. There they settled in a certain place, where they had been before, in the Forest of Windsor, for Fouke had a thorough knowledge of the area. Then they heard hunters and beaters blowing their horns and thereby they knew that the king was going hunting. Fouke and his companions armed themselves very richly and Fouke swore a great oath that even if it meant his death he would not refrain from avenging himself on the king, who had disinherited him forcibly and wrongfully, or from challenging him boldly for his rights and inheritance. Fouke had his companions remain where they were, and he himself, he said, would go and spy out adventures. (48, 24–38; 49, 1–2)

Fouke set off, and he met an old charcoal-burner carrying a shovel in his hand. He was dressed all in black, as befits a charcoal-burner. Fouke begged him in friendly fashion to give him his clothing and his shovel in exchange for money. 'Lord,' he said, 'willingly.' Fouke gave him ten besants and asked him kindly not to tell anyone about this. The charcoal-burner went on his way and Fouke remained behind. He dressed at once in the clothing which the charcoal-burner had given him, then he went over to his charcoal and began to tend the fire. Fouke saw a large iron fork and he took it in his hand and began to arrange his logs here and there. (49, 3–12)

Then the king with three knights on foot came to Fouke, where he was tending his fire. When Fouke saw the king, he recognized him easily and throwing down the fork, he greeted his lord. He knelt down before him most humbly. The king and his three knights laughed heartily over the charcoal-burner's manners and behaviour. They stayed there for a long time. 'Sir peasant,' said the king, 'have you seen any stag or doe pass this way?' 'Yes, my lord, some time ago.' 'What beast did you see?' 'My lord, a horned one with long horns.' 'Where is it?' 'Sire, my lord, I can easily take you to where I saw it.' 'Go on then, sir peasant, and we shall follow you.' 'Lord,' said the charcoal-burner, 'shall I take my fork with me? For if it were stolen, I should suffer a great loss.' 'Yes, peasant, if you wish.' (49, 13–26)

Fouke took the large iron fork in his hand and led the king away to shoot, for he had a very fine bow. 'My lord,' said Fouke, 'does it please you to wait, and I shall go into the thicket and make the beast come this way?' 'Yes,' said the king. Fouke darted swiftly into the thicket and ordered his company to capture King John swiftly, 'for I have brought him here with only three knights, all his retinue is on the other side of the forest'. Fouke and his household darted out of the thicket and let out a yell on seeing the king, whom they captured immediately. 'Lord king,' said Fouke, 'now I have you in my power. I shall pass sentence on just as you would have liked to do to me, if you had captured me.' The king trembled with fright, for he was terrified of Fouke. Fouke swore that he would die because of the way he had damaged and disinherited him and many worthy men in England. The king begged for mercy and beseeched him for the love of God to spare his life. He would restore to him in its entirety all his inheritance and whatever he had taken away from all his people, and he would grant him love and peace for the rest of his days. To this end he would in all things make such security as Fouke himself would devise. Fouke granted him all he had asked for, on condition that he would promise, in the presence of his knights, to keep this agreement.[42] (49, 27–39; 50, 1–8)

The king pledged his faith that he would keep the agreement with him and he was very happy that he could escape in this way. He returned to his palace and assembled his knights and his retinue, telling them word for word how Sir Fouke had deceived him. He told them he had made this oath under duress and therefore would not keep it, and he ordered them all to arm themselves swiftly in order to capture these felons in the park.

Then Sir James de Normandy, who was the king's cousin, asked to be allowed to have the vanguard, saying that the English, at least most of the nobles, were cousins of Sir Fouke and therefore traitors to the king. These traitors would not be willing to catch him. Then Ranulf, Earl of Chester, said: 'Upon my word, lord knight, saving the honour of our lord the king, but not yours, this is a lie.' He would have tried to strike him with his fist, but for the presence of the earl marshal. He said that they were not and had never been traitors to the king or his people. But he declared that all the nobles and the king himself were indeed cousins of the said Fouke. Then the earl marshal said: 'Let us get after Sir Fouke! Then the king will see who will be faint-hearted because of kinship.'[43] (50, 9–26)

Sir James de Normandy and his fifteen companion knights armed themselves most richly, all in white armour, and they were all nobly mounted on white horses. He hastened forward with this company in order to win esteem. John de Rampaigne had taken note of everything that had happened and recounted it to Sir Fouke, who could not escape in any other way than by battle. Sir Fouke and his companions armed themselves very richly and hurled themselves boldly against Sir James. They defended themselves vigorously and killed all his companions, apart from four, whose wounds were almost fatal. Sir James was captured and Sir Fouke and his companions armed themselves immediately with the arms of Sir James and the other Normans, and they mounted their fine horses, which were white, for their own horses were weary and lean. They put Sir James in Sir Fouke's armour and bound his mouth so that he could not speak. They placed his helmet on his head and rode towards the king. When he saw them, he recognized them by their armour and thought that Sir James and his companions were bringing Sir Fouke. Then Sir Fouke presented Sir James to the king, saying that he was Sir Fouke. When they saw this, the Earl of Chester and the earl marshal were very distressed. (50, 27–37; 51, 1–9)

The king, for the gift, ordered him to kiss him. Sir Fouke said that he could not waste time taking off his helmet, for he had to pursue the other Fitz Waryns. The king dismounted from his fine steed and ordered him to mount it, for it was swift in the pursuit of his enemies. Sir Fouke got down and mounted the king's horse. He made his way to his companions and they fled more than six leagues from there. They disarmed themselves there in a copse and bathed their wounds. They bandaged the wound of his brother William, who had been severely injured by one of the Normans. They thought he was dead and everyone was totally grief-stricken. The king ordered the immediate hanging of Sir Fouke. Then Emery de

Pin, a Gascon who was related to Sir James, came forward, saying that he would hang him. He took him and led him a short distance away. He had his helmet taken off and saw immediately that it was James. He unbound his mouth and James told him everything that had happened between himself and Sir Fouke. Emery went straight to the king, taking Sir James, who told him how Sir Fouke had served him. When the king realized he had been deceived, he was most distressed. He swore a great oath that he would never divest himself of his hauberk until he had captured these traitors. Fouke knew nothing of this. (51, 10–29)

The king, his earls and his barons followed the horses' hoofprints, until they almost reached the copse where Fouke was. When Fouke spotted them, he wept and mourned William, his brother, considering himself destroyed for ever. William begged them to cut off his head and take it away with them, so that the king, when he found his body, would not know who he was. Fouke said that he would not do so for the world. In tears he prayed most tenderly that God in his mercy should help them. You have never seen greater grief than they displayed between them. (51, 30–38)

Ranulf, Earl of Chester, led the way, and when he saw Sir Fouke he ordered his company to halt. He went privately to Sir Fouke and begged him for the love of God to surrender to the king. He would act as surety for him in life and limb and he would be fully reconciled with the king. Fouke said he would not do so for all the money in the world. 'My lord cousin, for the love of God, I beg you that when my brother, who is lying there, is dead, you bury his body so that wild beasts will not devour it, and ours too, when we die. Return to your lord, the king, and perform your service to him without hesitation and without regard for us who are of your blood. We shall now receive here the destiny which is ordained for us.' The earl, in tears, returned to his company. Fouke stayed behind, tenderly shedding tears of compassion for his brother, whom he was forced to abandon there. He prayed to God that he would succour and help him. (51, 39; 52, 1–14)

The earl ordered his retinue and his company to attack and they did so vigorously. The earl himself attacked Sir Fouke, but in the end the earl lost his horse and a large part of his retinue was killed. Fouke and his brothers defended themselves boldly, and as Fouke defended himself Sir Berard de Blois came up behind him and struck him on his side with his sword and he believed that he had killed him. Then Fouke turned round and struck him back on the left shoulder with both his hands, slicing through his heart and his lungs, and he fell down dead from his horse. Fouke had bled so profusely that he collapsed over his horse's neck in a faint and his sword fell from his hand. Then his brothers began to grieve tremendously. John, his brother, darted behind Fouke on his horse and held on to him so that he could not fall. They took flight because they had no strength to remain. The king and his retinue pursued them, but they could not catch them. They rode all night so that the next morning they came to the sea, to Mador the mariner. Then Fouke regained consciousness and asked where he was and in whose power. His brothers comforted him as best they could. They put him into a very fine bed in the ship and John de Rampaigne tended to his wounds. (52, 15–33)

The Earl of Chester had lost a very large number of men. Near him he saw William Fitz Waryn, who was on the point of death, and he took the body and sent it to an abbey to be cared for. At length he was discovered there and the king had him come before him at Windsor in a litter. There he had him thrown into a deep dungeon and was very angry with the Earl of Chester for having concealed him. The king said: 'Fouke is mortally wounded and I have this man. I shall get the others, wherever they are. I am certainly very distressed at Fouke's arrogance, for, had he not been so arrogant, he would have gone on living, and whilst he was alive there was no such knight on earth. So it is a great loss to lose such a knight.' (52, 34–39; 53, 1–5)

In the sea, near Spain, there is an island surrounded by high rocks and it has only one entrance. It is called Beteloye and is half a league long and the same distance wide. No man or beast dwelt there. On the sixth day they arrived at this island. Fouke began to sleep, for he had not slept for the previous six days. His brothers and his companions went ashore and he himself slept alone on the ship, which was secured to the rock. Then a dreadful wind got up and it broke the ship's ropes and carried the ship out on to the high sea. Then Fouke awoke and saw the stars and the firmament. He called to his brother John and his other companions, but no one replied. He saw that he was alone on the high sea. Then he began to weep and to curse his destiny, which was so harsh, and he grieved for his brothers. Then sleep took hold of him and his ship very soon arrived in the land of Barbary, at the city of Tunis. And there at that time was Messobryn, the King of Barbary, with four kings and six emirs, who were all Saracens. The king was leaning on a tower overlooking the sea and he saw this marvellous galley arriving at his land. He ordered two men-at-arms to go and see what it was. (53, 6–24)

The two men went on board the ship, but found nothing apart from the knight, who was still asleep. One of them kicked him and ordered him to wake up. The knight sprang up like a man in a fright and gave him such a blow with his fist that he fell overboard into the sea. The other man took flight and came to tell the king what had happened to him. The king ordered a hundred knights to go and seize this ship and bring the knight to him. The hundred knights, all armed, came to the ship and attacked it on all sides. Fouke defended himself boldly against them all, but in the end he surrendered, on condition that he would be well treated. They brought him before the king, who ordered him to be well cared for in a bed-chamber. (53, 25–35)

Isorie, the king's sister, used to come and visit him often and comfort him. She was a very beautiful and noble maiden and she noticed that he was wounded in the side. She asked him in friendly fashion to tell her his name, from what land he was and in what way he had been wounded. He replied that his name was Maryn le Perdu de France, and that he had a deep and tender love for a maiden, the daughter of an earl in his country. She gave a great appearance of loving him, but she loved someone else more. 'It happened one day that she and I were joined together in our great love and she held me very tightly in her arms. Then the other man turned up, whom she loved more, and he struck me here with his sword. Then they put me into a galley on the sea, as if I were dead, and the galley brought me to these parts.' 'Certainly,' said Isorie, 'this maiden was scarcely courtly.' She took her harp, which was magnificent, and played melodies and tunes to comfort Fouke, for she saw he was handsome and of courtly bearing. (53, 25–39; 54, 1–11)

Fouke asked the beautiful Isorie what the commotion was which could be heard in the hall before the king. 'Certainly,' she replied, 'I shall tell you. In the land of Iberia there was a duke who was called Duke of Carthage and he had a beautiful daughter, Ydoyne de Carthage. During the lifetime of her father, she lived in his castle in Carthage. Then a dragon came, which captured her and carried her to a high mountain at sea and kept her there for more than seven years, until a knight from England, by the name of Fouke Fitz Waryn de Metz, came to that mountain. He killed the dragon and returned her to her father. Soon afterwards, the duke died and she held the entire duchy. The king, my brother, sent messengers to her, saying that he would take her as his wife and she refused him. Because of the shame the king had suffered, he assembled a large number of men and destroyed her cities and demolished her castles. The maiden fled to a foreign kingdom in search of help. But now she has returned with a multitude of men and is beginning to wage a fierce war against the king. She is ready to do battle, army against army or knight against knight, so that if hers is beaten she would go to his land, and if ours is beaten, the king, my brother, would make good her losses in full. In respect of this, proud messengers have come today into our hall, and would that it pleased our god Mahomet that you were such a one as to dare to undertake the battle in the name of the king, my brother, for great honour would accrue to you.' 'Certainly, damsel, I am greatly beholden to my lord the king and especially to you, but I would never undertake a battle for Saracen against Christian, even if it cost me my life. But, if the king wishes to renounce his faith and become a Christian and be baptized, I shall undertake the battle and save his land and his people. I shall win for him the maiden about whom you have spoken to me.' Isorie went and told Messobryn, her brother, the King of Barbary, everything that Fouke, who called himself Maryn le Perdu de France, had promised her. The king agreed at once to everything he wished to arrange, if he could thus accomplish this business. (54, 12–38; 55, 1–5)

On the date which had been arranged for the battle, the king had Sir Fouke armed magnificently and Isorie herself served him with good will. The king and his Berbers, his emirs and all his other men were splendidly armed and they had many people with them. They brought forward his knight, Fouke, who was to do battle, and the duchess brought forward her man. The knights, who were fierce, spurred their horses and struck with their lances so that splinters flew over the fields. Then they drew their swords and struck each other boldly. Fouke struck his companion's horse and knocked it down dead. But he had intended to strike the knight. The knight, when he was on the ground, said: 'Wretched pagan, wretched Saracen of evil faith, may God in heaven curse you! Why have you killed my horse?' Fouke dismounted and they fought hard the whole day long. When it was almost evening, the knight said to Fouke: 'Sir pagan, you are strong and vigorous. Out of love, tell me, where were you born?' 'If you wish to know my nation, I shall not tell you, unless you tell me about your own first.' 'I grant that to you.' The knight told him that he was a Christian born in England, the son of Waryn de Metz, and called Philip the Red. He told him word for word, in the absolutely correct order, about his whole life and about his brothers and how the duchess came in a ship to the island of Beteloye and took them on board and saved them, for they had been there half a year and more. They ate their horses through hunger. 'When the countess had seen us, she recognized us immediately and supplied us with whatever we needed and she told us how she had come from England and looked for us there in order to support her war. Such is the hard life we have led!' Then Fouke said: 'Fair brother Philip the Red, do you not recognize me? I am Fouke, your brother.' 'You are certainly not, lord Saracen. Now you are trying to deceive me. In God's name, you will not do so!' Then Fouke gave him a true sign, which he recognized. Then they displayed great joy and put off the battle until the next day. Philip told the duchess that it was Fouke, his brother, with whom he had been fighting, with the result that, on the advice of Fouke, Philip and his other brothers, the king and all his household were baptized. The king married the duchess with great honour. (55, 6–39; 56, 1–3)

Fouke, his brothers and his household remained with the king for some time. Then they equipped themselves very richly to go to England. The king gave them gold, silver, horses, arms and all the riches which they would like to possess or desired. They filled their ship with a remarkable amount of riches. When they had arrived secretly in England, Fouke ordered John de Rampaigne to become a merchant and enquire where King John was and whether his brother William was alive or not. John decked himself out splendidly as a merchant and came to London. He stayed at the mayor's house and had himself served magnificently, and he became acquainted with the mayor and all his household. He gave them fine gifts and asked the mayor to make him known to the king, so that he might bring his ship ashore on the king's land. The language he spoke was jargon, but the mayor understood him easily. (56, 4–17)

The mayor brought him before the king in Westminster and the merchant greeted him very politely in his dialect. The king understood him easily and asked who he was and where he came from. 'Lord,' he said, 'I am a merchant from Greece and I have been to Babylon, Alexandria and India. I have a ship laden with merchandise, rich cloth, precious stones, horses and other riches, which could be of great value in this kingdom.' 'I am willing,' said the king, 'for you to bring yourself and your people ashore on my land and I shall be your surety.' They were ordered to remain for a meal. The mayor and the merchant ate together before the king. Then two sergeants-at-mace came and brought into the hall a tall, stout knight with a long black beard. He was poorly dressed and they placed him in the middle of the floor and gave him food. The merchant asked the mayor who he was and he replied: 'A knight named Sir William Fitz Waryn'. He told him the whole story of him and his brothers. When he heard his name, John was full of joy that he had seen him alive. But he was terribly distressed in his heart that he had seen him in such a sorry plight. The merchant went to Sir Fouke as soon as he could and told him the whole affair. He had the ship brought as close to the city as they could, and the next day the merchant took a white palfrey (there was none finer in the whole kingdom) and presented it to King John, who received it joyfully because it was so handsome. The merchant gave such generous gifts that he made everyone like him and he could do whatever he liked at court. (56, 18–38; 57, 1–3)

One day he took his companions and they armed themselves well and then donned their tunics, as befitted mariners. They went to Westminster, to court, where they were nobly received. They saw William Fitz Waryn, who was being taken by his guards towards the prison. The merchant and his companions, in spite of the guards, captured him by force and took him to their boat, which was floating very close by beneath the palace. They put him on board, and the guards raised the hue and cry and pursued them. The merchants were well armed and they defended themselves boldly. They escaped to their galley and sailed out towards the high sea. When Fouke saw William, his brother, and John de Rampaigne, who was the merchant, there is no need to ask if he was joyful. They kissed each other, and each told the other the story of his adventures and his misfortunes. When the king heard that he had been tricked by the merchant, he thought himself badly treated. (57, 4–18)

Fouke and his companions arrived in Brittany, where they remained half a year and more with Fouke's relatives and cousins. Then he decided that nothing would deter him from going to England. When he came to England, in the New Forest, where he used to live, he encountered the king, who was hunting a wild boar. Fouke and his companions captured him and his knights with him and took them to their galley. The king and all his men were very much afraid. There was a great deal of talking, but in the end the king put aside all his anger towards them and restored to them all their inheritance, promising them in good faith that he would proclaim peace for them throughout England. To this end he left his six knights with them as hostages, until the peace should be proclaimed. (57, 19–30)

The king went to Westminster and assembled earls, barons and clergy. He told them openly that he had of his free will granted his peace to Fouke Fitz Waryn and to his brothers and all their followers. He ordered that they should be honourably received throughout the whole kingdom and granted them their entire inheritance. (57, 31–35)

When Hubert, the archbishop, heard this, he was full of joy, and he immediately sent a letter to Fouke, to the Earl of Gloucester, to Ranulf, the Earl of Chester, and to Hugh, earl marshal, telling them to come to him in Canterbury with all speed. When they had arrived, they decreed that Fouke and his brothers should surrender to the king in London. Fouke, his brothers and the three earls, with their forces, prepared themselves as richly as they knew how and were able, and they came through London in noble apparel and knelt before the king in Westminster, surrendering to him. The king received them, restored to them all their holdings in England and ordered them to remain with him.[44] They did so for a full month. Then Fouke took his leave and stayed with the earl marshal. The earl gave him authority over Ashdown, Wantage and other lands. Fouke and his brothers armed themselves to their satisfaction and came to Abingdon. They removed from there everything they could find to sell and had it all carried and transported to Wantage, where they created a fair and a market town, which has since been held and still exists.[45] (57, 36–39; 58, 1–14)

Fouke took leave of the earl marshal and went to Earl Ranulf of Chester, who was preparing a large army to go to Ireland and defend his rights there. When they arrived, they saw a huge gathering of their enemies. The earl ordered them all to arm themselves and he had with him three young men, who were brothers and men of great valour and strength. They were armed and well mounted and Fouke was with them. Then they saw a hideous giant amongst their enemies. He was armed and on foot, hideous, black and horrible, taller by twelve feet than anyone else. He yelled out: 'Earl of Chester, send me the most valiant knight you have to defend your right.' The three young men, who heard him, went to him, one after the other, and he killed them straightaway with the axe he was holding. Then Fouke spurred his horse. He attempted to strike him with his lance, but the giant parried a little and struck Fouke, almost killing him. Fouke was very fearful of him and he kept his eye firmly on him so that he managed to run him through the body with his lance. He fell to the ground and in falling struck Fouke's horse and cut off two of its hooves. Fouke fell to the ground, then leaped up and drew his sword. He cut off the giant's head and took his axe back to Blancheville, where on marshy ground he had a strong and handsome castle built. Thus the earl conquered all his lands and castles in Ireland, and when he had stayed there and brought order to his lands he returned to England. (58, 15–38)

Fouke came to Blancheville, where he found Matilda, his wife, and his children, who were very glad that he had come. They all rejoiced together and then Fouke had his treasures and his riches brought there. He gave lands and horses very liberally to his men-at-arms and his friends and maintained his land with great honour. (58, 38; 59, 1–4)

Fouke decided that he had committed grievous sins against God, by killing men and by other great misdeeds. For remission of his sins, he founded a priory in honour of our Lady the Virgin Mary of the order of Grandmont, near Alberbury, in the wood on the River Severn. It is called the New Abbey.[46] Shortly afterwards Lady Matilda de Caus, his wife, died and she was buried in this priory. A good long while after this lady died, Fouke married a very noble lady, Lady Clarice d'Auberville, and by the one and the other lady he fathered fine and very valiant children.[47] (59, 5–15)

When Lady Joan, wife of Llywelyn, Prince of Wales, who was the daughter of King Henry of England, was dead, he asked Sir Fouke, because of his great reputation for prowess and bravery, for his daughter Eve. Fouke granted her to him and with great honour and solemnity they were married. But Llywelyn lived for only a year and a half afterwards. He died and was buried in Conway, without having produced an heir by Eve. Afterwards she was married to the Lord of Blancminster, who was a knight of great worth, courageous and bold.[48] (59, 16–24)

Fouke and Lady Clarice, his wife, were in bed together one night in their chamber. The lady was sleeping and Fouke lay awake thinking of his youth. He was heartily sorry for his sinful life. Then he saw in his bedroom such a great light that it was truly marvellous, and he wondered what it could be. Then he heard a voice, as if it were thunder in the air, saying: 'Vassal, God has granted you penance, which is worth more here than elsewhere.' At these words the lady awoke, saw the great light and covered her face in fear. Then this light disappeared, and after it Fouke could never see again, for he was blind for the rest of his life. (59, 25–35)

This Fouke was a good and generous host, and he had the highway diverted by his hall, at his manor of Alveston, so that no stranger would pass without receiving food or lodging, or other honour or goods of his. Merlin says that in Britain the Great a wolf will come from Blanche Lande. It will have twelve sharp teeth, six below and six above. It will have such a fierce look that it will chase the leopard away from Blanche Lande, such strength and power will it have. But we know that Merlin said this about Fouke Fitz Waryn. For each of you can be sure that in the time of King Arthur what is now called Blancheville was called Blanche Lande. For in that country there was a beautiful chapel of St Augustine, where Cahuz, son of Yvain, dreamed that he stole the candelabrum and that he encountered a man who wounded him with a knife and injured him in the side. As he slept, he called out so loudly that King Arthur heard him and awoke from his sleep. When Cahuz was awakened, he put his hand to his side and found there the knife which had wounded him right through. The Graal, the book of the Holy Vessel, tells us this. There King Arthur recovered his courage and his valour, when he had lost everything, his chivalry and his power. The wolf came from this land, as the wise Merlin said, and we have recognized the twelve sharp teeth by his shield. He carried a shield indented, as the heralds devised. On the shield are twelve teeth gules and argent. By the leopard King John can be recognized and well understood, for he bore on his shield the leopards of beaten gold.[49] (59, 36–39; 60, vv. 1–39; 61, vv. 1–7)

This Fouke remained blind for seven years and he bore his penance well. Lady Clarice died and was buried at the New Abbey. After her death Fouke lived for only one year. He died at Blancheville and was buried at the New Abbey with great honour. May God have mercy on his soul. The body lies close to the altar. May God have mercy on them all, the living and the dead! Amen. (61, 8–13)

NOTES TO THE TRANSLATION

These notes should be read in conjunction with the excellent notes in the Anglo-Norman Text Society (ANTS) edition (pp. 62–104). There are also substantial notes in the edition by Thomas Wright (pp. 185–231).

1. This account of the activities of Owain Gwynedd, here called Prince of Wales, is deficient on a number of counts. Owain Gwynedd was certainly prince of Gwynedd, but he did not take the title Prince of Wales. Nor was he ruler of Gwynedd at the time of the Conquest. His period of rule was from 1137 to 1170 (for a substantial account of his life see J.E. Lloyd, *A History of Wales*, II, pp. 487–535). The praise for Owain in the *Romance* is, however, justified, as he was certainly a strong and astute ruler. Henry II waged campaigns against him in 1157 and 1165 (see David Walker, *Medieval Wales*, pp. 45–48) and there may be a reflection of this in the *Romance*. But it would appear to be the border activities of Gruffydd ap Llywelyn, which took place between 1055 and 1063, which are being alluded to here. Walker calls Gruffydd 'undoubtedly the outstanding Welsh ruler of the eleventh century', but 'he was totally ruthless, his hands stained with the blood of rivals and opponents' (ibid., p. 18). Gruffydd succeeded to the kingdom of Gwynedd in 1039, but it was the death in 1055 of Gruffydd ap Rhydderch, ruler of Deheubarth (South Wales), which gave him the opportunity to impose his authority over a united Wales. He used ruthless tactics to achieve this aim and pursued an aggressive policy with regard to the English, launching raids against their southern borders (see K.L. Maund, *Ireland, Wales, and England in the Eleventh Century*, pp. 64–68). For a list of the 'authentic facts' in the *Romance*, as compared with its 'apocryphal events', see L. Brandin, 'Nouvelles Recherches sur *Fouke fitz Waryn*', pp. 22–24.

2. William the Conqueror in fact made only one visit to Wales, to St Davids in 1081. With reference to the early part of the text the ANTS editors write: 'The whole of this episode is fabulous, as far as the Conqueror is concerned. The settlement of the families in the Oswestry area, and the activities of Owain Gwynedd and his older contemporary Meredith ap Bleddyn of Powys, are simply transferred from the reign of Henry I to a period of half a century earlier' (p. 63). They add that in the account of Owain Gwynedd's depredations and conquests there also seems to be a reflection of the last years of Welsh independence in the thirteenth century (ibid.).

3. Roger de Bellême was in fact Roger de Montgomery, to whom the Conqueror gave the earldom of Shropshire some time after 1071. It was his son Robert who had the title 'de Bellême', which he inherited from his mother, Mabel Talvas, Roger's first wife. However, it is true, as stated in the *Romance*, that Roger founded (in 1087) Shrewsbury Abbey, which was, as the *Romance* says, dedicated to St Peter, and that Arnulf, his fifth son, established himself at Pembroke (in 1093). It is also true that Henry I disinherited and banished the family for good (in 1102) and that the unlicensed construction of the castle at Bridgnorth was the probable cause of the rupture (see Lynn H. Nelson, *The Normans in South Wales, 1070–1171*, pp. 118–21). J.F.A. Mason, in his article 'Roger de Montgomery and his Sons (1067–71)', states that 'Robert probably chose the site [at Bridgnorth] in 1100, and work could have begun in the

1101 building season' (p. 22, n. 2). For the character of Roger de Montgomery's sons, who in the *Romance* are called 'unruly and treacherous men', see Orderic Vitalis, III, pp. 138–50, Mason, pp. 24–28, and V. Chandler, 'The Last of the Montgomerys: Roger the Poitevin and Arnulf'. On adulterine castles see Charles Coulson, 'The Castles of the Anarchy', in E. King, *The Anarchy of King Stephen's Reign*, pp. 65–92 (on Bridgnorth see pp. 68–69).

4.   The origin of Ludlow Castle remains uncertain. The first reference to the castle dates from 1138, but 'the curtain wall of the inner bailey, its flanking towers and parts of the gatehouse-keep date from the 11th century' (David Lloyd, *Ludlow Castle: a History and a Guide*, p. 2). Derek Renn thinks that the castle may have been founded as early as 1075 (' "Chastel de Dynan": the First Phases of Ludlow', pp. 55, 58). There is no reason to think that Roger de Montgomery had anything to do with its construction, but Thomas Wright points out that in the thirteenth century there was evidently a common belief to this effect in the locality (p. 186). The site of the castle was on the manor of Stanton, which the Lacy family had held since 1066. The River Corfe and the River Teme, both of which are mentioned here, offered important protection for the castle. See Notes to the Introduction, n. 59.

5.   There are close analogies between the story of Geomagog, as recounted here, and the passage in Geoffrey of Monmouth's *Historia regum britanniae* in which the giant Gogmagog first attacks Brutus and then fights with Corineus, who ends up hurling him into the sea (*The History of the Kings of Britain*, trans. Lewis Thorpe, Harmondsworth: Penguin Books, 1966, pp. 72–73). See Timothy Jones, 'Geoffrey of Monmouth, *Fouke le Fitz Waryn*, and National Mythology'. Jones points out that the author of *Fouke Fitz Waryn* replaces the native British myth with a new Norman and Christian myth, one which 'justifies the Norman occupation of Wales, the Fitz Waryn family's claim to Whittington, Fouke's defiance of King John and his favoritism toward the Welshman Roger de Powys' (p. 235). Castle Bran is almost certainly Castell Dinas Brân, which lies on a steep hill near Llangollen. The new name for Castle Bran, given here as the Old Border (la Vele Marche), probably represents Wallie Marchia. King Bran, son of Donwal (or Brian Fitz Donwal), can be identified as Brennius, son of Dunvallo Molmutius (Dyfnwal Moelmud), in Geoffrey's *Historia* (pp. 88–91). See R.S. Loomis, 'Chastiel Bran, Dinas Brân, and the Grail Castle', in his *Wales and the Arthurian Legend*, pp. 42–52. Loomis examines a number of aspects of the Geomagog and Payn Peverel story, in particular the relationship with accounts of the Horn of Brân and the confusion between *cor* 'horn' and *tor* 'bull'.

6.   There is a further anachronism here. Payn Peverel's activities belonged principally to the reign of Henry I not to that of William the Conqueror. Henry gave him the honour of Bourn in Cambridgeshire. See below, note 9.

7.   Within the prose text of the *Romance* this prophecy, pronounced by the spirit of the defeated Geomagog, has been preserved in verse form (edition, p. 6). The prophecy refers to the struggle between the hero, Fouke III, designated as the wolf (the sharp teeth are an allusion to his arms), and King John, designated as the leopard. See note 49.

8.   Meredith (Maredudd) ap Bleddyn and Alan Fitz Flaald were certainly real people. Meredith (d. 1132) was ruler of Powys and he and his brothers directed a great deal of their activity against the Normans (Maund, p. 44). He was associated in 1102 with the rebellion of Roger de Bellême which caused Henry I to throw that family out of England (see above, note 3). Alan was a Breton knight who received his advancement at the hands of Henry I and became sheriff of Shropshire and lord of Oswestry in 1101. In the time of King Stephen, Meredith's son Madog seems to have possessed Oswestry during the exile of William Fitz Alan (Eyton, X, p. 321, see also II, pp. 107–12).

9. The Peverel family concerned are the Peverels of Dover and of Bourn (Cambridgeshire), not the Peverels of Nottingham or the Peverels of Essex. For the Cambridgeshire holdings of the Peverels see William Farrer, *Feudal Cambridgeshire* (passim, but especially the genealogy on p. 160). The ANTS editors inform us that 'there were three brothers at the court of Henry I, Hamo Peverel, who held lands in Shropshire in 1093–8, William of Dover, and Pain of Bourn, who was one of the founders of Barnwell Abbey' (p. 69). Payn Peverel was never lord of the Peak, as the *Romance* states. The William who built Whittington would be William II, nephew of Hamo and William I. His father was probably Robert, another brother, and as such he would, as the text says, have been the nephew of Payn. William II died in 1147 on the Second Crusade. See Eyton, II, pp. 104–07, and X, pp. 232–34, and Ordericus Vitalis, VI, pp. 518–19. The *Romance* goes on to tell us that William II Peverel had two nieces (Leland says two daughters), but in reality he had four sisters. 'If Waryn de Metz ever married one of them', write the ANTS editors, 'it must have been long before the period when William held his Shropshire lands, since Waryn's sons were already attesting deeds at this period' (p. 70). If Fouke I were related to the Peverels, who were staunch supporters of Matilda, this might explain the support given to her by the Fitz Waryns.

10. A Guy le Estrange (or le Strange), with his brothers John and Hamo, received lands from Henry II early in his reign. The Guy referred to in the *Romance* would seem to be the father of these brothers, but the relationship remains unclear. Eyton states that 'there is some reason to believe that the Fitz Warines and Lestranges were related', but he concludes that, if there is any truth in what the *Romance* says about the involvement of the Estrange brothers in a tournament attended by Owain, Prince of Wales, and William Peverel, the events described must have taken place between 1137 (the accession of Owain) and 1147 (the death of William Peverel). In reality, says Eyton, 'Warine de Metz must have been married long before' (III, pp. 123–24). John le Estrange, lord of Knockin and Ryton, appears later in the *Romance* as an ally of King John (see below, note 34).

11. The Welsh prince Yervard (Iorwerth) cannot have been the son of Owain (Yweyn), Prince of Wales. The author must be referring to the activities of Iorwerth Goch (Red Edward), son of Meredith ap Bleddyn, ruler of Powys. Iorwerth Goch was the brother of Madog ap Meredith and he was active in the period before the Anarchy. His father, whom the author of the *Romance* had mentioned earlier, was involved in the revolt of Roger de Bellême (see above, note 8). Iorwerth Drwyndwyn (Yervard Droyndoun in the Anglo-Norman text, p. 19, line 14) was, as the text says, the son of Owain Gwynedd (see above, note 1) and father of Llywelyn the Great. He bore the nickname Trwyndwn 'flat-nosed', and is said, because of his deformity, to have been excluded from all share in the succession (Lloyd, II, p. 550).

12. Eyton points out that in all probability Ludlow came into the hands of Henry I as an escheat of Lacy not by forfeiture of Robert de Bellême. He adds that Joce probably obtained Ludlow from Stephen or the Empress not from Henry I (V, p. 244). W.E. Wightman, in his book *The Lacy Family in England and Normandy 1066–1194*, states that the conflict between Joce de Dinan and the Lacy family over the possession of Ludlow Castle and the surrounding lands seems to have occurred between 1143 and 1148 (p. 187). It is not impossible, however, that it took place later, but it must have been earlier than 1162–63. The Lacy involved was almost certainly Gilbert, but it could just have been Robert (Wightman, ibid.). Joce was given, 'at some date not later than 1157–8' (Wightman, p. 188), an estate on the royal demesne of Lambourn in Berkshire, possibly as compensation for the loss of Ludlow (this land was taken over by Richard de Lucy in 1162–63). In the period around 1140 Joce certainly possessed lands in southern Shropshire, for a charter, dated 1140–42, in which Stephen makes a grant to Robert Beaumont, Earl of Leicester, mentions the fief of Joce de Dinan which

had belonged to Hugh de Lacy (see Wightman, pp. 180–81, and Henry C. Davis, 'Some Documents of the Anarchy', pp. 172–73). There is an interesting passage in *The Anglo-Norman Chronicle of Wigmore Abbey* which tells of a 'tres grant gere' ('very great war') between Sir Hugh de Mortimer and Joce de Dynan, lord of Ludlow Castle. We are told that Sir Joce was virtually imprisoned within his castle for fear of Sir Hugh, but that, thanks to the use of spies, he managed to capture Hugh and hold him prisoner until a ransom was paid (p. 428). The account in the *Romance*, in which the young Fouke rescues Joce from the Lacys, when he has been attacked on Dinham bridge, is accepted as factual by Derek Renn (' "Chastel de Dynan": the First Phases of Ludlow', p. 58). Renn (ibid.) thinks that Joce himself built this bridge (see Wright, edition pp. 186–87).

13. The scribe, who was associated with Hereford, probably intended to look into the question of the precise name before filling in the blank. There are at least four possible Roberts who held the office of Bishop of Hereford: Robert of Lorraine (1079–95), Robert of Bethune (1140s), Robert of Melun (1163–67) and Robert Foliot (1174–86). Meisel thinks that the most likely bishop was Robert Foliot (p. 134).

14. In his *Ludlow Castle: a History and a Guide* David Lloyd relates the story of Marion de la Bruere (p. 11). He concludes that it 'may well be founded on a true incident'. Marion's story has proved popular and it is related, for example, by Thomas Wright (*The History of Ludlow*, pp. 56–58) and A.G. Bradley (*In the March and Borderland of Wales*, pp. 180–83).

15. Roger de Powys and his brother Jonas were associated with Iorwerth Goch (see note 11) not with Iorwerth Drwyndwyn, who was a prince of Gwynedd. Roger and Jonas were established as castellans of Whittington and Overton in 1165, having first appeared in Shropshire in 1159.

16. Thomas Wright has a lengthy note on the road taken by Fouke as he escapes from the skirmish which takes place between Caynham and Ludlow. In the *Romance* he is said to go over or beyond Whitcliffe, which, says Wright, 'he would not have done by the present road from Ludlow to Leominster and Hereford' (p. 202).

17. There is no evidence that Fouke ever had the office of constable, but it is interesting to note that at approximately the same period as the manuscript was written this office was held by Fouke VI.

18. The Joan who married Llywelyn was the natural daughter of King John, not the daughter of Henry II, as stated here (her mother was Clementina). Henry had by his wife Eleanor a legitimate daughter called Joan, who married the King of Sicily in 1177. John's daughter Joan was betrothed to Llywelyn ap Iorwerth in 1204 and the marriage took place in 1206 or 1207, much later than is implied in the *Romance*. It is true, however, that Joan received the lordship of Ellesmere as her dower. See C. Given-Wilson and A. Curteis, *The Royal Bastards of Medieval England*, pp. 128–30.

19. Joce's eldest daughter Sybil(le) did not marry Payn Fitz John, but Hugh de Plugenai. Payn did marry a Sybil, but she was the daughter of Hugh de Lacy (see Wightman, pp. 175–76).

20. Fouke actually had a sixth son, Richard (see Meisel, p. 37).

21. There is a similar scene in the *chanson de geste*, *Renaud de Montauban* (also known as *Les Quatre Fils Aymon*). In this text Renaud, in a fit of rage, kills Charlemagne's nephew with a chessboard. See Philippe Verelst, *Renaud de Montauban, édition critique du ms. de Paris, B.N. fr. 764 (R)*. Gent: Rijksuniversiteit te Gent, 1988, vv. 273ff. See also L. Brandin, in Alice Kemp-Welch, *The History of Fulk Fitz-Warine*, pp. xiv–xvi, and T. Jones, 'Geoffrey of Monmouth, *Fouke le Fitz Waryn*, and National Mythology', n. 35. We may be dealing here with a typical attempt by a biographer to provide a reason to account for events in his subject's later life. Meisel, however, although she describes it as 'bizarre', finds the episode convincing by virtue of its very

implausibility and she is certain that there was some 'personal animosity' between Fouke and John (p. 135). But when and where would this episode have taken place? John spent his earliest years at Fontevrault Abbey. Between 1174 and 1182 he was brought up in the household of his eldest brother, Henry (see R.V. Turner, *King John*, p. 37).

22. The association between the Fitz Waryn family and the Hodnets is certainly based on fact. Wright claims that it is 'very probable' that they were related (p. 204). Baldwin was one of the outlaws pardoned by John in November 1203. He was a knight and a tenant of the Fitz Waryns, from whom he held, when he died, around 1225, the manors of Moston and Welbatch. Stephen, possible Baldwin's younger brother, also participated in the outlawry and was amongst those pardoned. See Eyton, VII, pp. 53–54, and Meisel, pp. 14, 89, 113–14.

23. Castle Baldwin ('chastiel Baudwyn') is Tref Faldwyn 'Baldwin's Town', Montgomery (Powys). In the original text, the words 'qe ore est apellee Mountgomery' ('which is now called Montgomery') have been added by the scribe above the line. Baldwin de Hodnet was hereditary seneschal of Montgomery Castle.

24. As John was on his way to the Welsh Marches, it is unlikely that he met John in Winchester. Painter suggests that a careless scribe has confused Winchester with Worcester: 'Only a scribal error conceals his knowledge of the place where the grant to Maurice [Morys] was made' (*The Reign of King John*, p. 50). But John was in Winchester on 6 and 7 May, 1201.

25. 'Audulf de Bracy was of Meole, near Shrewsbury. Several generations of the family bore the same Christian name of Auduf. The individual mentioned here was, in the time of King John, involved in a great litigation with his suzerain, Roger de Mortimer, of Wigmore, as to the tenure of the manor of Meole, which is still known as Meole-Brace' (Eyton, III, p. 12). Although the *Romance* indicates the Audulf shared Fouke's exile in Brittany during the period of outlawry, he is not one of the pardoned outlaws (for the list of names see Notes to the Introduction, n. 30). The litigation mentioned by Eyton seems to have taken place between 1203 and 1207.

26. The lord of the manor of Higford in King John's time was certainly a Sir Walter. But Eyton points out that Vyleyne / Emmeline de Higford, the hero's aunt, must have been Waryn de Metz's granddaughter not daughter. She must also have been Sir Walter de Higford's mother rather than wife (III, p. 13). She was already a widow before the period of Fouke's outlawry.

27. In the list of men pardoned with Fouke there appear a William Malveisin and a Ralph Malveisin (see Introduction, n. 30). Meisel reports that the Malveisins held the manor of Stallington from the Pantulfs (p. 83).

28. Hubert Walter was Archbishop of Canterbury from 1193 to 1205, so his participation in Fouke's outlawry and pardon was chronologically possible. But there is in fact no evidence that he was involved. C.R. Cheney, in *Hubert Walter*, makes no mention of the Fitz Waryn family. The *Romance* is certainly wrong in calling Hubert's brother Theobald le Botiler. Theobald (d. 1206) did not assume the name Le Botiler 'The Butler'. It was his son who did so in 1221. The title stems from the fact that Theobald went to Ireland with Henry II in 1217, as a result of which Henry conferred on him the office of chief butler of Ireland. He also accompanied John to Ireland in 1185. The author of the *Romance* is correct in stating that Theobald possessed lands in Ireland. In addition to numerous smaller territories he held the baronies of Upper and Lower Ormond. However, as he was still alive during Fouke's outlawry, Fouke could not have married his widow. The text is also incorrect in stating that Theobald's wife was called Matilda de Caus. Her name was Matilda le Vavasur. Matilda de Caus was her grandmother (Eyton, VII, p. 73). Fouke's marriage to Theobald's widow took place in 1207, four years after his outlawry. See Introduction, pp. 103–04.

29. It is not easy to know whether there is any truth in this story of the sons of noblemen joining forces with robbers in the early thirteenth century. But it is interesting to note that at about the time when the prose version was being copied the Folville gang was operating. In 1331, for example, the gang ambushed Richard Willoughby, justice of the king's bench, took him off to a nearby wood and forced him to pay 1300 marks to save his head. A. Harding, in his book *Law Courts of Medieval England*, points out that the Folvilles were gentry and he comments that the gang 'was typical of the period, when people were compelled to look for security in "local bands and private associations" ' (p. 91). Harding adds that 'this was a conflict not between poor and rich so much as between "outs" and "ins", between the rogues in the woods and rogues in authority' (ibid.). In this context one can see why the *Romance of Fouke Fitz Waryn* would have been popular. Concerning the ribalds, with whom the sons of noblemen are associated in the *Romance*, Thomas Wright comments that they 'formed a class, or caste, of society in the middle ages, consisting of persons who seem to have been considered out of the pale of the laws and of morality; they had no particular occupation, but lived upon the overflowings of people's tables, and were ready to perform any infamous act or outrage that might be required of them' (p. 211).
30. Concerning the pass of Ness ('le pas de Nesse') Wright states: 'Ness is a parish about seven miles to the north-west of Shrewsbury, through which the road runs from that town to Oswestry and Whittington. The scene of this adventure was perhaps the neighbourhood of the hill called Ness-cliff, which overlooks the road, and in the state of the country at that time was probably the best position along the road for laying in ambush to intercept a party going to Shrewsbury' (p. 212).
31. The events alluded to here correspond well to the known facts, although no details are available of Fouke's involvement in them. The ANTS editors (p. 91) point to an interesting passage in the *Brut y Tywysogyon* 'The Red Book' for the year 1202. The passage states that Llywelyn ap Iorwerth moved an army from Powys to subdue Gwenwynwyn, who, although related to him, was his enemy in action. In due course churchmen and monks made peace between Llywelyn and Gwenwynwyn (trans. T. Jones, Cardiff: University of Wales Press, 1955, p. 185). Gwenwywyn (d. 1216), prince of southern Powys, was, as the *Romance* states, the son of Owain Cyfeiliog (d. 1197). David Walker, in his book *Medieval Wales*, confirms that the events recounted in the *Romance* are not without some foundation: 'As early as 1202, Llywelyn ap Iorwerth signalled his intention to harass Powys, but for a while King John found it expedient to encourage Gwenwynwyn as a makeweight against Gwynedd. By 1208 the prince of Powys had come into open conflict with John for which he paid dearly. Summoned to the king's court in 1209, he was forcibly detained and his lands were declared forfeit, and in the aftermath southern Powys was invaded by Llywelyn' (p. 97). In 1211 Gwenwynwyn's lands were restored to him, but Llywelyn soon increased his influence in Powys. He obtained Gwenwynwyn's homage and succeeded in driving him into exile in England (Walker, p. 99). See also D. Stevenson, 'The Politics of Powys Wenwynwyn in the Thirteenth Century', pp. 40–44.
32. For the marriage of Joan and Llywelyn see note 18. Walker states that 'neither homage nor marriage could prevent conflict between Llywelyn and John' and he adds that John 'could play one off against the other' (*Medieval Wales*, p. 93). At first John supported Llywelyn, but in 1211 he switched to Gwenwynwyn, once he had been re-established in Powys. The account in the *Romance* of John's attack on Llywelyn would seem to reflect the events of 1211 and 1212. W.L. Warren, in his book *King John*, states that John was in no mood to tolerate an ambitious Welsh chieftain and he describes as follows the two efforts John made to subdue Llywelyn in 1211: John 'gathered an army and Llywelyn's Welsh rivals and marched on the castle of Deganwy. He was too precipitate: he had not reckoned with the difficulties of fighting in moun-

tainous country. Llywelyn and his men withdrew with their property into the fast-nesses of Snowdonia and left John's army nothing to fight but famine: even eggs were hard to come by and the troops resorted to eating horseflesh – a serious matter in the days when the horse was a man's most valuable possession. John retired, but only to prepare himself better. In July he set out again from Oswestry with a larger army and abundant provisions, and marched down the vale of Llangollen and the river Conway to Bangor, building forts as he went. Llywelyn was cowed and sent his wife to plead with her father. John agreed to make peace, but he imposed crushing terms' (p. 198). However, in June 1212 Llywelyn recruited his former rivals, including Gwenwynwyn, and launched an attack on the forts which John had built in 1211. John decided that once and for all he would solve the Welsh problem, but his projected assault on Wales never materialized, because of rumours of a conspiracy (Warren, ibid., p. 200).

33. King John was not in Shrewsbury during the period of Fouke's outlawry. He was there, however, in late January 1209.

34. On Gam Elen (Gué Gymele) see G. Price, 'Le Gué Gymele in Fouke Fitz Warin'. Price suggests that the Welsh form ford or ffordd 'road' had been misinterpreted as 'ford' and translated as gué. Gué Gymele would be Ffordd Gam Elen 'the crooked road of Elen'.

35. John le Estrange (or Lestrange) seems to have been the grandson of Guy Lestrange (see note 10). It is certainly true that he was a staunch supporter of King John. The Dictionary of National Biography reports that 'he served in 1214 under King John in Poitou, and between 1233 and 1240 was successively appointed by Henry III constable of the castles of Montgomery, Shrewsbury, Bridgnorth, and Chester. He spent a long life in defending the Welsh border as a lord marcher, and during the rebellion of Simon de Montfort stood fast to the crown' (XI, p. 996). In the third year of Henry III's reign he obtained permission to rebuild the castle of Knockin, which would suggest that it had been destroyed, as the Romance states, in border warfare. See Wright, p. 215, and Eyton, X, p. 259.

36. It is true that Sir Henry de Audley (Staffordshire) was a faithful supporter of John. Henry founded the Audley family and built Redcastle (Chastiel Rous) in 1232. See Eyton, VII, pp. 183, 185.

37. On Thomas Corbet and the Corbet family see Janet Meisel, Barons of the Welsh Frontier: The Corbet, Pantulf, and Fitz Warin Families, 1066–1272, pp. 3–22, 60–75. The Corbets were barons of Caus in Shropshire and, in John's reign, the barony was held by Robert Corbet (d. 1222), father of the Thomas Corbet (d. 1274) mentioned in the Romance. Robert was, in Meisel's words, 'an unusually peaceable, reverent, and nonbelligerent baron' (p. 13), but, as the Romance indicates, Thomas was a rebel: 'His activities as a rebel against King John were conspicuous enough to cause his father to lose his seisin of Caus' (Meisel, p. 14). It is possible that he and Fouke Fitz Waryn fought together. Both the Fitz Waryns and the Hodnets were vassals of the Corbets. Meisel states that Thomas 'seems to have been born before 1177' (p. 13).

38. Eyton states that 'Hawise, born about 1208, must have married William Pantulf, baron of Wem before 1226. William Pantulf died in 1233 and Fulk fitz Warine pur-chased the wardship and marriage of his infant heirs' (VI, pp. 75–77, IX, pp. 168–69). See Rotuli de finibus, I, p. 237.

39. It is true that Fouke's daughter Joan by Matilda de Caus married Henry de Pembridge. Pembridge is a castle five miles north of Monmouth. See Wright, p. 217, and the ANTS edition, p. 94.

40. On the Fountain of Maidens ('Fontaigne dé Puceles') see the note in the ANTS edition (p. 94), which offers the possible identification of the location as the Afon Morwynion 'Maidens' River', a tributary of the Dee to the west of Llangollen. This river joins the Dee at Carrog, around twenty miles from Alberbury.

41. Gerald of Wales (Giraldus Cambrensis) refers to 'the pleasant conjecture that Saint Patrick and other saints purged the island of all harmful animals' (*The History and Topography of Ireland*, trans. J. O'Meara, Harmondsworth: Penguin Books, 1982, p. 50).

42. Wright (pp. 219–20) compares this episode with an equivalent episode in *The Romance of Eustace the Monk*.

43 Sir James of Normandy seems to be an imaginary figure, but Ranulf, Earl of Chester, was one of the wealthiest and most respected magnates of King John's reign. In spite of occasional quarrels, he remained true to the king and was one of the royal *familiares* (see R. V. Turner, *King John*, pp. 17, 73). Wright suggests that Ranulf, 'being so much connected with the border, could not but feel an interest in the Fitz Warines' (p. 220). In the spring of 1203, whilst Fouke was still an outlaw, John grew suspicious of Ranulf, seemingly because of the desertion of his brother-in-law, lord of Fougères in Brittany. John accused Ranulf of plotting with the disaffected Bretons, but he soon regained confidence in him (Turner, p. 123, Warren, *King John*, pp. 108–09). The earl marshal at the time of Fouke's outlawry was Hugh Bigod. ˙

44. On Fouke's pardon see the Introduction, pp. 102–03, and n. 30. There is no evidence that Hubert Walter had any part in the pardon, which was due to the Bishop of Norwich and the Earl of Salisbury. But Wright suggests that because of the powerful positions he occupied Hubert 'may still have been the real and primary mediator' (p. 224). The *Romance* is certainly wrong in indicating that Fouke received his pardon at Westminster, as the king was in Normandy at the time.

45. The overlordship of the manor of Wantage belonged to the earls marshal of England and it was originally granted to Fouke by William Marshal's son, William II, shortly before 1222, not as early as the *Romance* states and not by Hugh (presumably intended to be Hugh Bigod, who married William Marshal's eldest daughter). It is, however, true that Fouke was given the right to hold a fair at Wantage (Wright states that 'it was the usual custom to include in such grants a fair as well as a market', p. 229). The ANTS editors (p. 102) quote *The Victoria History of the Counties of England, Berkshire*: 'In 1224 Fulk Fitz Warin made an agreement with the Abbot of Abingdon by which the abbot's fair at Shellingford came to an end for the benefit of Fulk's fair at Wantage' (IV, 267, see also p. 321).

46. Eyton places the foundation of the New Abbey at Alberbury 'about the year 1220' (VII, p. 92). David George et al., *St Michael and All Angels Church, Alberbury: a 700th Celebration*, give the date as 'between 1221–1226' and they state that 'Augustinian in origin, it was soon transferred to the French order of Grandmontines' (p. 3). This happened 'before 1232' according to *The Victoria History of the Counties of England, A History of Shropshire*, II, p. 47. The order of Grandmont was a Benedictine order founded at Grandmont (Normandy) around the year 1076. The order flourished in thirteenth-century England, but as a result of disputes between monks it began to decline in France from 1184. See R. Graham, 'The Order of Grandmont and its Houses in England', and in *English Ecclesiastical Studies*, pp. 228–29, 243–45. See also Wright, p. 229, and the ANTS edition, p. 102.

47. Matilda de Caus is, as we have seen (note 28), a mistake for Matilda le Vavasur. Nothing much is known of Fouke's second wife, Clarice d'Auberville (see Eyton, VII, pp. 76–79).

48. Llywelyn's wife Joan died in 1137. Nothing is known of his second wife Eve. Llywelyn became a monk at the Cistercian Abbey of Aberconway, which he had founded, in April 1240. He died and was buried there soon afterwards. Just who the lord of Blancminster was is not clear. Both Whitchurch and Oswestry bore the name Album Monasterium (Blancminster). Eyton (VIII, p. 87) points to a certain Eva de Oswaldistre, who may have been Eve de Blancminster. She was in her second widowhood in 1282. See ANTS edition, p. 103.

49. Like the earlier prophecy (see note 5), this passage has been preserved in verse form (edition, pp. 60–61). On this occasion the prophecy is attributed to Merlin. To the designation of Fouke III as wolf and King John as leopard is added the story of Cahuz, a story which has been adapted by the author of the *Romance* from the Arthurian romance *Perlesvaus* (ed. W.A. Nitze and T.A. Jenkins, 2 vols, Chicago: University of Chicago Press, 1932, reprint New York, 1972, I, pp. 26–39, notes pp. 209–10). See Michel Zink, 'Le Rêve avéré: la mort de Cahus et la langueur d'Arthur du *Perlesvaus* à *Fouke le Fitz Waryn*'.

BIBLIOGRAPHY

Editions

Brandin, Louis. *Fouke fitz Warin: roman du XIVe siècle*. Paris: Champion (Classiques Français du Moyen Age, 63), 1932.

Hathaway, E.J., P.T. Ricketts, C.A. Robson, and A.D. Wiltshire. *Fouke le Fitz Waryn*. Oxford: Blackwell (Anglo-Norman Text Society, 26–28), 1976.

Michel, Francisque. *Histoire de Foulques Fitz-Warin, publiée d'après un manuscrit du Musée Britannique*. Paris: Silvestre, 1840.

Moland, L. and C. d'Héricault. *Nouvelles françoises en prose du XIVe siècle, publiées d'après les manuscrits avec une introduction et des notes*. Paris: Jannet, 1858. Contains Wright's text (pp. 15–114) and an introduction (pp. xvi–xlv).

Stephenson, Joseph. *Gesta Fulconis Filii Warini*, in *Radulphi de Coggeshall Chronicon anglicanum*. London: Longman, etc. (Rerum britannicarum medii aevi scriptores), 1875, pp. 277–415. Also contains a translation of the text.

Wood, A.C. *Fulk Fitz-Warin: Text and a Study of the Language*. London: Blades, 1911. M.A. thesis, University of London.

Wright, Thomas. *The History of Fulk Fitz Warine, an Outlawed Baron in the Reign of King John, edited from a manuscript preserved in the British Museum, with an English translation and illustrative notes*. London: The Warton Club, 1855.

John Leland's Synopsis

In *Joannis Lelandi antiquarii de rebus britannicis collectanea*, ed. Thomas Hearne. 6 vols, Oxford: E Theatro Sheldoniano, 1715, 2nd ed. London: G. and J. Richardson, 1770, 3rd ed. London: Benjamin White, 1774. Reprint of 1774 edition, Farnborough, Hants: Gregg International, 1970. See vol. I, pp. 230–37.

See also F. Michel, pp. 101–12, and L. Brandin, *Romania*, 55 (1929), pp. 26–32.

Translations

Guiton, P.A. *Histoire de Foulques Fitz Garin, edited and annotated*. London: Blackie and Son, 1924. This translation was 'specially written for use in schools' (p. v).

Kemp-Welch, Alice. *The History of Fulk Fitz-Warine Englished by Alice Kemp-Welch with an Introduction by L. Brandin Ph.D.* London: De La Mare Press (The King's Classics), 1904.

Jordan, Leo. *Das Volksbuch von Fulko Fitz Warin*. Leipzig: Deutsche Verlagsactiengesellschaft (Romanische Meistererzähler), 1906.

See also J. Stephenson and T. Wright (references above).

Chronicles and Archival Material

The Anglo-Norman Chronicle of Wigmore Abbey, ed. J.C. Dickinson and P.T. Ricketts, *Transactions of the Woolhope Naturalists' Field Club, Stroud*, 39 (1969), 414–45.

Calendar of Patent Rolls, Preserved in the Public Record Office, AD 1232–47. London: His Majesty's Stationery Office, 1906.

Calendar of Patent Rolls, Preserved in the Public Record Office, AD 1258–66. London: His Majesty's Stationery Office, 1910.

The Cartulary of Haughmond Abbey, ed. U. Rees. Cardiff: University of Wales Press, 1985.

The Cartulary of Shrewsbury Abbey, ed. U. Rees. 2 vols, Aberystwyth: The National Library of Wales, 1975.

Close Rolls of the Reign of Henry III, Preserved in the Public Record Office, AD 1231–34. London: His Majesty's Stationery Office, 1905.

Matthew Paris [Matthaei Parisiensis], *Chronica majora*, ed. H.R. Luard, 7 vols, London: Longman, etc. (Rerum britannicarum medii aevi scriptores), 1872–84.

Orderic Vitalis, *The Ecclesiastical History*, ed. M. Chibnall. 6 vols, Oxford: Oxford University Press, 1969–80.

Pleas before the King or his Justices (1198–1212), ed. Doris M. Stenton. 4 vols, London: Bernard Quaritch (for the Selden Society), 1952–67.

The Red Book of the Exchequer, ed. H. Hall. 2 vols, London: Her Majesty's Stationery Office, 1896–97.

Regesta regum anglo-normannorum: 1066–1154, vol. III, ed. H.A. Cronne, R.H.C. Davis and H.W.C. Davis. Oxford: Clarendon Press, 1968.

Roger of Hovedon, *Chronica*. In *Chronica Rogeri de Houedene (A.D. 732–1201)*, ed. William Stubbs. 4 vols, London: Longman, etc. (Rerum britannicarum medii aevi scriptores), 1868–71.

The Roll of the Shropshire Eyre of 1256, ed. A. Harding. London: Selden Society, 1981.

Rotuli de finibus. In *Rotuli de oblatis et finibus in Turri Londinensi asservati, tempore regis Johannis*, ed. Thomas Duffus Hardy. London: The Commissioners of the Public Records, 1835, pp. 197–605.

Rotuli de liberate ac de misis et praestitis regnante Johanne, ed. Sir Thomas Duffus Hardy. London: Eyre and Spottiswoode, 1844.

Rotuli litterarum clausarum in Turri Londinensi asservati, ed. Sir Thomas Duffus Hardy. 2 vols, London: Eyre and Spottiswoode, 1834–44.

Rotuli litterarum patentium in Turri Londinensi asservati, ed. Sir Thomas Duffus Hardy. London: Publications of the Commissioners of the Public Records, 1835 (vol. I, pars i, 1201–1216).

Rotuli de oblatis. In *Rotuli de oblatis et finibus in Turri Londinensi asservati, tempore regis Johannis*, ed. Thomas Duffus Hardy. London: The Commissioners of the Public Records, 1835, pp. 1–196.

William of Newburgh, *Historia rerum anglicarum*. In *Chronicles of the Reigns of Stephen, Henry II and Richard I*, ed. Richard Howlett. 2 vols, London: Longman, etc. (Rerum britannicarum medii aevi scriptores), 1884–85, II, pp. 415–583.

William Rishanger, *Chronica et annales, regnantibus Henrico Tertio et Edwardo Primo, A.D. 1259–1307*. In *Chronica monasterii S. Albani*, ed. H.T. Riley. London: Longman, etc. (Rerum britannicarum medii aevi scriptores), 1865.

Items Devoted in Full or in Part to Fouke Fitz Waryn

Benecke, Ingrid. *Der gute Outlaw.* Tübingen: Niemeyer, 1973.

Brandin, Louis. 'Nouvelles Recherches sur *Fouke Fitz Waryn*', *Romania*, 55 (1929), 17–44.

Carrington, Tim. 'Fulk Fitz Warine', in *Shropshire Legends and People.* Shrewsbury: Shropshire Promotions, n.d., pp. 1–2.

Francis, Elizabeth A. 'The Background to *Fulk FitzWarin*', in *Studies in Medieval French Presented to Alfred Ewert.* Oxford: Oxford University Press, 1961, pp. 322–27.

Haydon, Laura. 'The Morphology of a Medieval Adventure Romance: *Fouke Le Fitz Waryn*'. M.A. dissertation, Birkbeck College, University of London, 1990.

Holmes, Urban T. 'The Adventures of Fouke Fitz Warin', in *Medium Aevum Romanicum: Festschrift für Hans Rheinfelder*, ed. H. Bihler and A. Noyer-Weidner. Munich: Max Hueber, 1963, pp. 179–85.

Jones, Timothy. 'Geoffrey of Monmouth, *Fouke le Fitz Waryn*, and National Mythology', *Studies in Philology*, 91 (1994), 233–49.

Keen, Maurice. 'The Romance of Fulk Fitz-Warin', in *The Outlaws of Medieval Legend.* London and Henley: Routledge and Kegan Paul – Toronto and Buffalo: University of Toronto Press, 1961, revised ed. 1977, revised paperback edition, London and New York, Routledge and Kegan Paul, 1987, pp. 39–52.

Levy, Brian J. '*Fouke le fitz Waryn*: de l'historicité incertaine aux valeurs plus littéraires d'un roman lignager anglo-normand', in *Histoire et littérature au Moyen Age: actes du colloque du Centre d'Etudes Médiévales de l'Université de Picardie (Amiens 20–24 mars 1985)*, ed. D. Buschinger. Göppingen: Kümmerle (Göppinger Arbeiten zur Germanistik, 546), pp. 251–62.

Martin, E.M. 'A Shropshire Lad of the Middle Ages', *Fortnightly Review*, 114 (1923), Part I, 966–75, Part II, 81–94.

Meisel, J. *Barons of the Welsh Frontier: The Corbet, Pantulf, and Fitz Warin Families, 1066–1272.* Lincoln, Nebraska, and London: University of Nebraska Press, 1980.

Morris, Joseph. 'The Family of Fitz-Warine', *Archaeologica Cambrensis*, new series, 3 (1852), 282–91. Reprinted in *Transactions of the Shropshire Archaeological and Natural History Society*, 5 (1882), 241–50.

Painter, Sydney. 'The Sources of *Fouke fitz Warin*', *Modern Language Notes*, 50 (1935), 13–15.

Pensom, Roger. 'Inside and Outside: Fact and Fiction in *Fouke le Fitz Waryn*', *Medium Aevum*, 63 (1994), 53–60.

Paris, Paulin. 'Anonyme, auteur de *L'Histoire de Fouke Fitz-Warin*', in *Histoire Littéraire de la France*, 27 (1877), pp. 164–84.

Price, Glanville. '*Le Gué Gymele* in *Fouke Fitz Warin*', *Modern Language Review*, 57 (1961), 220–22.

Ross, David J.A. 'Where did Payn Peverell defeat the Devil? The Topography of an Episode in *Fouke le Fitz Waryn*', in *Studies in Medieval French Language and Literature Presented to Brian Woledge in Honour of his 80th Birthday*, ed. Sally B. North. Geneva: Droz (Publications Romanes et Françaises, 180), 1988, pp. 135–43.

Schmolke-Hasselmann, Beate. 'Füchse in Menschengestalt: die listige Heldin Wistasse le Moine und Fouke Fitz Waryn', in *Third International Beast Epic, Fable and Fabliau Colloquium, Münster 1979, Proceedings*, ed. J. Goossens and T. Sodmann. Cologne: Böhlau (Niederdeutsche Studien, 30), 1981, pp. 356–79.

Southam, S. Clement. 'A Shropshire Robin Hood', *Transactions of the Shropshire Archaeological Society*, 2nd series, 9 (1897), 1–20.

Stephenson, G.G. 'The Value of the Romance *Fulk Fitz Warren* as a Source for Thirteenth-Century English History'. B. Litt. thesis, University of Oxford, 1953.

Tedder, H.R. 'Fulk Fitzwarine', in *The Dictionary of National Biography*, VII, Oxford: Oxford University Press, 1973, pp. 223–24.

Watson, G.W. et al. 'FitzWarin', in *The Complete Peerage of England, Scotland, Ireland, Great Britain and the United Kingdom*. 13 vols, London: St Catherine's Press, 1910–40, V (1926), 495–513.

Wilshere, Alan. 'A Syntactical Study of Fouke Fitz Waryn'. Ph.D. thesis, London, 1965.

Zink, Michel. 'Le Rêve avéré: la mort de Cahus et la langueur d'Arthur du *Perlesvaus* à *Fouke le Fitz Waryn*', *Littératures* (*Mélanges René Fromilhague*), 9–10 (1984), 31–38, reprinted in idem, *Les Voix de la consience: parole du poète et parole de Dieu dans la littérature médiévale*. Caen: Paradigme, 1992, pp. 137–143.

Other Items Consulted

Auden, Thomas. 'The Rebellion of Robert de Belesme', *Transactions of the Shropshire Archaeological Society*, 3rd series, 1 (1901), 107–18.

Baugh, G.C., and D.C. Cox. *Shropshire and its Rulers: a Thousand Years*. Shrewsbury: Shropshire Libraries, 1979.

Bradley, A.G. *In the March and Borderland of Wales*. London: Constable, 1905.

Bussey, Valerie. 'A Woman's Love and Betrayal Led to Ludlow Castle being Captured in the Night', *The Shropshire Magazine*, July 1952, 39.

Cathwall, William. *History of Oswestry*. Oswestry: George Lewis, reprint Oswestry: Gallery Books, 1987.

Chandler, Victoria. 'The Last of the Montgomerys: Roger the Poitevin and Arnulf', *Historical Research*, 62 (1989), 1–14.

Cheney, C.R. *Hubert Walter*. London: Nelson, 1967.

Collins, Ernest. *Whittington Castle and its Story*. Whittington: Mary Morris, n.d.

Crane, Susan. *Insular Romance: Politics, Faith and Culture in Anglo-Norman and Middle English Literature*. Berkeley: University of California Press, 1986.

Dannenbaum, Susan. [=Susan Crane] 'Anglo-Norman Romances of English Heroes: "Ancestral Romance"?', *Romance Philology*, 35 (1981–82), 601–08.

Davies, William. *The History of Whittington*. Oswestry: E. Edwards, n.d.

Davis, Henry C. 'Some Documents of the Anarchy', in *Essays in History Presented to Reginald Lane Poole*. Oxford: Clarendon Press, 1927, reprint, 1969, pp. 168–89.

Davis, R.H.C. 'Treaty between William Earl of Gloucester and Roger Earl of Hereford', in *A Medieval Miscellany for Doris Mary Stenton*, ed. P.M. Barnes and C.F. Slade. London: Pipe Roll Society, 1962, pp. 139–45.

Eyton, R.W. *Antiquities of Shropshire*. 12 vols, London: John Russell Smith, 1854–60.

Faraday, Michael. *Ludlow 1085–1660: a Social, Economic and Political History*. Chichester: Phillimore, 1991.

Farrer, William. *Feudal Cambridgeshire*. Cambridge: Cambridge University Press, 1920.

———. *Honors and Knights' Fees*. 3 vols, London: Spottiswoode, Ballantyne and Co., 1923–25.

Garbet, Sam. *The History of Wem*. G. Franklin, 1818, reprint Shrewsbury: John Thornhill, 1982.

George, David, Marion Halford and Sir Michael Leighton. *St Michael and All Angels Church, Alberbury: a 700th Celebration*. Pontesbury, Shropshire: Alberbury 700 Committee, 1987.

Gibson, Alexander G. *Whittington Castle: its History, Legend and Romance; 'A Tale of Other Days'*. St Mary's, Isles of Scilly: Gibson and Sons, n.d.

Graham, Rose. 'Alberbury Priory', *Transactions of the Shropshire Archaeological Society*, 4th series, 11 (1928), 257–95.

———. *English Ecclesiastical Studies: Being some Essays in Research in Medieval History*. London: Society for Promoting Christian Knowledge, 1929.

Haines, George H. *Shropshire and Herefordshire Villages*. London: Hale, 1974.

Harding, Alan. *England in the Thirteenth Century*. Cambridge: Cambridge University Press, 1993.

———. *The Law Courts of Medieval England*. London: Allen and Unwin, 1973.

Holt, J.C. *Magna Carta and Medieval Government*. London and Roncverte: The Hambledon Press, 1985.

Hope, W.H.St.J. 'The Castle of Ludlow', *Archaeologia*, 61 (1908), 257–324.

King, Edmund (ed.). *The Anarchy of King Stephen's Reign*. Oxford: Clarendon Press, 1994.

Legge, M. Dominica. *Anglo-Norman Literature and its Background*. Oxford: Oxford University Press, 1963, reprint Westport, Connecticut: Greenwood Press, 1978.

Levy, Brian J. 'The Ancestral Romance in Mediaeval French with Special Reference to Anglo–Norman Literature'. Ph.D. Dissertation, University of Edinburgh, 1966.

Lloyd, David. *Ludlow Castle: a History and a Guide*. Telford: Printex Press, no date given.

Lloyd, F. 'Whittington Castle', in *Documents Concerning the Parish of Whittington*. Shrewsbury: Local Studies Library, 1987, document q.

Lloyd, John E. *A History of Wales, from the Earliest Times to the Edwardian Conquest*. 2 vols, 2nd ed. London, etc.: Longman, Green and Co., 1912.

Loomis, Roger Sherman. *Wales and the Arthurian Legend*. Cardiff: University of Wales Press, 1956.

McCall, Andrew. *The Medieval Underworld*. London: Hamish Hamilton, 1979.

Mason, J.F.A. 'Roger de Montgomery and his Sons (1067–71)', *Transactions of the Royal Historical Society*, 5th series, 13 (1963), 37–62.

Maund, K.L. *Ireland, Wales, and England in the Eleventh Century*. Woodbridge, Suffolk: The Boydell Press, 1991.

Morris, George. 'Shropshire Genealogies Shewing the Descent of the Principal Proprietors of the County of Salop from the Time of William the Conqueror to the Present Time'. 8 vols, I, pp. 395–412 (unpublished MS, no date).

Morris, Joseph. 'Genealogical Manuscripts Connected with the County of Salop, based on the Heralds' Visitations of Shropshire, with notes and additions'. 10 vols, VII, pp. 3612–18, IX, pp. 4401–03 (unpublished MS, no date).

Nelson, Lynn H. *The Normans in South Wales, 1070–1171*. Austin, Texas, and London: University of Texas Press, 1966.

Owen, H., and J.B. Blakeway. *A History of Shrewsbury*. 2 vols, London: Harding, Lepard and Co., 1825.

Painter, Sydney. *The Reign of King John*. Baltimore: The Johns Hopkins Press, 1949.

Phillips, Graham, and Martin Keatman. *Robin Hood and the Man behind the Myth*. London: Michael O'Mara Books, 1995.

Prestwich, Michael C. 'Geoffrey de Geneville or Joinville', in *The Dictionary of National Biography: Missing Persons*. Oxford: Oxford University Press, 1993, p. 247.

Reeves, A. Compton. *The Marcher Lords*. Llandybïe: Christopher Davies (A New History of Wales), 1983.

Renn, Derek. ' "Chastel de Dynan": the First Phases of Ludlow', in *Castles in Wales and the Marches: Essays in Honour of D.J. Cathcaret King*, ed. J.R. Kenyon and R. Avent. Cardiff: University of Wales Press, 1987, pp. 55–73.

Revard, Carter. 'Richard Hurd and MS. Harley 2253', *Notes and Queries*, 224 (1979), 199–202.

Round, J. Horace. 'The *Geste* of John de Courcy', in *Peerage and Pedigree: Studies in Peerage Law and Family History*. 2 vols, London: James Nisbet, 1910, II, pp. 258–306.

Rymer, Thomas. *Foedera, conventiones, literae, et cujuscunque generis acta publica*. 4 vols in 7, London: Eyre and Strahan, 1816–69.

Statham, Samuel P.H. *The History of the Castle, Town, and Port of Dover*. London: Longmans, 1899.

Stevenson, D. 'The Politics of Powys Wenwynwyn in the Thirteenth Century', *Cambridge Medieval Celtic Studies*, 7 (1984), 39–61.

The Victoria History of the Counties of England, Berkshire. 4 vols, vols I–II, London: Constable, 1906–07, vols III–IV, London: St Catherine Press, 1923–24.

The Victoria History of the Counties of England, A History of Shropshire. Vol. I, ed. W. Page, London: Constable, 1908, vol. II, ed. A.T. Gaydon, Oxford: Oxford University Press, 1973, vol. III, ed. G.C. Baugh, Oxford: Oxford University Press, 1979, vol. VIII, ed. A.T. Gaydon, Oxford: Oxford University Press, 1968, vol. XI, ed. G.C. Baugh, Oxford University Press, 1985.

Sykes, Harry. *The Story of Whittington Castle*. Oswestry: Woodall, Minshall, Thomas and Co., 1902.

Turner, Ralph V. *King John*. London and New York: Longman (The Medieval World), 1994.

Usher, G.A. 'The Career of a Political Bishop: Adam de Orleton', *Transactions of the Royal Historical Society*, 5th series, 22 (1972), 33–47.

Ward, Harry L.D. *Catalogue of Romances in the Department of Manuscripts in the British Museum*. 2 vols, London: British Museum, 1883–93.

Warren, W.L. *King John*. London: Eyre & Spottiswoode, 1961, reprinted with corrections, 1964.

Weston, Jessie L. 'Notes on the Grail Romances', *Romania*, 43 (1914), 403–26.

Wightman, W.E. *The Lacy Family in England and Normandy 1066–1194*. Oxford: Clarendon Press, 1966.

Williams, Daniel. 'The Peverils and the Essebies 1066–1166: a Study in Early Feudal Relationships', in *England in the Twelfth Century: Proceedings of the 1988 Harlaxton Symposium*, ed. D. Williams. Woodbridge, Suffolk: The Boydell Press, 1990, pp. 241–59.

Wright, Thomas. *Historical and Descriptive Sketch of Ludlow Castle and of the Church of St Lawrence, Ludlow*. 17th ed., Ludlow: George Woolley (Woolley's Ludlow Guide), 1924.

———. *The History of Ludlow and its Neighbourhood, Forming a Popular Sketch of the History of the Welsh Border*. Ludlow: R. Jones – London: Longman and Co. and W. Pickering, 1852.

The Romance of Eustace the Monk

INDEX OF PERSONAL NAMES

References are to page numbers in the Translation. Forms in parentheses are the Old French forms which differ from those in the English translation.

Morel (Moriel), pp. 56–57. A horse stolen by Eustace from the Count of Boulogne.

Omer, St, p. 62. Bishop and saint (d. c.699). Also known as Audomarus.

Peter, St, p. 70. Leader of the apostles and saint (d. c.64).

Philip (Phelippe), King, p. 66. Philip Augustus, King of France 1180–1223.

Raoul (Raous) de Tournelle, p. 77. A companion of Eustace.

Remi, St., pp. 58, 74. Bishop and saint (d. 533). Also known as Remigius.

Renaud (Renaus, Renaut), Count, pp. 64, 67, 76. Renaud de Dammartin, Count of Boulogne. Also called simply the Count of Boulogne (pp. 54, 55 etc.) or the Count of Dammartin (p. 59).

Richard (Richier), St, p. 64. Saint (d. 720).

Romer, p. 62. The name of a donkey.

Romerel, p. 73. The leader of the forces defending the Channel Islands.

Simon (Symon), p. 56. Pseudonym adopted by Eustace the Monk.

Simon (Symon) de Boulogne, p. 55. See Notes to the Translation, n. 9.

Simon (Symon), St, p. 77. First-century apostle and saint.

Spanish (horse), p. 68.

Travers, p. 53. One of the three thieves in the fabliau *De Haimet et de Barat* by Jean Bodel.

Varlet (Varlés) de Montagui, p. 77. A companion of Eustace.

Vincent (Vincens), p. 57. A monk from the abbey of Clairmarais.

Virgin Mary (Marie, la Sainte Puciele, Warie), pp. 56–57, 59, 67–68, 72.

Walet (Wales) de Coupelle, pp. 56, 70. A vassal of the Count of Boulogne.

William de Fiennes, p. 71. Eustace's rescuer.

William (Guillaumes, Willaumes) de Montcavrel, pp. 56, 68, 70. A vassal of the Count of Boulogne.

Winnoc (Vinape, Winape), St, p. 74. Abbot and saint (d. c.717). Also known as Wunnoc or Winnow.

The Romance of Eustace the Monk

INDEX OF PLACE NAMES

References are to page numbers in the Translation. Forms in parentheses are the Old French forms which differ from those in the English translation. A number of locations are difficult to identify. *See* Conlon, pp. 123–29, and Berger and Petit, pp. 193–99. Cross-references to the Index of Personal Names are provided where relevant.

INDEX OF PERSONAL NAMES

References are to page numbers in the Translation. *See* the Index of Proper Names in the ANTS edition (pp. 126–35). Forms in parentheses are the Anglo-Norman forms which differ from those in the English translation.

INDEX OF PLACE NAMES

References are to page numbers in the Translation. *See* the Index of Proper Names in the ANTS edition (pp. 126–35). Forms in parentheses are the Anglo-Norman forms which differ from those in the English translation. Cross-references to the Index of Personal Names are provided where relevant.

some one of which Marion could have taken her name' (pp. 193–94).
Burgundy (Borgoyne), p. 137.

Canterbury (Canterburs, Caunterburs, Caunterbury), pp. 154, 156, 164.
Carreg-y-nant (Carreganant), p. 164. Welsh place-name.
Carthage (Cartage), pp. 170–72, 177. Probably Cartagena on the east coast of Spain.
Caus, Shropshire, pp. 156, 163, 181. See Matilda de Caus.
Ceiriog, River, p. 136. A tributary of the River Dee.
Chester (Cestre), Cheshire, pp. 132–33, 136, 148, 174–76, 180–81. See Ranulf, Earl of Chester.
Clerfountayne, p. 152. See Aaron de Clerfountayne.
Colchester (Colecestre), p. 154. Essex. See Jordan de Colchester.
Conway (Aberconewey), p. 182. Cistercian abbey.
Cornwall (Cornewayle), p. 133.
Corve, River, p. 133. Shropshire.
Cosham, p. 154. See Thomas, Peter and William of Cosham.
Croes Oswallt (Arbre Osawald), p. 135. Shropshire.

Dee, River, p. 136. Cheshire.
Denmark (Denemarche), p. 169.
Dinorben (Dynorben), p. 161.
Dover (Dovere, Dovre), pp. 164, 172. Kent.
Dynan, pp. 132–33, 138–39, 141–49. Dinham, the old name for Ludlow. See Joce de Dynan and Notes to the Translation, n. 4 and n. 12.

Ellesmere, pp. 136, 146, 148–49. Shropshire (about five miles north of Whittington).
England (Engletere, Engleterre), pp. 132, 135, 141–42, 146, 148, 150, 152–54, 156, 159, 166–67, 170, 172–73, 178–82.
Ethiopia (Ethiopie), p. 162.
Ewyas, pp. 138, 141, 143. Herefordshire. The seat of Walter de Lacy's barony.

Ffordd Gam Elen. See Gam Elen.
Fountain of Maidens (Fontaigne dé Puceles), p. 164.
France (Fraunce), pp. 148, 151, 165–66, 177–78. See Gerard de France and Philip, King.

Galloway (Galewey), p. 137. Scotland.
Gam Elen (Gué Gymele), Fford, p. 160. See Notes to the Translation, n. 34.
Gloucester (Gloucestre), pp. 147–48, 180.
Gothland (Gutlande), p. 169. Sweden.
Greece (Grece), p. 179.

Hartland (Hertlande), pp. 142–43. Devonshire.
Hereford (Herford), pp. 142, 148.
Higford (Huggeford), pp. 152, 164. Shropshire. See Walter de Higford.
Hodnet (Hodenet), pp. 150–52, 154, 164. See Baldwin de Hodnet.
Holy Land, the (la Terre Sainte), p. 150.

Iberia (Yberie), pp. 170, 177.
India (Ynde le Majour), p. 179.
Ireland (Irlaund, Irlaunde, Yrland, Yrlande, Yrlaunde), pp. 141, 146, 156, 169, 181.

Kent, p. 154.
Key, Castle, pp. 145, 147. See Keyenhom.
Keyenhom, p. 145. Caynham (Shropshire), an Iron Age camp or entrenched hill, situated about two miles east of Ludlow (see Wright, p. 198).
Knockin (Knokyn), p. 161. Shropshire (eight miles south-south-east of Oswestry).

Lacy, pp. 138–41, 143, 148–49. See Walter de Lacy.
Lambourn (Lambourne), p. 148. Berkshire.
Lannerch (LLannerth), p. 159. Llannerch Hudol (Powys).
Linney (Lyneye), p. 145. The part of Ludlow immediately to the north of the castle.
London (Londres, Loundres), pp. 132, 136, 149–50, 179–80.
Lorraine (Loreygne), p. 135.

ADDITIONAL BIBLIOGRAPHY
(paperback edition)

(i) *The Romance of Eustace the Monk*

Editions and Translations

Holden, A. J., and J. Monfrin. *Le Roman d'Eustache le Moine: nouvelle édition, traduction, présentation et notes*, Ktemata, 18. Louvain, Paris and Dudley, MA: Peeters, 2005.

Kelly, Thomas E. 'Eustache the Monk', in *Medieval Outlaws: Ten Tales in Modern English*, ed. Thomas H. Ohlgren. Stroud, Gloucestershire: Sutton Publishing, 1998, pp. 61–98; revised and expanded edition, West Lafayette, IN: Parlor Press, 2005, pp. 100–50.

———. 'From *Eustache the Monk*', in *Robin Hood and Other Outlaw Tales*, ed. Stephen Knight and Thomas Ohlgren, TEAMS Middle English Texts series. Kalamazoo, MI: Medieval Institute Publications, 2000, pp. 668–86.

Lecco, Margherita. *Saggi sul romanzo del XIII secolo, vol. II: Wistasse le Moine (studio letterario, con edizione del testo, traduzione italiana, commente e note)*. Alessandria: Edizioni dell'Orso, 2007.

Mousseigne, Édouard. *Eustache le Moine: pirate boulonnais du XIIIe siècle*. Lille: Voix du Nord, 1996.

Studies

Angeli, Giovanna. 'Le Comique cruel dans *Wistasse* et *Trubert*', in *'Ce est li fruis selonc la letre': mélanges offerts à Charles Méla*, ed. Oliver Collet, Yasmina Foehr-Janssens and Sylvanie Messerli. Paris: Champion, 2002, pp. 23–40.

Busby, Keith. 'The Diabolic Hero in Medieval French Narrative: *Trubert* and *Wistasse le Moine*', in *The Court and Cultural Diversity: Selected Papers from the Eighth Triennial Congress of the International Courtly Literature Society, The Queen's University of Belfast 26 July – 1 August 1995*, ed. Evelyn Mullally and John Thompson. Cambridge: D. S. Brewer, 1997, pp. 415–26.

Lecco, Margherita. '*Wistasse rossignol*: l'intertesto tristaniano nel *Wistasse le Moine*', *Romance Philology*, 59 (2005), 103–20.

Williams, Alison J. *Tricksters and Pranksters: Roguery in French and German Literature of the Middle Ages and the Renaissance*, Internationale Forschungen zur allgemeinen und vergleichenden Literaturwissenschaft, 49. Amsterdam: Rodopi, 2000.

(ii) *The Romance of Fouke Fitz Waryn*

Editions and Translations

Kelly, Thomas E. '*Fouke fitz Waryn*', in *Medieval Outlaws: Ten Tales in Modern English*, ed. Thomas H. Ohlgren. Stroud, Gloucestershire: Sutton Publishing, 1998, pp. 106–98; revised and expanded edition, West Lafayette, IN: Parlor Press, 2005, pp. 165–247.

———. 'From *Fouke le fitz Waryn*', in *Robin Hood and Other Outlaw Tales*, ed. Stephen Knight and Thomas Ohlgren, TEAMS Middle English Texts series. Kalamazoo, MI: Medieval Institute Publications, 2000, pp. 687–723.

Studies

Allen, Rosamund. 'The Loyal and Disloyal Servants of King John', in *The Court Reconvenes: Courtly Literature across the Disciplines: Selected Papers from the Ninth Triennial Congress of the International Courtly Literature Society, University of British Columbia 25–31 July 1998*, ed. Barbara K. Altmann and Carleton W. Carroll. Cambridge: D. S. Brewer, 2003, pp. 264–73.

Burgess, Glyn S. 'Fouke Fitz Waryn III and King John: Good Outlaw and Bad King', in *Bandit Territories: British Outlaws and their Traditions*, ed. Helen Phillips. Cardiff: University of Wales Press, 2008, pp. 73–98.

———. 'I kan rymes of Robyn Hood, and Randolf Erl of Chestre', in *'De sens rassis': Essays in Honor of Rupert T. Pickens*, ed. Keith Busby, Bernard Guidot and Logan E. Whalen, Faux Titre, 259. Amsterdam and New York: Rodopi, 2005, pp. 51–84.

———. 'Women in the *Fouke le Fitz Waryn*', in *'Por le soie amisté': Essays in Honor of Norris J. Lacy*, ed. K. Busby and C. Jones, Faux Titre, 183. Amsterdam: Rodopi, 2000, pp. 75–93.

Cavell, Emma. 'The Burial of Noblewomen in Thirteenth-Century Shropshire', in *Thirteenth Century England XI*, ed. Janet Burton, Phillipp Schofield, Karen Stöber and Björn Weiler. Woodbridge: Boydell, 2007, pp. 174–92.

Jones, Timothy Scott. 'Redemptive Fictions: The Contexts of Outlawry in Medieval English Chronicle and Romance'. Dissertation, University of Illinois at Urbana-Champaign, 1994.

Osborn, Marijane. 'The Real Fulk Fitzwarine's Mythical Monster Fights', in *Words and Works: Studies in Medieval English Language and Literature in Honour of Fred C. Robinson*, ed. Peter S. Baker and Nicholas Howe. Toronto: University of Toronto Press, 1998, pp. 271–92.

Revard, Carter. 'Scribe and Provenance', in *Studies in the Harley Manuscript*, ed. Susanna Fein. Kalamazoo, MI: Medieval Institute Publications, 2000, pp. 21–109.

Rock, Catherine A. 'Romances Copied by the Ludlow Scribe: *Purgatoire Saint Patrice, Short Metrical Chronicle, Fouke le Fitz Waryn*, and *King Horn*'. Dissertation, Kent State University, 2008.

Stephenson, D. '*Fouke le Fitz Waryn* and Llywelyn ap Gruffydd's Claim to Whittington', *Transactions of the Shropshire Archaeological and Historical Society*, 77 (2002), 26–31.

Williams, Alison. *Tricksters and Pranksters* (see above).

———. 'Manipulating the Past for the Sake of the Future: Optimistic Perspectives in the Outlaw Romance *Fouke le Fitz Waryn*', *New Zealand Journal of French Studies*, 28 (2007), 19–31.

Printed and bound by CPI Group (UK) Ltd, Croydon, CR0 4YY

09/06/2025

14685719-0003